Contemporary Maritime Piracy

Recent Titles in
Contemporary Military, Strategic, and Security Issues

Energy Security Challenges for the 21st Century: A Reference Handbook
Gal Luft and Anne Korin, editors

An Introduction to Military Ethics: A Reference Handbook
Bill Rhodes

War and Children: A Reference Handbook
Kendra E. Dupuy and Krijn Peters

Military Justice: A Guide to the Issues
Lawrence J. Morris

Military Space Power: A Guide to the Issues
Wilson W.S. Wong and James Fergusson

American Missile Defense: A Guide to the Issues
Victoria Samson

Private Armed Forces and Global Security: A Guide to the Issues
Carlos Ortiz

Women in the United States Armed Forces: A Guide to the Issues
Darlene M. Iskra

War Crimes, Genocide, and the Law: A Guide to the Issues
Arnold Krammer

NATO: A Guide to the Issues
Brian J. Collins

Geopolitics: A Guide to the Issues
Bert Chapman

Strategic Communication: Origins, Concepts, and Current Debates
Christopher Paul

Contemporary Maritime Piracy

International Law, Strategy, and Diplomacy at Sea

James Kraska
Foreword by Brian Wilson

Contemporary Military, Strategic, and Security Issues

AN IMPRINT OF ABC-CLIO, LLC
Santa Barbara, California • Denver, Colorado • Oxford, England

Library of Congress Cataloging-in-Publication Data

Kraska, James.
Contemporary maritime piracy : international law, strategy, and diplomacy at sea / James Kraska ; foreword by Brian Wilson.
p. cm. — (Contemporary military, strategic, and security issues)
Includes bibliographical references and index.
ISBN 978-0-313-38724-1 (hardback : acid-free paper) — ISBN 978-0-313-38725-8 (ebook) 1. Piracy—Southeast Asia. 2. Piracy—Africa, East. 3. International criminal law. I. Title. II. Series.

K5277.K73 2011
345'.0264—dc22 2011008005

ISBN: 978-0-313-38724-1
EISBN: 978-0-313-38725-8

15 14 13 12 2 3 4 5

This book is also available on the World Wide Web as an eBook.
Visit www.abc-clio.com for details.

Praeger
An Imprint of ABC-CLIO, LLC

ABC-CLIO, LLC
130 Cremona Drive, P.O. Box 1911
Santa Barbara, California 93116-1911

This book is printed on acid-free paper ∞

Manufactured in the United States of America

For my wife

Contents

Foreword

At any given time, more than a dozen ships and their crews are under the control of pirates, being held for ransom. Most of the victims will be released, but some will suffer torture and all will be emotionally scarred by the experience. The devastating impact of piracy on mariners and their families has, unfortunately, been a hallmark of this timeless and quite resilient crime. For more than 2,000 years, piracy has existed wherever there is maritime commerce and a lack of security, ranging from mere nuisance to destabilizing threats.

With two decades of maritime security experience, Commander Kraska is uniquely qualified to examine piracy. I had the pleasure of working with him in the Pentagon from 2004 through 2008, when U.S. government piracy policy was being developed, along with maritime security initiatives (in multinational venues) that sought to increase legal authorities and partnering capabilities. As the oceans policy advisor for the Director of Strategic Plans and Policy on the Joint Staff, Commander Kraska had a leading role in efforts that improved the ability of the U.S. armed forces to more effectively respond to illicit maritime activity.

Piracy directly affects only a small percentage of international shipping, but indirectly the crime impacts thousands of vessels through increased insurance premiums and changed trade routes. Satisfying the demands of pirates has historically resulted in payment of billions of dollars in tribute and ransom, and this money provides support to illicit organized crime syndicates. Ransoms have been paid, in part, because doing so has been expeditious and appears to be cost beneficial. This shortsighted approach, however, has enabled piracy to continue, and at times thrive, for generations.

The methods of pirates and the responses from states date to the Greek and Roman Empires, as well as to the early United States, and they have relevance today. For three centuries, the Barbary corsairs pillaged the North

African coastline. Barbary success can be attributed to the close proximity to a lucrative trade route, an ability to fight in the location and at the time of choosing, and access to sanctuary. The Barbary pirates were defeated only when their sanctuary was removed with overwhelming force. A long-term solution to contemporary piracy in the Horn of Africa requires regional commitments and sustained international support to address the lawlessness in Somalia. The fact that piracy even occurs, despite the focus of the strongest navies in history, highlights the nature of this asymmetric crime and the challenge of patrolling the vast oceans. The operating space of Somali pirates, for example, is at least four times the size of the state of Texas.

My first substantive exposure to maritime piracy occurred during assignment as the oceans policy advisor to the Under Secretary of Defense (Policy). Reports that Somali pirates had hijacked an Indian-flagged dhow with a crew of 16 mariners in 2006 triggered a successful rescue by the guided missile destroyer, USS *Winston S. Churchill* (DDG 81). The operational aspects of regaining control of the dhow were challenging, but once the pirates were in custody, multiple legal and policy questions were raised. What was the legal authority for detaining pirates? Who would investigate the case? Where would the pirates be held, and by whom? What about the Indian crewmembers, all of them witnesses to the crime, and what would happen to their ship and cargo? The 10 pirates responsible for hijacking the dhow were ultimately tried, convicted, and imprisoned in Kenya. The difficult logistics, investigation, and disposition questions in piracy interdiction, however, would occupy policy makers going forward.

In 2008, the United Nations Security Council turned its attention toward combating piracy, calling on flag, port, and coastal states to cooperate in actions off the Somali coast. As the 2006 *Churchill* interdiction illustrated, it is especially important that once an attack is disrupted at sea, states coordinate to provide real-time disposition and logistics assistance with respect to the suspected pirates, victims, and witnesses. Commander Kraska was a principal author of the below provision contained in United Nations Security Council Resolution 1816 (2008), which called upon states to

> cooperate in determining jurisdiction, and in the investigation and prosecution of persons responsible for acts of piracy and armed robbery off the coast of Somalia . . . and to render assistance by, among other actions, providing disposition and logistics assistance with respect to persons under their jurisdiction and control, such as victims and witnesses and persons detained as a result of operations conducted under this resolution.

This Security Council provision did not compel a state to accept suspected pirates, victims, or witnesses from a warship, but it provided political support to help to solve a vexing operational challenge. For many states, the resolution filled a critical policy void, providing a political basis for greater action. More broadly, the resolution set the tone for increased international partnership and cooperation.

The United Nations Security Council would approve six additional resolutions over the next three years condemning piracy off the Somali coast, more than on any other maritime issue. Counterpiracy operations foreshadow a new period of diplomatic and operational collaboration, from information sharing to multinational and regional meetings that address legal and jurisdictional challenges.

Alignment within a government is equally critical. The dramatic rescue of Captain Richard Phillips, the master of M/V *Maersk Alabama*, by U.S. Special Operations Forces in 2009 was a seminal event in countering maritime piracy. The attack on the *Alabama* was the first successful hijacking of a U.S.-flagged vessel by pirates in more than 150 years. The response to the attack on the ship involved coordination among multiple departments within the U.S. government and was conducted under the procedures sets forth in the presidentially approved Maritime Operational Threat Response (MOTR) plan. The plan has been used more than 750 times since its inception to integrate federal agencies and departments in the response to maritime threats, which could include, in addition to piracy, drug trafficking, human smuggling, illegal fishing, and terrorism. Following the *Maersk Alabama* incident, plans were developed to create an office to manage the MOTR process, culminating in the establishment of the Global MOTR Coordination Center in 2010.

Most threats occurring in the maritime domain involve multiple nations, and the international response to piracy has also spawned "whole of world" initiatives at the United Nations and the International Maritime Organization to enhance operational antipiracy collaboration. One prominent example is Shared Awareness and Deconfliction (SHADE) meetings for more than 30 nations involved in counterpiracy patrols off the Somali coast. SHADE represents a pioneering and strategically invaluable venue to discuss best practices and operational activities. Earlier in the decade, the Regional Cooperation Agreement on Combating Piracy and Armed Robbery against Ships in Asia (ReCAAP) entered into force. ReCAAP was the first treaty dedicated solely to combating piracy, and it established the Information Sharing Centre (ISC) in Singapore. The ISC compiles and disseminates piracy-related information among member states.

Piracy is a global concern. Partnering, alignment, and diplomatic efforts have reduced the threat, but it still exists. Short of systemic improvements on the ground, attention must remain focused on holding pirates accountable for their criminal action and removing sanctuary. Piracy will remain a challenge because the operating space of the oceans is simply too large for any one nation to effectively patrol. This volume provides a comprehensive analysis of the U.S. and international antipiracy tools at our disposal. As *Contemporary Maritime Piracy* underscores, piracy will not end with the current Somali attacks. But the myriad national, regional, and international efforts that have arisen over the past few years have better positioned nations to address piracy and other maritime threats. The book is an essential reference for grasping where we have been in developing counterpiracy policy, law, and strategy, and the study provides a compelling glimpse of where we need to go.

Captain Brian Wilson, U.S. Navy (Retired)

Acknowledgments

When the luxury cruise ship *Seabourn Spirit* was attacked on a leisure voyage from Yemen to Kenya by Somali pirates in the fall of 2005, I was serving as oceans policy adviser for the Director of Strategic Plans & Policy, Joint Staff in the Pentagon. The ship had a large number of American citizens on board, and suddenly the gathering problem of piracy off the Horn of Africa became an important issue inside the Pentagon. The U.S. Navy had forces deployed in the western Indian Ocean and maintained routine patrols in the region to ensure freedom of navigation and to counter terrorism. But the Somali Basin is far from the normal operating area in the Arabian Gulf, and the tyranny of time, distance, and space meant that U.S. and allied warships could not deter many of the piracy attacks against merchant shipping.

The U.S. Fifth Fleet, which is located in Bahrain, did not have sufficient assets to provide continuous coverage of the Horn of Africa. Furthermore, even when U.S. naval forces successfully interdicted pirates at sea, as the USS *Churchill* did only two months after the *Seabourn Spirit* incident, they were left with a raft of difficult legal, political, and diplomatic problems. In order to deepen and complement U.S. naval capabilities in the fight against piracy, the commander of U.S. Central Command sought assistance from the Joint Chiefs of Staff to intercede with the Office of the Secretary of Defense and the Department of State. Piracy policy landed in the oceans policy portfolio, and I was lead for efforts by the U.S. armed forces to answer the call. Pentagon efforts included work with the State Department to negotiate a United Nations Security Council resolution against piracy off the coast of Somalia, which would declare that the crime was a threat to international peace and security. The resolution authorized states to use "all necessary means" under Chapter VII of the UN Charter in addressing the threat of maritime piracy. Following 18 months of seemingly endless intragovernmental and diplomatic discussions and rejoinders, UN Security Council Resolution 1816 was adopted at Turtle Bay.

A bevy of additional legal and political instruments to enhance the effectiveness of navy counterpiracy operations were needed, including bilateral agreements for the transfer and prosecution of suspected pirates, revision of outdated recommendations and guidance promulgated by the International Maritime Organization (IMO), and development of tactical guidance to U.S. operational commanders that were involved in the interdiction of suspected pirates. Specifically, commanding officers of warships sought protocols for the collection and handling of evidence, detention of suspected pirates, repatriation of victims and witnesses, and steps they could take to aid in the preparation of trial. Working in tandem with Captain Brian Wilson and then Captain David Gruber, my counterparts in the Office of the Secretary of Defense, we sought endorsement from the Vice Chairman of the Joint Chiefs of Staff and the Under Secretary of Defense for Policy to begin the process of "building out" U.S. and international law and policy, updating stale authorities to address contemporary maritime piracy.

The Pentagon efforts to burnish the legal and diplomatic "toolkit" marked the period of 2005–2009 as a renaissance in the development of maritime security protocols and authorities. As the legal and policy tools in the counterpiracy toolkit multiplied, it became apparent that there was value in producing a single volume that captured the most important elements. In 2009, when Steve Catalano, Senior Editor for Military History and Security Issues at Praeger Publishers, approached me to write such a book, I could not resist. I thought the study would have both practical utility and prove beneficial to scholars. Likewise, at the end of the process of editing and rewriting, I thank Steve and his team at Praeger, including Valentina Tursini, for their attention to the manuscript, and especially to Carmel Huestis for her incredibly exacting copyedit. Any shortcomings, of course, remain my own.

Research in this volume has been heavily influenced by my interaction with students and faculty at the U.S. Naval War College. The student body at the Naval War College includes both U.S. and foreign military officers and U.S. representatives of other departments and agencies who are serving in a one-year program leading to the award of the Master of Arts degree in National Security and Strategic Studies. I learn as much from these accomplished and seasoned midlevel and senior civilian professionals and military officers of all five branches of the armed forces as they do from me. They bring a wealth of policy acumen and operational and tactical experience to the legal and diplomatic aspects of maritime security.

Many of the War College students have operated in waters imperiled by piracy; they have flown fixed-wing reconnaissance missions over water and land, and conducted Lilly pad rotary-wing interdiction operations against pirates and terrorists at sea. They have operated throughout the world's oceans, boarded ships on the high seas, and conducted missions for the control and protection of civil shipping. Having worked with foreign vessel masters and crews, they understand how diplomacy and law unfolds in the oceans. They have operated with partner nations and developed coalition rules of engagement (ROE). In short, they are tested in the "real world." In the words of the iconic legal scholar Dean Roscoe Pound, these experienced students understand the difference between "law in books" and "law in action."[1] While in the classroom, they never failed to deliver a dose of reality to anodyne legal and diplomatic concepts.

I also wish to thank Professor John Norton Moore, the Walter L. Brown Professor of Law, and Director of the Center for Oceans Law & Policy and the Center for National Security Law at University of Virginia School of Law. As a mentor in rule of law, oceans law and policy, national security law and international law, Professor Moore has left an indelible mark on my thoughts about countering maritime piracy. Professor Moore also has provided a number of ideas for consideration in the fight against piracy, including a plan to curtail the payment of ransoms that is analogous to U.S. and international policy against payment of ransoms to free diplomatic hostages.

Professor Myron H. Nordquist, Associate Director at the Center for Oceans Law & Policy, has been instrumental in contributing to the concepts in this book. He has invited me to participate in numerous valuable conferences and meetings concerning oceans law and policy, and as a former U.S. Marine and expert in the international law of the sea, he always provides savvy and thoughtful judgment on issues of maritime security.

No book on contemporary maritime piracy could be written without recognizing the great influence of Dr. Martin Murphy and Dr. J. Peter Pham, whom I consider the deans of modern counterpiracy scholarship. Murphy is the preeminent navalist and renowned expert on irregular maritime security and warfare; Pham is the leading expert on the strategic and security consequences of African politics. Both men are brilliant scholars, and together, their writings constitute collected "masterworks" of essential thought on contemporary maritime piracy. If this volume supplements their work by adding a thorough analysis of the international diplomatic and legal dimensions of piracy, it will have succeeded.

This study has benefited from the mentoring and suggestions of numerous additional scholars, including Ted McDorman, Faculty of Law, University of Victoria; Robert C. Beckman, Director of the Centre for International Law (CIL) and the head of its program in Ocean Law and Policy and Associate Professor in the Faculty of Law, National University of Singapore; Dr. Samuel P. Menefee, Maury Fellow, Center for Oceans Law & Policy and Senior Associate of the Center for National Security Law, University of Virginia School of

Law; J. Ashley Roach (CAPT, JAGC, USN, ret.), formerly of the Office of the Legal Adviser in the U.S. Department of State; and Dr. Frank Wiswall, *Honoris Causa* Vice President, Comité Maritime International and the International Maritime Law Institute, who was involved in development of the 1988 "Achille Lauro" Convention.

I am especially indebted to Brian Wilson (CAPT, JAGC, USN, ret.), former oceans policy adviser for the Office of the Under Secretary of Defense for Policy and now Deputy Director, Global Maritime Operational Threat Response (MOTR) Coordination Center located at U.S. Coast Guard Headquarters. Captain Wilson wrote the foreword to this volume, and no one has more experience in developing interagency solutions to complex maritime problems. It is an honor to have his deft pen and sharp mind provide a prologue to the book. Captain David Gruber, JAGC, USN, also a former oceans policy adviser for the Office of the Under Secretary of Defense (Policy), helped to form my views on piracy in the "early days" of 2006 while we worked together in the Pentagon—consulting with each other several times a day—to develop a unified Department of Defense counterpiracy policy. Dave's observation in 2006 that the United States and the international community do not need a piracy policy so much as they need a Somalia policy rings more true than ever.

This work has benefited immensely from the rest of the academic community of the U.S. Naval War College. Mrs. Alice Juda and the entire staff of the Naval War College Library were fantastic in helping me to locate sources. Professor Dennis Mandsager (CAPT, JAGC, USN, ret.), Chair of the International Law Department, Center for Naval Warfare Studies, U.S. Naval War College, and Professor Raul "Pete" Pedrozo (CAPT, JAGC, USN, ret.), International Law Department, Naval War College, both served as staff judge advocates for U.S. Pacific Command, and they bring a wealth of experience and operational law wisdom to the problems of maritime security that continually reshape my views. Professor Mandsager and Robert C. "Barney" Rubel (CAPT, USN, ret.), Dean of the Center for Naval Warfare Studies, U.S. Naval War College, have created an academic environment that promotes teaching and scholarly research and that funds engagement with other experts, making the Department and Center an ideal place for practical research and theoretical inquiry. "Pete" Pedrozo is a wealth of knowledge and experience in international law, and this volume benefited particularly from his insight.

Finally, Vice Admiral (select) James P. "Phil" Wisecup (USN), President, U.S. Naval War College, and Ambassador Mary Ann Peters (ret.), Provost, U.S. Naval War College, have provided the strategic leadership that makes the institution the preeminent center of excellence for addressing a variety of strategic and security issues. This work would not have been possible without their strong leadership and support for scholarly inquiry. This study reflects the views of the author alone and does not represent the official policy or position of the Department of Defense.

With the murder by Somali pirates of four Americans, Jean and Scott Adam and Phyllis Macay and Bob Riggle, on board the yacht *Quest* in February 2011, there is renewed urgency in the fight against piracy. The *Quest* hijacking precipitated a review of U.S. counterpiracy policy by the Obama administration, and it is clear that more must be done on land and at sea. It is my hope that this short volume helps to inform that effort to eradicate piracy from the seas.

Naval War College,
Newport, Rhode Island
April 2011

Note

1. Roscoe Pound, *Law in Books and Law in Action*, 44 American Law Review 12, 13 (1910). Pound admonished his students, "Let us not become legal monks." At 36.

Abbreviations

ADMM	ASEAN Defense Ministers Meeting
AIMS	Africa Integrated Maritime Strategy
AIS	Automatic Identification System
AK	Avtomat Kalashnikova (Soviet and Russian 7.62 mm assault rifle)
AMISOM	African Union Mission in Somalia
AOR	Area of Operations
ASEAN	Association of Southeast Asian Nations
ASG	Abu Sayyaf Group
ASLP	Archipelagic Sea Lanes Passage
ASWJ	Ahlu Sunna wal Jama
AU	African Union
BIMCO	Baltic and International Maritime Council
BMP	Best Management Practices
CDEM	Construction, Design, Equipping and Manning
CGPCS	Contact Group on Piracy off the Coast of Somalia
CLIA	Cruise Lines International Association
CMF	Commander, Maritime Forces
CMI	Comité Maritime International
COP	Common Operating Picture
CS/PD	Strategic Communications and Public Diplomacy
CSDP	Common Security and Defense Policy, EU
CSO	Company Security Officer
CTF	Combined Task Force
DDG	Guided Missile Destroyer
EDF	European Development Fund
EEZ	Exclusive Economic Zone
EiS	Eye in the Sky
EMPS	Marine Environmental Management and Protection System
ETA	Estimated Time of Arrival
EU	European Union

EUMC	European Union Military Committee
FRAGO	Fragmentary Order
FY	Fiscal Year
GCC	Gulf Cooperation Council
GDP	Gross Domestic Product
GMCC	Global MOTR Coordination Center
GOA	Gulf of Aden
GT	Group Transit
IBIA	Interferry International Bunker Industry Association
IBTA	International Bulk Terminals Association
ICC	International Chamber of Commerce
ICC	International Criminal Court
ICS	International Chamber of Shipping
ICTR	International Criminal Tribunal for Rwanda
ICTY	International Tribunal for the Former Yugoslavia
IGP&I	International Group of P&I Clubs
ILC	International Law Commission
IMB	International Maritime Bureau
IMCA	International Marine Contractors Association
IMO	International Maritime Organization
IMRF	International Maritime Rescue Federation
INTERCARGO	International Association of Dry Cargo Ship-owners
INTERPOL	International Criminal Police Organization
INTERTANKO	International Association of Independent Tanker Owners
IOCS	International Outreach and Coordination Strategy
IPTA	International Parcel Tankers Association
IRTC	Internationally Recommended Transit Corridor
ISAF	International Sailing Federation
ISC	Information Sharing Centre
ISF	International Shipping Federation
ISPS	International Ship and Port Facility Security Code
ITF	International Transport Workers' Federation
ITLOS	International Tribunal for the Law of the Sea
IUU	Illegal, Unreported, and Unregulated Fishing
JHC	Joint Hull Committee
JWC	Joint War Committee, Lloyds Market Association
LNG	Liquefied Natural Gas
LPG	Liquefied Propane Gas
LRAD	Long Range Acoustic Device
LRIT	Long Range Identification and Tracking
MARLO	Maritime Liaison Office Bahrain
MDA	Maritime Domain Awareness
MEH	Marine Electronic Highway
MEND	Movement for the Emancipation of the Niger Delta
MEPC	Marine Environmental Protection Committee

MLA	Maritime Law Association (United States)
MOTR	Maritime Operational Threat Response Plan
MOU	Memorandum of Understanding
MOWCA	Maritime Organization of West and Central Africa
MSC	Maritime Safety Committee
MSCHOA	Maritime Safety Centre—Horn of Africa
MSP	Malacca Straits Patrol
MSSIS	Maritime Safety and Security Information System
MTSA	Maritime Transportation Security Act of 2002
NATO	North Atlantic Treaty Organization
NAVFOR	Naval Force
NDAA	National Defense Authorization Act
NOC	Naval Operations Concept
NOTMAR	Notice to Mariners
NSC	National Security Council
OAS	Organization of African States
OAU	Organization of African Union
OCIMF	Oil Companies International Marine Forum
OEF	Operation Enduring Freedom
P&I	Protection and Indemnity
PA	Public Affairs
PIU	Project Implementation Unit, Djibouti Code of Conduct
PRC	Piracy Reporting Centre, International Maritime Bureau
PSC	Political and Security Committee, Council of the EU
RCC	Rescue Coordination Center
ReCAAP	Regional Agreement on Combating Piracy and Armed Robbery against Ships in Asia
RMSI	Regional Maritime Security Initiative
ROE	Rules of Engagement
RPG	Rocket Propelled Grenade
SAR	Search and Rescue
SCI	Seamen's Church Institute
SHADE	Shared Awareness and Deconfliction
SIGTTO	Society of International Gas Tanker and Terminal Operators
SLOC	Sea Lines of Communication
SOLAS	1974 Safety of Life at Sea Convention
SPINS	Special Instructions
SPM	Self-Protective Measures
SSA	Ship Security Assessment
SSAS	Ship Security Alert System
SSO	Ship Security Officer
SSP	Ship Security Plan
SUA	1988 Convention for the Suppression of Unlawful Acts against the Safety of Maritime Navigation
TFG	Transitional Federal Government

TINA	Royal Institution of Naval Architects
TWIC	Transportation Worker Identification Credential
UKMTO	United Kingdom Maritime Trade Operations
ULCC	Ultra Large Crude Carrier
UNCLOS	1982 United Nations Convention on the Law of the Sea
UNODC	UN Office on Drugs and Crime
UNSC	UN Security Council
UNTS	United Nations Treaty Series
USCG	United States Coast Guard
USN	United States Navy
USTS	United States Treaty Series
VLCC	Very Large Crude Carrier
VRS	Voluntary Reporting Scheme
WFP	World Food Program
WG	Working Group
WSC	World Shipping Council
YTW	Yemeni Territorial Waters

INTRODUCTION

The Oceans and the Genealogy of Piracy

Maritime piracy is an historic problem, but after two decades of decline it has surged in recent years. The International Maritime Organization (IMO), a specialized agency of the United Nations (UN), has recorded 5,667 piracy attacks against international shipping since 1984.[1] In 2009, the London-based international organization received 406 reports of piracy and armed robbery against ships, an increase of 106 or 24.6 percent from 2008.[2] Similarly, the International Maritime Bureau (IMB), a branch of the International Chamber of Commerce and the industry organization that tracks piracy attacks, reports that worldwide there were nearly 3,000 attempted or successful maritime piracy attacks during the period 2000–2009.

Today the areas at greatest risk of piracy are the Horn of Africa, including offshore Somalia, the Gulf of Aden (GOA), the western Indian Ocean, the Arabian Sea, and the Red Sea. In Asia, the waters surrounding Indonesia, Malaysia, and India are the highest threat corridors. Of the 980 successful maritime piracy incidents during the five-year period of 2005–2009, 527 involved theft of goods on board a ship. Hijacking and kidnapping, the model of piracy made infamous by the Barbary pirates of old and contemporary pirates off the coast of Somalia, occurred 159 times during the same period. In 2009, 867 seafarers were captured and held for ransom off the Horn of Africa.

In the first six months of 2010, there were 33 ships attacked in the GOA, compared to 86 during the corresponding period of 2009, although the number of attacks in the wider Somali basin and Indian Ocean has remained essentially level, at 49 and 51, respectively. Furthermore, while Somali pirates hijacked 27 ships with 544 seafarers taken for ransom in the first half of 2009, they seized 30 vessels and 495 crew members over the same period in 2010. Somali pirates successfully hijacked 45 ships in 2009 and 49 ships in 2010.

Of the 2010 figures, 10 successful attacks occurred in the Gulf of Aden and 7 in the internationally recognized transit corridor, which offers security escorts by coalition warships. As of January 24, 2010, Somali pirates were holding 26 ships and their crews for ransom.

Most maritime pirates seek to steal goods or cash on board a ship, seize the ship and its cargo for resale, or take the master and crew hostage and hold them for ransom. Stealing cash, equipment, electronics, clothes, or even the ship itself, is the favored model of piracy in most of the world, including Southeast Asia, South Asia, South America, and the Gulf of Guinea in West Africa. For the most part, piracy involves armed robbery beyond the territorial sea of a coastal state, and it is generally apolitical, except perhaps in the Gulf of Guinea. Along the coastline of Nigeria, insurgents use piracy as a means to compel redistribution of the country's oil wealth. Drilling rigs and offshore installations have been attacked and foreign oil workers have been kidnapped. Nigerian pirates seek to siphon wealth from the country's oil industry as a means of altering the political map of the country, but in most places piracy is a crime of opportunity and gain, not a political act.

Maritime piracy is a function of a lack of governance on land.[3] Consequently, the most successful efforts to suppress piracy are shore-based political solutions.[4] Whether securing the Hansa trade in the Baltic Sea in the 14th century, or protecting merchant shipping along the Suez Canal route in the GOA in the 21st century, establishment of peace, good government, and the rule of law on land is the best method of maintaining order at sea.[5] But although piracy emerges from the land, its effects reverberate throughout the seas. Through the ages and around the world, the varied nature of maritime piracy has been shaped by the social, political, and economic milieu of the region and of the era. The fertile geography of the vast oceans of the planet has served as the backdrop, a perilous expanse of anonymity.[6]

The Evolution of the Order of the Oceans

The oceans are a continuous, global body of water comprising 71 percent of the surface of the Earth.[7] The unified world ocean has an area of more than 139 million square miles (361 million square kilometers) and a total volume of 322,280,000 cubic miles (1,347,000,000 cubic kilometers), comprising 97 percent of the water on the planet.[8] Frozen seawater trapped at the North and South Poles accounts for another 2.2 percent of the world's water.[9] Relatively little is known about seabed topography, as only 10 percent of the seafloor has been mapped with advanced instrumentation—mostly in the coastal zone.[10]

With a relatively free interchange of water and aquatic life among the oceans, we should think in terms of the seas as being a single, unfathomable, and vast body of water. The interconnected quality of the seas has made the oceans an essential route for regional cabotage (intracontinental) shipping and transcontinental voyages, including commercial trade; a regular domain of military training, maneuver, and strategic mobility; and a vector for migration, smuggling, and trafficking; and the transmission of disease.[11]

As a sphere principally useful for mobility—shipping is by far the most efficient method of transporting large quantities of heavy cargo and material long distances—the oceans have had a profound effect on world politics, demographics, and economics. Large population centers emerged along oceans and rivers. Furthermore, in ancient time as well as the present, the oceans serve as the planet's geopolitical fulcrum. Early civilizations emerged along the Nile delta and the fertile Tigris-Euphrates watershed. In the modern period, Tokyo, New York, and London provided pathways to the sea. Today most of the world's large, primate cities lie along the coastlines. Most of the fish congregate near the shore, where they can be more easily caught for food, and most of the shipping runs along the coast. Three-quarters of the world's population now assembles along the shorelines. Although the global oceans are interconnected to form one immense body of water, the social and political density of regional and coastal seas means that most piracy occurs within 200 miles of the shore. The unity of the oceans is the simple physical fact underlying the dispositive value of sea power to shape events on the land.[12]

In the ancient world, Greek civilization and the Roman Empire coalesced around the Mediterranean Sea. The Ottoman expansion during the Dark Ages relied on control of the eastern Mediterranean—an advance that appeared unstoppable until it was vanquished in the mighty sea engagement at Lepanto in 1571.

Natural Law and the Oceans

The vastness of the maritime domain and the importance of the seas to world order drove states to fashion universal principles for sail and steam—common principles that could be used to administer the ungoverned space. The rules concerning the oceans predate modern international law and the rise of modern diplomacy. Oceans law was a precursor to the 1648 Peace of Westphalia, which ended the bloody Thirty Years War in Europe and prominently led to development of *jus gentium* or the modern law of nations. Frederick III, who ruled from 1440 to 1483, was the last emperor crowned in Rome by the pope. The weakening of the ecclesiastical order, which was accelerated by the Protestant Reformation, encouraged the development of a new source of authority to govern states that was based in law and not on the Church.[13] The cooperation among the cities and territories of the Hanseatic League, founded in 13th-century German lands and the Italian city-republics, provided early impetus for the development of international diplomacy. But the emergence of transcontinental travel by sail undertaken by a tiny group of seafaring pioneers revolutionized oceans law and diplomacy.

In the late 15th century, the Portuguese and Spanish empires asserted control over the immeasurable and unexplored oceans of Africa, the Americas, and Asia. The voyages of Christopher Columbus ignited a controversy over ownership of the newly discovered continents in the west. The division of the world ocean into two spheres—one controlled by the Kingdom of Castile (Spain), the other by Portugal—was memorialized by Pope Alexander VI in the papal bull *Inter Caetera* in 1493, and adjusted slightly in favor of Portugal in the Treaty of Tordesillas the following year. Using a meridian located 370 leagues west of the Cape Verde Islands, which were already owned by Portugal, the two Latin powers laid claim to all of the sea and land area of the New World.

Latin bipolar hegemony was extended to the east, as separate spheres for Spain and Portugal were demarcated in Asia with the Treaty of Saragossa in 1529. The Treaty of Saragossa recognized Portuguese ownership of the Moluccas Islands (in modern-day Indonesia) and Spanish ownership of the Philippine Islands. The land and sea west of Indonesia was granted to Portugal, opening the way for Portuguese "ownership" of outposts in India, such as Goa, and Africa. The oceans and land surrounding the Philippines and westward to the New World, excepting present-day Portuguese-speaking Brazil, were recognized as under suzerainty of Spain.

The Columbian exchange—the epochal exchange of animals, plants, humans, and cultures between Europe and the New World—transpired over sea links. With the rise of Protestantism in Central Europe, however, the power of the Latin Catholic kingdoms waned. The Dutch War of Independence against Spain, also called the Eighty Years War (1568–1648), was a revolt of the Dutch Provinces against Spain, sovereign of the Hapsburg Netherlands. The war overlapped and broadened into the devastation of the Thirty Years War (1618–1648)—the Bourbon and Hapsburg rivalry that engulfed Central Europe. The Thirty Years War was perhaps the bloodiest in European history, and it inspired Italian theologian Alberico Gentili (1452–1608) and Dutch jurist Hugo Grotius (158–1645) to collect and publish collected laws of war and peace. The treatises these early masters produced reflected the accepted rules applicable to the global commons.

The rise of the Dutch Provinces and British world hegemony were global phenomena that leveraged the power of fleets the world over, and made possible only by international sea transportation. In perhaps the most memorable legal work of the early 17th century, Grotius repudiated Portugal's claim of entitlement to the waters of present-day Indonesia in Southeast Asia. The concept of a liberal world order formed the basis for his classic treatise on the freedom of the seas. Grotius championed unrestrained access to all the oceans for the Dutch United Provinces, and his work marked the rise of the first maritime power outside of Latin Europe. Although the concept of freedom of the seas was inherited from Rome and already was part of the lexicon, Grotius and Gentili added a veneer of natural law theology, arguing that the sea was by its very nature open to all men and its use common to all.[14]

Spain and Portugal proved unable to earn international acceptance for their vast claims over the seas. As the Iberian powers extracted great hordes of gold and silver from the New World and began founding agricultural colonies in the Americas, French, Dutch, and British sea raiders disregarded the papal bull and began targeting rich treasure fleets heavily laden with specie bound for the coffers of Spanish and Portuguese courts. Flouting the Treaty of Tordesillas, France, the nascent Dutch Republic, and eventually England, began to enter "Spanish" and "Portuguese" waters, disrupting the carrying trade and developing colonies in the New World.

Excluded from the original and restrictive Iberian maritime bargain, the newcomers adhered to a liberal view of the oceans based on freedom of the seas. At the same time, the concept of free seas was meaningless unless users also could be secure in their enjoyment of the oceans. Thus, freedom of the seas became inextricably bound to safety and security—freedom from attack by pirates in peacetime and from privateers and belligerent warships in time of war.

The Anglo-Saxon tradition embraced freedom of the seas as a natural component of the new world public order. The Dutch, British, and Americans were concerned with what today we would call "global governance," or the maintenance of the world system, rather than the narrow and parochial pursuit of national interest—"provincial myopia" in the words of the brilliant scholar Myres S. McDougal.[15] The liberal order of the oceans that prevailed as the law of the maritime commons throughout the modern period of the state system—from the 16th century until the present—encourages international engagement.

The globally accepted norm of free seas provided stability and predictability in international affairs, facilitated an explosion in commerce and cosmopolitan social and economic growth, and provided an enduring basis for the maintenance of minimum world public order.[16] The commitment to preserving freedom of the seas was backed by overwhelming sea power, and by making the issue a priority for Anglo-Saxon-American diplomacy. The liberal order of the oceans assumed iconic status, and all maritime powers championed the concept.

The connection between freedom of the seas and the understanding that such freedom had to include safety and security was a continual feature of the international law of the sea, and it would resurface during World War I and World War II, when Allied nations insisted that freedom of the seas included the right to be free from harm while transiting the oceans. The rise of American power, and during the Cold War the near-parity position of the Soviet Union, was a function of strategic sea power, which included the Kremlin's massive arsenal of ballistic missile submarines. A Soviet-American condominium based upon mutual interests recognized the oceans as a global commons, open to all nations. The two superpowers worked in tandem at the Third United Nations Conference on the Law of the Sea from 1973 to 1982 to enshrine broadly permissive rules for freedom of navigation and overflight throughout the seas. At the apex of the superpower rivalry, the two nations met at Jackson Hole, Wyoming, and affirmed the principle of freedom of navigation, even within the 12-nautical-mile territorial sea.[17]

While ensuring strategic stability, freedom of the seas fueled an explosion in world trade. During the past 50 years, container shipping and world trade have facilitated the rise of globalization, which is transforming the political and economic landscape of the planet. The order of the oceans has not been without challenge, however. Piracy is important today because it threatens to disrupt communication links among nations, impeding the flow of world trade in oil, oats, and automobiles, and every other imaginable product and commodity. Because the liberal world order is dependent upon free and unfettered use of the oceans, maritime piracy is hostile to political stability and economic prosperity. Once again, prosperity and liberty are irreconcilably bound to freedom of the seas.

Genealogy of the Crime of Piracy

The Latin word *pirata* is derived from *transire, a transeundo mare,* which signified a maritime knight or an admiral or commander at sea. *Pirata* means "to attempt" or "to attack." In Greek, the word *peirato* suggests something that is semi-sovereign, a description that captures the ancient dilemma over whether piracy was closer to naval warfare or merely a maritime crime. *Pirata* represents the historical genesis for a number of words in modern English, including the prefix *per*, which means, "to try" or "to risk." The words "peril," "experience," "expert," "empire," and, of course, "pirate" all are derived from the Latin original. Like the word "Viking," the word "piracy" denotes not just criminal marauding, but a seafaring way of life based upon maritime violence.

Historically, efforts to suppress maritime piracy were characterized as acts of littoral warfare rather than constabulary or police action. The Roman consul Pompey (106 B.C.–48 B.C.) was issued a commission by the Roman senate to conduct a military campaign against pirates operating in the waters surrounding the Aegean islands, Crete, the Dodecanese Islands, and throughout Asia Minor. Early Mediterranean pirates were not viewed as criminals or outlaws, but rather enemies to be crushed in battle. Pompey's military genius defeated the brigands in fairly short order, but rather than killing or imprisoning them, he treated the survivors humanely. The remaining pirates and their communities were resettled to pursue legitimate work as farmers.

Later, Greek historian and philosopher Plutarch (circa A.D. 46–120), who eventually became a Roman citizen and was renamed Lucius Mestrius Plutarchus, recounted the Roman Empire's continuing war against piracy in the eastern Mediterranean. With Rome dominating the Mediterranean Sea, the view of piracy as having the same character of warfare persisted for 1,000 years. Only relatively recently has maritime piracy been regarded as a crime of plunder and depredation at sea, rather than a tool of military conquest.

It was not until the rise of England in the early modern period that nations began to move away from thinking about the concept of piracy as a form of warfare. With the introduction of the granting of letters of marque and reprisal, governments issued licenses authorizing private vessels (privateers) to attack and capture enemy vessels. In 1688, for example, King James II (1633–1701) abdicated the throne of England and fled to France and then to Ireland. He granted letters of marque to a network of privateers that preyed on English shipping as part of his campaign to regain the English throne, which had been seized by William of Orange during the Glorious Revolution. Captured ships could be brought before admiralty courts and condemned and sold for profit, providing incentive for private ships to supplement naval fleets in targeting enemy shipping. Freelance pirates who did not operate under authority of such a letter of marque became associated with outlawry.

By 1700 the English statute against piracy defined the act as a crime that could only be committed by "subjects or denizens of the kingdom," not foreign governments. This modern approach reflected a view that already had become popular among the Renaissance lawyers, including Catholic theologian Gentili, who defined piracy as unlawful violence—outlawry—essentially armed robbery at sea. Presciently, Gentili suggested that whether an act constitutes piracy or warfare depends on whether the acts are committed on behalf of a government that is recognized in international law.

Gradually however the notion that piracy reflected private motives of individuals acting outside of the sanction of the state, rather than a political struggle or warfare conducted by the state, gained greater traction. Piracy did not occur when a government acted against the merchant ships of a belligerent power during wartime because such attacks were merely part of the international conflict. In order for an attack to be piracy, all shipping, and even lucrative targets on the beach, had to be equally vulnerable. Whether a ship belonged to a neutral state or a belligerent, it sailed at risk of assault by pirates. Pirates were the criminals of all mankind.

The United States inherited the English common law against piracy. Still, the issue of whether piracy was an act of war or a criminal act was slow to resolve within the young republic. During the era of the Barbary pirates, George Washington viewed piracy as illegal state-sponsored conduct. President Jefferson also focused on dealing with the Barbary States using a mixture of military force and payment of tribute. Similarly, during the American Civil War, the Union maintained that the Confederate states were conducting an unrecognized belligerency at sea by licensing privateering commerce raiders to target Northern shipping. One hundred years later, as late as 1975, President Ford would characterize the unprovoked Cambodian attack on the U.S.-flagged merchant vessel *Mayaguez* as a piracy attack. Although today the term "piracy" is appropriate only for attacks committed by nongovernmental gangs, it is still used as a shorthand description for any despicable act of violence in the oceans.

Despite the American claims connecting piracy to state action and tantamount to naval warfare, U.S. law adopted the British view that piracy was indeed a crime committed by individuals rather than an act of war committed by a state. The first U.S. statute on piracy, which dates to 1790, represented the emergent view that piracy was not an offense against the law of nations, but rather a felony committed on the high seas.

Both the United States and the United Kingdom bypass jurisdictional questions, permitting courts to prosecute any person who has committed an act of piracy, regardless of nationality. The natural law position that emerged from the Renaissance Mediterranean held that international law applies to individuals, even though the law of nations lacks an effective international enforcement mechanism to bring people before a court. In a natural law view, states must step in to prosecute individual pirates because the international community has no ability to do so. The positivist legal tradition disagreed with this position. Believing that international law applies only among states, positivists maintained that maritime piracy is only a part of state or municipal criminal law, not a universal crime "injurious to God" and a violation of the law of nations.

Notes

1. IMO Doc. MSC.4/Circ.164, Reports on Acts of Piracy and Armed Robbery against Ships, December 3, 2010, at 2.
2. IMO Doc. MSC.4/Circ.152, Reports on Acts of Piracy and Armed Robbery against Ships—Annual Report 2009, March 29, 2010, at 2.
3. Martin N. Murphy, *Solving Somalia*, Proceedings of the U.S. Naval Institute 30, 31, 33–34 (July 2010).
4. J. Peter Pham, *The Somali Solution to the Somali Crisis*, 6 Harvard Africa Policy Journal 71, 72–75 (2009–2010).
5. David K. Bjork, *Piracy in the Baltic: 1375–1398*, 18 Speculum 39, 40 (January 1943).
6. William Langewiesche, *The Outlaw Sea: A World of Freedom, Chaos, and Crime* 1–8 (2005).
7. From the Greek word, Ὠκεανὸς, or *okeanos* ("Oceanus").

8. Matthew A. Charette and Walter H.F. Smith, *The Volume of Earth's Ocean*, 23 Oceanography 112–114 (June 2010).

9. Table 1, *Physics FactBook: An Encyclopedia of Scientific Essays* (Glen Elert, ed., 2001), http://hypertextbook.com/facts/2001/SyedQadri.shtml.

10. Charette and Smith, *The Volume of Earth's Ocean*, at 112–114.

11. The bubonic plague or "Black Death" is thought to have entered Venice via trading vessels from farther along the eastern Mediterranean. Similarly, Europeans introduced smallpox and other infectious diseases into the Americas, devastating the native populations. See, e.g., Jared Diamond, *Guns, Germs and Steel: A Short History of Everybody for the Last 13,000 Years* 195–215 (2005).

12. John Halford Mackinder, *Britain and the British Seas* 12 (2d ed. 1907).

13. Lori F. Damrosch, et al., *International Law: Cases and Materials* xxviii (4th ed. 2001).

14. See, e.g., Alberico Gentili, *Il De Iure Belli Libri Tres* 24 (Oxford: Clarendon Press: John C. Rolfe, trans. 1933 [1612]) and Theodor Meron, *Common Rights of Mankind in Gentili, Grotius and Suarez*, 85 American Journal of International Law 110, 113–114 (1991).

15. Myres S. McDougal and Florentino P. Feliciano, *Law and Minimum World Public Order: The Legal Regulation and International Coercion* 844–845 (1961).

16. McDougal and Feliciano, *Law and Minimum World Public Order*, at 854 and Thomas W. Fulton, *Sovereignty of the Sea* 544–545 (1911).

17. Union of Soviet Socialist Republics—United States: Joint Statement with Attached Uniform Interpretation of Rules of International Law Governing Innocent Passage, done at Jackson Hole, Wyoming, September 23, 1989, 28 International Legal Materials 1444, 1445 (1989). See also, Erick Franckx, *Further Steps in the Clarification of the Soviet Position on the Innocent Passage of Foreign Warships through Its Territorial Sea*, 19 Georgia Journal of International and Comparative Law 535 (1989) and John W. Rolph, *Freedom of Navigation and the Black Sea Bumping Incident: How Innocent Must Innocent Passage Be?* 135 Military Law Review 137 (Winter 1992).

CHAPTER 1

From Antiquity to the Golden Age

The development of the contemporary understanding of the concept of maritime piracy runs through the Mediterranean Sea of ancient Greece and Rome, the Baltic and North Atlantic, modern and medieval Europe—the Latin West and Orthodox East, the Islamic world, the littoral waters of the Asia-Pacific, and the "golden age" of Caribbean piracy.

Early piracy was used as a method of warfare to seize luxury goods, valuable commodities, and slaves from rival powers. The ill-gotten wealth often was traded to inland communities for finished goods. Piracy was a tool of warfare and state policy, as well as a criminal endeavor committed by nonstate groups who pillaged for private gain. Since piracy could arise as a form of crime or as a warfare strategy, the original definitions of piracy were quite flexible.

Historically, virtually any form of violence or depredation committed at sea was considered maritime piracy.[1] Most people living in seaside communities along the shores of the Adriatic Sea, the Black Sea, and the Mediterranean Sea practiced, either deliberately or in self-defense, what we would consider as "piracy." Even communities that were not directly engaged in piracy often willingly provided supplies or safe havens to the sea raiders, trading with bandits either out of filial, tribal, or religious sympathy, or even strictly for the commercial benefits of business. There is no single template for what crimes constitute piracy, and the evolution of the term has followed a meandering course.

Piracy in Antiquity—Greece and Rome

In the Western world, piracy was a constant feature of the political geography of ancient coastal communities situated along the Mediterranean coastline. In the west the story of piracy begins in the second millennium BC in the Minoan-Mycenaean world. In the first half of the era, Minoan civilization dominated the microcosm of the eastern Mediterranean. As long ago as the Mycenaean civilization, raiding communities strung along the Greek shores and on the island of Crete became wealthy from piracy and plunder, as well as legitimate trade by sea. The ancients claim the mythical king Minos was first to form a navy.[2] It is said he used naval forces to defeat piracy, assert control over the Aegean, and establish settlements on most of the Cycladic islands, where he appointed his sons to govern.[3] But Minoan civilization gave way to the Peloponnese and central Greece.[4]

By the 15th century BC the leading city of Mycenae dominated the Aegean Sea, and the era from 1600 BC to 1100 BC is called the "Mycenaean Period." During the 13th century BC, "sea peoples" of the Aegean and Adriatic attacked the coastal communities of the Hittite Empire in Asia Minor and Egypt. The sea peoples laid waste to many of the ports and villages along the eastern Mediterranean. The reach of the Mycenaean extended at least to Africa. Ancient inscriptions on the tomb of Pharaoh Ramses III "the Great" at Medinet Habu (City of Habu) and the vast temple complex at Karnak in modern Luxor, Egypt, describe incursions by sea raiders from the north. A massive naval battle was fought in 1186 BC off the Nile Delta, in which a marauding flotilla of sea peoples suffered disastrous defeat by the Egyptian fleet. The decisive victory by Ramses the Great led to the rapid decline of the threat of the sea peoples to coastal communities in the eastern Mediterranean and North Africa.

The Greek city-states and the Phoenicians were also maritime civilizations of early classic antiquity. The Phoenicians, which were based in the Levant, spread through the western Mediterranean as far west as Spain. Providing naval forces to the Achaemenid Persian Empire, the Phoenicians blurred the line between naval warfare and piracy.

Reliable records of maritime piracy, however, do not survive until the emergence of the Greek city-states. The Greeks traveled throughout the Black Sea and as far south as the Red Sea. In the *Odyssey*, Homer describes the island of Crete as a hotbed of piracy. The city-state of Athens rose as the dominant naval power in the fifth century BC and began to counter maritime piracy from Crete. Alexander the Great ushered in an era of Macedonian rule, and the period was marked by an emphasis on land warfare in the Near East and Egypt. In the second century BC, the Greek maritime city-state of Rhodes finally conducted a decisive war against the pirates on Crete, clearing the island of safe havens.

The Roman Empire expanded through continuous and preemptive application of the doctrine of "just war," a series of defensive invasions and preventive aggression designed to protect Rome and keep the peace.[5] The war against the Illyrians near the end of the third century BC, for example, was waged to protect nearby Italian and Greek cities along the Adriatic. The Romans conducted a series of punitive expeditions against pirates along the Dalmatian coast on the Adriatic (present-day Croatia) during the second century BC, but the corsairs were not completely cleared from the seas until their defeat by the Roman general Pompey the Great (Gnaeus Pompeius Magnus) in the mid-first century. Similarly, the Romans conquered the Balearic Islands in 123–122 BC between Spain and Algeria by claiming the goal of suppressing piracy, although the historian Livy describes the inhabitants as a peaceful people who were prone instead to "spending the summer lying around naked."[6]

At the end of the second century BC, Rome was preoccupied with defending against incursions by Germanic tribes that were pressing along the northern border. Rome did, however, conduct an extended campaign against piracy in the eastern Mediterranean Sea, encouraged by allies such as Rhodes, to bring greater safety to the region. The need to impose a semblance of security in the eastern Mediterranean and the quest for glory, however, provided the impetus for periodic campaigns against maritime piracy in the Mediterranean. By the dawn of the first century BC, Rome began to emerge as the undisputed great power in the west. Although the Roman Empire was a militaristic and imperialist superpower, it also took seriously its image as the benefactor and protector of weaker states.

Until the Roman Empire pacified the Mediterranean, the sea was essentially ungoverned, creating a hospitable environment that made piracy thrive.[7] Archeologists have discovered ample evidence of early Roman writings, such as those found on an enormous monument at Delphi, that the empire had a well-developed code of law to deter and punish piracy.[8] Under the law, Roman consuls were instructed to ensure that kings in alliance with Rome, such as the ruler in Rhodes, withhold the use of territories from pirates.

Pompey the Great led Rome's greatest counterpiracy naval campaign, which was targeted at the Cilicians. The Cilicians were among the most notorious pirates of the ancient world. Based in Asia Minor, or present-day Turkey, they harried the coastal communities of the Levant and disrupted maritime trade from the Middle East to Europe. In 102 BC, when Marcus Antonius was still a middle-level city magistrate or praetor with his eye on the title of consul, Rome's highest magistracy, he led an expedition into Cilicia to suppress piracy. As a result of his victory, Antonius was elected to consulship in 99 BC.

Rome tended to attach the term "pirate" to anyone who opposed the empire, so it is difficult to dissect the motives for counterpiracy. Rome occupied the area of Cilicia in Asia Minor, ostensibly to deny pirates the ability to operate from a safe haven and ensure the safety of the sea lanes in the eastern

Mediterranean. Like most of Rome's defensive invasions, however, the absorption of Cilicia into the empire also had undeniable imperialist overtones. Was the imperial goal to promote freedom of navigation or expansion of the empire?

The war against Mithridates VI, king of Pontus and Armenia Minor in northern Anatolia (Turkey), epitomized the dual purpose of Rome's war against piracy. Mithridates ruled from about 119 BC to 63 BC, and he fought a series of battles against Rome between 89 BC and 63 BC. Cilician and Cretan pirates allied themselves with Mithridates, who besieged Roman-occupied Rhodes. But on land, the Roman army was supreme and gradually drove Mithridates out of Greece. Rome also invaded and occupied the island of Crete in order to sever the cooperation between Mithridates and the maritime pirates on the island.

In 74 BC a young aristocrat, Gaius Julius Caesar, was sailing to the island of Rhodes to undertake academic study, and during the voyage pirates set upon his ship. Caesar was captured and held for 38 days. He was released upon payment of ransom. Following his captivity, Caesar raised a small fleet at Miletos and tracked down the pirates, capturing most of them. The pirates were imprisoned at Pergamon near the Aegean coast in present-day Turkey. When Marcus Junius Silanus Torquatus, the Roman governor of Asia, failed to take action against the seafaring marauders, Caesar returned to their hideout and had the remaining brigands crucified.

When the Cilicians supported the slave revolt led by Spartacus in 73–71 BC, Rome renewed measures to sweep the seas of pirates. Gaius Verres, the governor-general of Sicily from 73 BC to 71 BC, was prosecuted by Cicero for widespread public corruption and dereliction of duty for failing to aggressively suppress maritime piracy. Verres was charged with absconding with public funds raised for the purpose of constructing a fleet to deal with the threat of escalating piracy.

Without increased Roman naval patrols, the pirates grew in strength and expanded their bold attacks westward to threaten the Italian coast. Communities along the Tiber River suddenly were vulnerable and the sea lines of communication between Rome and North Africa, Sardinia, Sicily, and Corsica were unsafe. At risk of having the capital city of Rome cut off from the critical wheat-producing areas that provided grain for the masses, in 67 BC Pompey the Great was offered an imperious or military dictatorship to rid the entire region of pirates. Nearly two decades later, Julius Caesar would become a rival of Pompey in the Roman Civil War.

In 49 BC Caesar would cross the Rubicon River to march on Rome and challenge Pompey.[9] But in 67 BC Pompey was regarded as Rome's leading general and savior of the republic. General Pompey was afforded sweeping antipiracy authority and vast resources to make the sea lanes safe, and he accomplished the mission in just 90 days. Leading a force of 500 ships and 120,000 Roman troops, Pompey divided his fleet among more than a dozen defensive zones, and positioned a large naval force around Cilicia, which is located along the northeastern shore of the Mediterranean Sea in modern-day Turkey.

Then his fleet started at Gibraltar and swept eastward toward Cilicia—killing pirates and driving them ahead of him as he went. The ships in the west were in the position of the hammer, and the fleet blockading Cilicia served as the anvil. Logistics bases in Rhodes, Cyprus, and Syria supplied the Roman fleet. The pirate ships could not match the small, fast Roman biremes in combat, and the cordon around Cilicia prevented escape by sea. Pompey landed marines at Cilicia and drove the pirates into the main pirate fortress of Coracesium on the Alanya peninsula.

The Cilician pirates made their last stand at the mountaintop Crow's Nest, where they were defeated in detail. Five hundred pirate ships were destroyed and 10,000 pirates were either killed in battle or executed. The counterpiracy campaign was wildly successful. The Mediterranean Sea was cleared of pirates for the first time in history, and Roman shipping would enjoy the security of the *Pax Romana* or "Roman Peace" until the fall of the empire in the west.

Caesar's heir, Gaius Julius Octavian, the future emperor Augustus, defeated a naval challenge by Sextus Pompeius, Pompey's surviving son, during 43–36 BC. Calling Pompeius a "pirate," for conducting maritime attacks against Rome from bases in Sardinia and Sicily, Augustus defeated him. Another rival, Mark Antony, was also defeated, and Augustus consolidated the empire's power under his monarchy. Once internal security was achieved throughout the empire, Augustus continued to provide maritime constabulary control over the Mediterranean Sea. Order was brought to the Mediterranean Sea, but as the empire declined in the west, a powerful new host of pirates emerged from the north.

Vikings and Nordic Raiding

Viking raiders began to move out of Scandinavia in the late Roman era.[10] These groups were chiefly from Denmark, Norway, and Sweden, and the people were relatively tall and often had red or blonde hair. The Vikings invaded scattered regions in Eastern and Western Europe. Coastal communities in England, Scotland, Ireland, and France lived in constant fear of Viking raids. Scandinavian seaborne pirates established numerous sites throughout Britain beginning in the late eighth century.

By about 800, the Danes established a strong central authority in Jutland, and they began to reach beyond their own territory for land, trade, and plunder. In Norway, rugged mountainous terrain and deeply indented fjords formed strong natural boundaries, separating communities and impeding development of a central government. Norway was divided into as many as 30 smaller kingdoms.

Vikings from throughout Scandinavia built oared long ships and deployed them on raiding expeditions, initiating what we today call the "Viking Age." The Viking Age of conquests coincided with a medieval warming period that stretched from about 800 to 1300, until the world cooled once again during the Little Ice Age, which lasted from about 1250 to 1850. During the warmer era, melting pack ice opened up the Baltic Sea and North Atlantic Ocean. The harsh Scandinavian climate made the northern region unable to support an expanding population, leading the Vikings to seek conquest and settlement abroad. The northern sea rovers were traders, colonizers, and explorers as well as plunderers, who settled the Faroe Islands, Iceland, parts of Scotland, Greenland, and even an area of Newfoundland in North America. A republic was founded in Iceland, which was governed by an annual assembly of elected officials called the *Althing*.

The Baltic Sea and North Atlantic Ocean were also theaters of medieval piracy. First, the notoriously harsh winters mean that large snowfalls block the roads. Second, even during the summer months, the dense forests and mountainous terrain make travel by land challenging. Finally, the high north was lightly settled, with vast distances separating communities. As a result, travel by sea was much faster, safer, and less expensive than land routes. The Scandinavians proved exceptionally proficient seafarers. Norse raiders both traded and looted along the coast of Western Europe as far south as the British Isles, and even made their way via river into Southern and Eastern Europe.

Striking seaside communities unexpectedly and with impunity, Vikings cultivated a fearsome reputation. Sometimes entire regions or seaside villages might be spared from pillage in exchange for the payment of tribute, called *danegeld*. Viking long ships were sleek and fast war machines, technologically advanced and well designed in comparison to other galleys. Agile long ships were deployed for reconnaissance and hit-and-run attacks. At full speed, long ships might go as fast as 14 or 15 knots—decisive in battle. The ships were constructed for expeditionary warfare. Long ships had a shallow draft, so they could enter inshore waters and river deltas, and be beached for amphibious assaults on land. For example, Vikings penetrated deep into Ireland by sailing up the River Shannon, building a harbor 60 miles (100 kilometers) from the coast. Although they were open vessels, long ships could travel great distances. But Vikings tended to use "knar" vessels for conducting long-distance trade, as the ships were wider and had a deeper draft than long ships.

By the end of the ninth century, Scandinavian raiders had established large-scale settlements in Britain, and asserted political rule over much of the British Isles. Settlers of Celtic Scotland and Ireland were from present-day

Norway. Vikings also pillaged the windy coastline of the European mainland, and sent a large force as far as the gates of Paris.[11] In 911, the Vikings conquered Normandy, which would later lead to Norman-French rule in England.

In 793, Viking raiders, probably from Norway, attacked the Lindisfarne monastery. The assault ignited a series of similar attacks that occurred over the following decades, as many monasteries in the north were destroyed. Iona was burned in 802, with the survivors fleeing to Kells with a Christian gospel, the Book of Kells. The raids continued sporadically until the 850s, when Viking armies stepped up their campaigns by embarking on a conquest of Britain.

The Vikings began to winter in England and were able to marshal large military forces sufficient to extort great sums of tribute from the British. In 991, for example, Danish Vikings were paid 4,500 kilograms of silver. Within 20 years, payment of danegeld rose to 22,000 kilograms of silver. In 1016, the Viking military leader Cnut or Canute the Great rose to power as king of England. By 1027, Cnut ruled Denmark, Norway, and parts of Sweden as well.

But Viking power began to wane after 1066, when, just one month before the Battle of Hastings, an English army under Saxon king Harold Godwinson turned back an invasion by the king of Norway, Harald Harada III, at the Battle of Stamford Bridge. Godwinson was subsequently defeated within four weeks by William I, or William the Conqueror, Duke of Normandy. William became known as William I of England after he seized control of the islands in 1066. William was a descendant of Scandinavian settlers in northern France, and his arrival across the Channel ended two centuries of rule by Danish and Norwegian Vikings throughout large tracts of England. The emergence of two newly unified territories—England and Scotland—was an indirect result of Scandinavian involvement in the affairs of Britain. The experience of the Vikings and their military conquest of Normandy, France and then the British Isles illustrate piracy as a method of warfare.

Ancient and Medieval Piracy in Asia—China and Japan

Piracy was ubiquitous throughout Asian history, and seafarers and coastal villages along the Indian Ocean, South China Sea, and East China Sea were vulnerable to attack and pillage. But in Asia, piracy was less a form of maritime warfare as it developed in the West, and more often associated with freelancing criminal gangs, or vast illicit enterprises that formed enormous secret societies. Large pirate havens along the southern coast of China, for example, could be relatively isolated from the rest of the empire, hidden behind entangling jungle and impenetrable, jagged mountains.

The pirates sought gold, silver, and slaves, but would also take anything of value, including rice. Japanese pirates in particular were renowned for rape, murder, and pillage of coastal towns. Observers living at the time recorded numerous instances of torture of men, women, and even infants.[12] Records show that many of the people arrested for piracy in Fujian and Guangdong had actually been victims who were abducted by pirates and impressed as a form of conscript labor into a life of crime.[13] The victims and the pirates usually emerged from the same marginal, poverty-stricken seaside communities of fishermen or sailors—people who were inescapably poor, unattached, and living on the edge.[14] Some seafarers would rotate in and out of piracy as a survival strategy, temporarily abandoning legitimate pursuits in order to get through hard economic times.

The *wokou* were Japanese pirates who raided the coastlines of China and Korea beginning in the 13th century until their decline in the 16th century. The Chinese term "wokou" is a combination of two ideographs: "wō" (倭), meaning "Japanese," and "kòu" (寇), referring to "bandit" or "invader." The word "wokou" in Korean is translated as "waegu" and in Japanese, as "wako." The term "wokou" is still used in China and Korea as a derogatory name for Japanese pirates.

The wokou or wako were lordless samurai (*ronin*), soldiers, merchants, and smugglers, and later many of them originated in China rather than Japan. Most wokou came from Tsushima and Hizen, southwest of Pusan across the Korean Strait. Attacks occurred intermittently against Korea and China for centuries. Japanese pirates conducted raids on the Korean peninsula and across the Yellow Sea in China. Pirates also emerged along the southern coast of China, and some Chinese posed as Japanese wokou, going so far as to operate from Japan in order to terrorize fellow Chinese.

The first wokou operating from Japan pillaged seaside towns in Korea during the early 13th century, as invading Mongols drew Korean soldiers away from the coasts to fight on the northern border. One of the first wokou raids occurred in the summer of 1223 on the southern coast of Korea, weakening the Goryeo dynasty. Mongol control of Korea was secured in 1273 through a strategic marriage between the Korean crown prince and the daughter of Kublai Khan. The Mongols turned the table on Japanese pirates, attacking their safe havens in Tsushima, Iki, and Kyushu. Staging from Korea, the Mongols invaded Japan outright in 1274 and 1281—on the latter occasion, the famous typhoon *kami kaze* ("divine wind") tore through the Mongol fleet, saving Japan from conquest.[15]

By 1350, Japanese wokou were once again launching large pirate raids against Korea, contributing to the collapse of the Goryeo dynasty. The Joseon dynasty rose to power in 1392 and began striking back hard against the wokou, especially those operating from the island of Tsushima between Korea and Japan. In the late 14th and early 15th centuries massive defensive attacks by Korea against wokou bases on Tsushima destroyed hundreds of pirate ships and freed large numbers of Korean captives. The largest of these assaults, known in Japan as the Oei Invasion, landed 17,000 Korean troops on Tsushima, forcing the wokou to enter into peace negotiations. The Koreans were more effective than the Chinese at resisting Japanese wokou. Unlike Chinese vessels, Korean naval ships were well built. Shipboard artillery was a Korean innovation, and as early as 1380 wokou pirate fleets were stalked by Korean warships and sent to the bottom of the sea.

Japanese pirates accelerated attacks on China in the 1350s. The mainland was a tempting target since the power of the Yuan dynasty was declining quickly.[16] From the chaos of famine, peasant revolt, and plagues raging throughout China, Zhu Yuanzhang (1328–1398) founded the Ming dynasty. At least initially, the Ming organized effective resistance to Japanese pirates. In 1378 and 1380 the shogun Ashikaga Yoshimitsu tried to open trade with China, but was rebuffed. But within a short time, 400 wokou samurai were involved in a plot with a Chinese conspirator to assassinate the Ming emperor. The samurai visited China under the pretense of paying tribute, but they had hidden gunpowder and swords in wax candles. The plot was discovered.[17] In response the Ming dynasty forbid civil trade with Japan in an effort to expel the wokou.

Instead of stemming the power of the wokou, however, the ban on trade drove Chinese merchants to the black market and into a cooperative relationship with the Japanese pirates. The wokou and their Chinese counter-parts began to cooperate in the early 16th century. Wokou mixed with Chinese seafarers, and the groups operated throughout East Asia and the Yangtze River delta. Sometimes local Chinese served as guides and scouts for the pirates—often coerced into service in order to save their own lives.

As Japan descended into war among rival shogunates or *bakufu*, the Ming Empire consolidated its power around an enormous army. The Ming rulers also cut off foreign trade except for the imperial tribute system of exchange, in which luxury goods and military supplies were obtained from abroad. Foreign travel was also outlawed. While the ban was not completely effective at keeping wokou at bay, it helped to insulate Chinese merchants from maritime piracy.[18]

In terms of population and territory, China was much stronger. Conventional metrics of Chinese power, however, belied the vulnerability of isolated coastal communities to resist wokou raids. The wokou inflicted severe hardship and misery on the villages they assaulted, and the pirates had such a fearsome reputation that Chinese soldiers garrisoned to protect communities sometimes would flee in the face of impending attack.

The Wokou era from 1522 to 1574 during the mid-Ming dynasty of China marks the first of three great pirate epochs of the late imperial period. From

1440 to 1550 there had been only 25 wokou raids against China; but in the nine years from 1551 to 1560, there were 467 attacks.[19] The pirates consisted of both Chinese and Japanese, and the reach of their attacks fanned out from the Korean peninsula to include the coast of China as far south as Hainan Island.

But piracy in Asia reached its zenith during the Haikou era of the Ming-Qing transition from 1620 to 1684 and the Yangdao period of the mid-Qing, which stretched from 1780 to 1810. Piracy emerged from the social demographic and economic conditions of China, and the nature of piracy evolved throughout the centuries. The bans restricting international trade with China always provided an opportunity for adventurous foreigners and clandestine merchants to turn to piracy.[20] As population along the South China coast burgeoned and ports began to open to foreign trade in the late 17th century, however, a large number of marginally employed sailors and fishermen, and the laboring poor, came to dominate maritime piracy.

Imperial inattention and lack of resources allowed piracy to flourish. In each wave of Asian piracy, the Chinese emperor always was preoccupied with a more pressing matter of security. During the middle and late Ming dynasty, for example, officials were riveted to the northern border, where Mongol and Manchu armies threatened the dynasty. In the Qing era, internal rebellions and military campaigns in Vietnam diverted attention from the great pirate leagues operating along the southern coast.

The most powerful pirate fleets in East Asian history were those of the Chinese pirates in the Qing or Manchu dynasty, which ruled from 1644 until the early 20th century. By the 19th century, Chinese pirates grew increasingly powerful and they had a widespread effect on black market trade for the Chinese economy. The pirates thrived on China's junk trade, which was a vital mode of Chinese commerce, particularly in Fujian and Guangdong provinces on the South China Sea.

Native Chinese pirate fleets also exacted payment of tribute and extortion and dominated many of the seaside villages. One of the largest criminal organizations was formed in 1804, when Zheng Yi, who had inherited a pirate fleet from a deceased cousin, combined efforts with a prostitute that he took as his wife, Zheng Yi Sao. The couple launched successful attacks from Canton to Macau under the banner of the "Red Flag Fleet." When Zheng Yi passed away in 1807, his wife took over the operation.

Zheng Yi Sao became one of the most powerful and famous female pirate "admirals," leading a powerful coalition. It is believed that she controlled 17,000 followers and 1,500 ships.[21] After eluding capture by Portuguese and British bounty hunters and the Chinese government, Zheng Yi Sao was offered general amnesty in 1810 if she would retire from piracy. The female pirate admiral accepted the terms of amnesty. She opened a gambling house and smuggled opium, until she died at the age of 69 in 1844. Once Zheng Yi Sao retired, Chinese piracy suffered a precipitous decline.[22] The defeat of Zheng Yi Sao and other leaders of the Guangdong piracy confederation resulted from an ancient strategy, which combined annihilation and appeasement—punishing retribution and liberal offers of amnesty—or what we would call a "carrot-and-stick" approach.[23]

Faith Slavery and the Barbary Corsairs

In the Middle Ages and during the early modern period, the Ottoman Empire became particularly adroit at employing piracy at the strategic level to supplement the caliphate's treasury and conquer large areas. The Ottoman Turks and their North African principalities used maritime piracy as a method of warfare against the Christian kingdoms of the West. Barbary corsairs from North Africa—and then Islamic fleets from Arabia and Turkey—conducted a continuous campaign of terror against the European shores of the Mediterranean from virtually the inception of Islam until the 19th century.

After the fall of Constantinople by Mehmet in 1453 and the loss of the Aegean Sea that followed with the collapse of the Byzantine Empire, the island of Rhodes—nestled only 8 miles from the Asian shore—was defended against Ottoman attacks by the Knights of Saint John. Initially the Ottoman Empire had little interest in warfare at sea, preferring to lay siege to land strongholds in the Balkans.

In a turn toward amphibious operations, however, in 1521 Suleiman the Magnificent, ruler of the Ottoman Empire in Istanbul, successfully invaded the Christian stronghold at Rhodes. The successful attack ended in a negotiated capitulation by the Christian forces. The surrender also ignited a naval war in the Mediterranean that raged for 50 years, with the Holy League marshaling forces to defend Europe against the Ottoman Turks. The conflict for the eastern Mediterranean culminated in the failure of the siege of the fortresses at Malta in 1565, and the destruction of the Ottoman fleet at a mighty naval engagement in 1571 just south of the town of Lepanto, now Naupaktos, in western Greece.

The Turkish defeat at Lepanto broke the myth of Muslim invincibility and stopped the Ottoman advance into Europe. Lepanto also was the last major naval battle fought by galleys, and the battle foreshadowed the introduction of naval technology in the West that would gradually emerge to dominate the seas. Portugal deployed a small number of galleasses—massive towed gunships with unrivalled firepower. The effectiveness of the galleass at Lepanto presaged the rise of the heavy-gun galleons that would colonize the globe.

The incidence of Muslim piracy expanded dramatically in the early 16th century, as the Ottoman Empire tried to wrest North Africa from Spain. At the same time, toward the end of the century, the seafaring city-states became harder to control from Istanbul. Algiers, Tunis, Tripoli, and Morocco remained Ottoman entities, but they exercised greater autonomy and issued permission—essentially letters of marquee—for pirates to operate from their ports.

Two brothers led the piracy campaign against Southern Europe. The Barbarossa brothers, Aruj and Khayr ad-Din, were born on the Greek island of Lesbos, but converted to Islam and resettled in Tunis. The Barbarossa brothers operated under the protection of the ruler of Tunis, who received one-fifth of their booty. In 1518, a force of 10,000 soldiers dispatched by Charles crushed the naval forces of the Barbarossa brothers at Algiers, killing Aruj. Khayr ad-Din, however, lived until 1546, and conducted numerous attacks against Christian communities along the Mediterranean coastline of Spain, Italy, and Greece. Three years before he died, Khayr ad-Din pillaged the Italian province of Reggio di Calibria. The governor's 18-year-old daughter was captured during the raid and forcibly married to the legendary corsair.

James I called the raiders "the enemies of God and Man."[24] During the century from 1580 to 1680, it is estimated that 850,000 Christian slaves were taken from the shores of Europe and from European ships, and forcibly carried to North Africa by Barbary corsairs. In doing so, the Barbary pirates sent raiders far from home to find victims. In one raid in 1627, for example, Algerian corsairs kidnapped more than 400 men, women, and children from villages on the coast of Iceland.[25]

In 1631, more than 100 Protestant settlers were taken from Baltimore, County Cork, Ireland. In the 1620s Moroccan pirates were hunting for slaves in the Thames estuary, only 30 miles from London.[26] More broadly, between 1530 and 1780, marauders from the semi-independent principalities of Morocco, Algiers, Tunisia, and Tripoli plied the waters of the Mediterranean Sea, and enslaved well over 1 million Europeans.[27]

Although Muslims were more systematic and successful in their use of Christian slaves, some Christian armies also used Muslims as slaves in the early modern period. Operating from their base at Rhodes, and later in Valetta, Malta, the crusading order of the Knights of Saint John, for example, conducted a continuous campaign of piracy and enslavement of Muslims to stem Islamic expansion westward.

Muslim slaves were used by the Knights of Saint John to row galleys and as heavy labor in the construction of stone fortifications, or they were regarded as chattel and sold for profit. The slave market in Valetta was perhaps as busy as those in Algiers and Constantinople.[28] Slaves captured in battle or taken from seaside villages were used as rowers in both Christian and Muslim navies, chained to galley benches to row the warships. The life of a rower was a particularly cruel and reprehensible existence. Galley slaves were chained to their oars, living their life where they sat. They ate, slept, and defecated on a one-foot-wide bench—often chained for months at a time, or until they collapsed from exhaustion and were thrown overboard to drown.

Muslims did not capture Europeans because of their white race. Instead, the Ottomans were interested in obtaining what one eminent scholar calls "faith slaves," placed into bondage as part of the calling of Holy War in Islam. Slavery of this nature was one aspect of sea raiding. Although it is much less well known today than the black African slave trade to the Americas, which came later, faith slavery left an indelible impression on the culture and society of Europe and North Africa.

During the period of European slavery, the greatest literature in Europe—from Cervantes to Moliére to Voltaire, as well as the popular stage—was replete with references to slavery at the hands of the "roguish Turks."[29] In the Western mind, the concept of Islamic piracy was bound to the idea of slavery; only later would African slavery displace faith slavery in Western political and social consciousness. But contemporary histories have tended to downplay the magnitude and horror of European slavery since it lies outside the dominant historical narrative of a colonial West and a victimized South and East.

> The doubts and disdain that many modern scholars have expressed in dealing with European enslavement narratives may tell us more about our present-day mind-set than about the actions and experiences of the past. We are, by and large, uncomfortable seeing white Europeans as anything other than the dominators of this historical era. Our master narrative of the early-modern, Atlantic world, built on the foundations of colonialism and the enslavement of blacks by whites, has little or no place for white Europeans as victims, powerless and at the mercy of those whom scholars now prefer to call "The Subaltern Other."[30]

For three centuries European states intermittently offered feeble naval resistance against Barbary hostage taking and abduction slavery. More often, however, the European states adopted an appeasement strategy of the payment of tribute, essentially protection money, to mollify the Barbary rulers and to try to reduce the number of European vessels that were seized for ransom. The Spanish were perhaps the most successful in raising ransom and exchanging payment for Islamic slaves captured by Spain. The Catholic Church and other charitable organizations routinely were involved in negotiating the release of Christian captives.

By the close of the 18th century, maritime relations between the European powers and the Islamic world dramatically improved with the increase in both the quantity and quality of Western warships. Despite an uptick in corsair activity in the tumultuous 1790s, Professor Robert C. Davis estimates that the number of faith slaves captured by Muslim pirates was, by the end of the 18th century, only 10 percent of what it had been 100 years before.[31]

The American Experience

The new nation of the United States entered the stage to play a central role in the effort against Barbary pirates. As long as the United States remained a colony of the English Crown, American vessels fell under the protection of the guns of the Royal Navy. Merchant ships were protected by the payment of tribute from London. After independence and the 1783 Treaty of Paris, however, the new country was particularly vulnerable to Barbary raiders because it lacked a powerful navy or the means to pay large tribute. France, later feeling abandoned by the United States' peace treaty with England, similarly declined to protect American commercial shipping. American ships were in peril. The issue was brought to the fore by the case of the *Betsey*.

Soon after American independence, in October 1784, Moroccan raiders captured on the high seas an American merchant brig, taking the crew hostage.[32] The 300-ton brig *Betsey* was sailing 100 miles off the shores of North Africa. The ship was interdicted by saber-carrying pirates dressed in turbans and pantaloons, taking the Americans to the slave markets of the independent monarchy of Morocco. Soon afterward, the U.S.-flagged ships *Dauphin* and *Maria* also were captured by Moroccan corsairs.

In the fall of 1784, Jefferson served as U.S. ambassador to France. In that post he had proposed that the United States and European nations form a counterpiracy coalition, but the governments on the Continent were unsupportive of the idea and continued paying tribute to the Barbary kingdoms. Following the European state practice, the United States authorized a payment of $80,000 to Morocco for the release of 11 prisoners.[33] The crew of the *Betsey* was released, but Tangiers continued to hold hostages from other captured U.S. ships.

Still more captures of U.S. merchant ships by other Barbary corsairs followed. America was unable to retaliate. Moreover, the British were keen not only to deprive the former colonies of protection, but London actually was complicit with the North African beys and pashas to expose American shipping to attack in order to aid domestic British industry from U.S. market competition.

The United States sent emissaries to negotiate with Algiers and Tripoli, but the discussions did not make any progress. John Adams represented the country in talks in London with the ambassador of Tripoli. Terms under consideration were that the United States would make an annual payment to Tripoli of 30,000 guineas for safe passage of American vessels.[34] The same agreement likely could have been made with Tunis, but it was apparent that Algiers and

Morocco would demand even more money—most likely double the amount demanded by Tripoli and Tunis.

Algiers was the most powerful of the Barbary principalities, and buying its "goodwill" was expected to cost in excess of $660,000.[35] Adams believed bribery was the only option for peace, but Jefferson disagreed. Jefferson, generally one of the most pacific presidents in American history, had grown frustrated with the high demands and national humiliation. George Washington and Jefferson both supported creation of a navy to protect U.S. shipping from Mediterranean corsairs. But under the Articles of Confederation, the United States had no legal mechanism to fund construction of warships.

In May 1787, representatives from 12 of the 13 colonies met in Philadelphia to consider forming a new constitution, which would permit creation of a strong standing navy. James Madison, a leader of the constitutional convention, suggested that weakness invites aggression. The enslavement of Americans in Algiers was one of the motivating forces for creating a new constitutional union. Despite fear of the expansion of central power, James Madison and John Jay argued in the *Federalist Papers* that the threat of Mediterranean corsairs made imperative creation of a strong union and powerful navy. The Constitution was adopted on March 4, 1789, forming a consolidated nation that was capable of defending its overseas commercial interests.

Jefferson was appointed as the Secretary of State, with the task of finding a solution to the Barbary piracy. Most Americans still opposed using force, and Jefferson continued to negotiate with Algiers for release of U.S. hostages. In December 1790, Jefferson recommended that the United States go to war, but the Senate rejected the option. Instead, the Congress approved payment of additional ransom money, and Jefferson dutifully proffered the tribute. Jefferson planned to send the legendary John Paul Jones as a courier to Algiers with $25,000—a paltry sum. Jones had achieved notoriety as an indefatigable naval captain in the Russian navy, achieving victories over the Ottoman fleets, but he became ill and passed away before he could make the trip.

Patience was growing thin in the U.S. government over the plight of American captives in North Africa. The sense of national insult was palpable. Some merchant ships hired Spanish or Dutch gunboats to guard their voyages through the Mediterranean Sea. The country once again debated creation of a naval fleet. The dispute over construction of a navy served as a fulcrum for the larger debate over the wisdom or folly of a strong central government. James Madison and Thomas Jefferson, who feared federal power, actually opposed the shipbuilding plan. The Federalist leader John Adams supported the plan. But legislation to create a navy and build six frigates passed by a vote of 50 to 39, upon the condition that warship construction cease once peace was achieved. President Washington signed the bill into law on March 27, 1794, thereby establishing the U.S. Navy.

Meanwhile additional ransom negotiations ensued, with churches and benevolent societies collecting money for the release of the hostages. On September 5, 1795, the United States and Algiers reached agreement for release of American captives for the exacting price of one 36-gun frigate, and $600,000 in goods, including 25 chests of tea, sugar, penknives, and other luxuries. The 77 surviving Americans were delivered to Philadelphia in 1797, creating a media sensation.

Tripoli and Tunis, seeing the great benefits of aggression, stepped up attacks on U.S. shipping. The United States reached ransom agreements with the two regencies, making payment in specie, as well as artillery, shot, and powder. After securing three treaties of peace, albeit at tremendous cost and great national shame, the Congress returned to a policy of appeasement. In March 1799, the United States sent consuls to the three principalities to serve as permanent envoys. At the same time, however, the country launched three frigates with a total of 124 guns, the *United States*, the *Constitution*, and the *Constellation*. The ships were outfitted with elements of the newly created Marine Corps, which served as expeditionary infantry.

President Jefferson was sworn into office in 1801, and the question of Barbary piracy occupied his first cabinet meeting on March 15, 1801. Jefferson had long believed paying tribute was beneath the dignity of the new nation, but previously he had been overruled in the use of force by presidents George Washington and John Adams.[36] The cabinet unanimously concurred in dispatching four of the six frigates to Gibraltar to protect American shipping in the region.

The president also sent naval expeditions to the eastern Atlantic and Mediterranean Sea to protect American shipping.[37] The U.S. expeditionary force was led by Captain Richard Dale, a former first lieutenant aboard the *Bonhomme Richard* under the command of John Paul Jones. Dale departed Hampton Roads on June 1, 1801, and arrived in the Mediterranean four weeks later. The orders were to sortie U.S. forces "so as best to protect our commerce and chastise their insolence—by sinking, burning or destroying their ships and vessels wherever you shall find them."[38] The arrival of the U.S. squadron off the coast of Tripoli on July 24 greatly worried the pasha, who made overtures to sue for peace.[39]

A week later, the U.S. schooner *Enterprise* under the command of Andrew Sterrett defeated, without a single U.S. casualty, a much larger cruiser from Tripoli.[40] This action immediately burnished the image of the new American navy, providing the backdrop for the declaration of a blockade of Tripoli by William H. Eaton, the U.S. consul in Tunis. For three months, and without U.S. ships near Tripoli, the principality was successfully blockaded by the simple force of the pronouncement of the U.S. consul in Tunis. Merchant vessels were deterred from entering port by fear of U.S. interception, underscoring the power of perception and coercive naval diplomacy. Captain Dale applauded Eaton's ingenuity, and completed his deployment in April 1802. The ineffectual Captain Richard Morris followed Dale. Morris dithered for more than a year despite orders from the president to blockade Tripoli. President Jefferson would refer to the period of missed opportunity and inaction as the "period of two years' sleep."[41]

The adventurous Eaton next suggested that the United States locate Hamet, the elder brother of the Yusuf, the Bashaw of Tripoli, and use him as leverage against the corsair ruler to secure a peace treaty. Professor Robert F. Turner recounts the proposal was first raised officially in a letter to Secretary of State James Madison on September 5, 1801.[42] In 1805, Eaton put the plan into motion. Lieutenant Isaac Hull was sent to Alexandria, Egypt, with a small band of Marines on a covert mission to make contact with Hemet and propose the operation.

The bashaw's elder brother agreed to depose Yusef, and 12 U.S. Marines recruited a motley force of 500 mostly Arab and Greek mercenaries for the operation. In March 1805, the makeshift army embarked on an inhospitable 500-mile march across North Africa to Tripoli, picking up additional volunteers as it made its way through the Western Desert. The desert crossing proved extremely difficult, but the force finally reached Bomba, where the fighters were resupplied from provisions sent by U.S. warships *Hornet* and *Argus*. Marching 60 more miles, the army arrived at Derne, the second largest city in Tripoli, and the population welcomed Hamet as the rightful leader. The governor of Derne, however, chose to fight, and the city was taken by force. Soon after, an army of 1,200 soldiers from Tripoli arrived to retake Derne, but they were scattered by accurate American artillery fire.

Meanwhile, U.S. Commodore Edward Preble blockaded the port of Tripoli. In 1803, the frigate *Philadelphia* was grounded off the coast of Tripoli by strong winds and subsequently captured by the corsairs. Three months later, and under cover of night, Lieutenant Stephen Decatur led a dramatically successful raid that burned the ship to the water as it lay at anchor with the Barbary fleet. Not a single American was lost in the engagement, which killed scores of pirates.

Decatur's heroic action stirred Lord Admiral Horatio Nelson to remark it was the "the most bold and daring act of the age."[43] Soon Tripoli agreed to a peace, ending the system of payment of annual tribute. Next, Decatur demanded Algiers stop seeking tribute. The Bey of Algiers quickly relented, as did the other Barbary principalities. The Europeans followed suit, refusing to continue payment to the corsairs, and the entire system of tribute collapsed. The systematic enslavement of European and American seafarers, and European seaside villagers, that had persisted for three centuries collapsed.[44]

The business model of the Barbary pirates was successful, and their impact on the security and commerce of the United States was substantial. The going rate for the release of a single Christian was about $4,000 per person—equivalent to roughly $1.5 million today. Holding a ship for ransom often would yield a payoff of $29 million in today's currency. The U.S. Navy lost the frigate *Philadelphia,* along with her captain and crew, at a time when the entire American fleet had just six warships. When U.S. ransom payments and tribute topped $1 million annually, it equaled 20 percent of the entire federal budget, or about three-fourths of a trillion dollars in today's money. The American experience ended Barbary piracy, but the system of European privateers persisted for decades.

European Privateers

European privateers have their origin in the discovery of the New World. After Columbus's claim of the Americas for Spain in 1492, the Caribbean quickly became a busy center of European trade and colonization for North and South America. By the middle of the 16th century, all the major European powers were vying for colonies, trading outposts, and influence in the West.

In the 1493 Treaty of Tordesillas the non-European world was divided between the Spanish and the Portuguese kingdoms along a north-south line 270 leagues west of Cape Verde, giving Spain control of the Americas (except Brazil) and the Portuguese control of the African and Indian coasts, to the Moluccas islands in present-day Indonesia. The boundary line demarcating Spanish and Portuguese "territory" was the longitudinal line of 36° 47 west, which ran through South America. The agreement later was reinforced with a papal bull issued by the pope to memorialize the treaty. Everything to the west of the line, including areas yet to be discovered, was ceded to Spain; everything east of the line, including Brazil, certain African possessions, and parts of India and Asia, belonged to Portugal.

Spanish conquistadors subjugated large indigenous empires in the Americas, extracting enormous wealth in gold, silver, and gems. Hernando Cortez landed on the coast of Mexico in 1519 with a force of 500 men and 13 horses carried in 11 ships. In less than two years, he toppled the Aztec Empire and claimed Mexico for the king of Castile in Spain. In 1513, another conquistador named Francisco Pizarro had crossed the Central American isthmus and conquered the Incan Empire, founding the city of Lima, the capital of Peru. These men took control of vast native civilizations and began to transfer to Europe enormous amounts of gold and silver specie from Mexico and Peru. The Spanish mined staggering amounts of silver bullion from the mines of Zacatecas in Mexico and Potosí in present-day Bolivia. The riches were sent back to Spain in heavily laden treasure fleets.

The French, English, and Dutch, however, were unwilling to recognize Spanish and Portuguese seizure of the New World and Asia. The northern coast of South America was regarded as the "Spanish Mainland," or "Spanish Main," and key early settlements included Cartagena in present-day Colombia, Porto Bello and Panama City on the Isthmus of Panama, Santiago on the southeastern coast of Cuba, and Santo Domingo on the island of Hispaniola. The meaning of the Spanish Main gradually became synonymous with the entire Caribbean basin, all controlled at least nominally by Spain.

Huge Spanish silver shipments from the New World attracted pirates and French privateers like François Leclerc and Jean Fleury. In 1523 the French corsair Fleury seized three caravels filled with treasure bound for Spain. The treasure ships were vulnerable as soon as they left port in the Caribbean, throughout the journey across the mid-Atlantic, and in their predictable approach to Seville. News of the French success caused a wild sensation as the rest of Europe became aware of the full scale of Spain's plunder and conquest.

In 1526 Spain adopted a convoy system to protect the treasure fleets, but by then raiders from several nations were already preying on specie-laden Spanish ships. The successful attack by Fleury ignited two centuries of privateering by seafarers from England and other countries that targeted Spanish treasure fleets in the Spanish Main. The Spanish regarded foreign vessels in the Spanish Main as interlopers, since the kingdom of Castile claimed title to all of the land and sea. The first English interloper to operate in the Spanish Main appeared in 1527.

Queen Elizabeth issued peacetime letters of reprisal or wartime letters of marque to English seafarers who operated against Spanish treasure shipping. The privateer was granted a license by the Crown, which allowed him to attack the shipping of another state. In international law, privateers were considered enemy combatants rather than pirates. In return for the legal protection, the state issuing the letter of marque earned a percentage of any profits seized by the privateer. In turn, the privateer was an agent of the state and was permitted to attack only the vessels from enemy states that were identified in the letter of marque.

But while the English regarded privateers like Sir Francis Drake as national heroes, and some privateers became fabulously wealthy, the Spanish regarded them as pirates. If Spain captured a privateer, it might banish him to the galleys to row until death, or hang him in a public square. But France remained the great rival to Henry VIII in England, and so England and Spain maintained an uneasy alliance that tended to restrain early English privateering against the treasure fleets. Meanwhile, the French conducted continuous forays into the Spanish Main whereas the English often were forbidden to cross the line set forth in the Treaty of Tordesillas.

Enforcing Seville's claim to the Spanish Main was another matter. Despite being the wealthiest state in Europe, Spain could not afford to maintain an army and navy sufficient to control such an immense area. Spain also was unable to enforce its exclusionary, mercantilist trading laws, which permitted only Spanish merchants to trade with the New World colonists in the Americas. Consequently, there was a continuous flow of smuggling between America and Europe. Spain's precarious legal framework also was susceptible to new attempts at Caribbean colonization in peacetime by England, France, and the Netherlands. The European wars among the great powers of the early modern period also spilled over into the New World, and were marked by widespread piracy and privateering throughout the Caribbean. These trends tended to eat away at Spanish dominance, contributing to a slow but unmistakable decline in Spanish power.

The implicit alliance between England and Spain even survived Henry VIII's separation from the Catholic Church in the mid-1530s. With the accession of his daughter Elizabeth I in 1558, however, relations between England and Spain soured. Elizabeth was a devout Protestant who viewed Spain as both a religious and a political threat. The queen issued a letter of reprisal to John Hawkins. The peacetime letter of marque granted a subject the right to recover property from a foreign sovereign. Hawkins nursed grievances against the Spanish, and he embarked in 1562 to break the Spanish monopoly on trade in the New World.

The British joined the French and the Dutch in a protracted campaign to steal the wealth flowing from the New World to the Iberian Peninsula. While the French and Dutch began to intercept and capture Spanish treasure fleets loaded with gold and silver specie in the 1520s, the English did not get involved until the emergence of privateers called the "sea dogs" in the second half of the 16th century.

British sea dogs such as Hawkins and Francis Drake began their attacks 40 years after the French and Dutch. In 1570 Queen Elizabeth I granted Francis Drake a letter of reprisal to attack Spanish shipping under the pretext of seeking redress and reimbursement for losses he claimed to have suffered at the hands of the Spanish. Drake transited through the Straits of Magellan and sailed up the Pacific Coast of South America, going as far north as San Francisco. Along the way the famous captain plundered Spanish towns and captured a Spanish ship carrying 25,000 pieces of eight.

Drake also captured the vessel *Our Lady of the Conception* in early 1579 off the Pacific coast of South America. The ship contained 14 small chests in its hold, and each was filled with silver pieces of eight, gold bars and disks weighing 80 pounds each. The vessel also held 26 tons of silver cast in solid 80-pound ingots. The total value of the capture was about 200,000 pounds, which was more than half the annual income of the English Crown.[45]

The work of the privateers heavily influenced the course of virtually perpetual war on the continent of Europe. The vast wealth that Spain was funneling from the New World funded the effort to put down the Dutch campaign for independence. By the mid-1560s the Dutch were in rebellion, and while Incan and Aztec gold and silver were used to arm the Spanish, wealth seized by Elizabeth I's privateers was supplying Dutch rebels with money and troops. In 1585, after decades of seething hostility, the two kingdoms of England and Spain finally slipped into war. British sea captains operating under the direction of Queen Elizabeth stepped up their far-reaching raids on Spanish shipping, and turned in their peacetime letters of reprisal for wartime letters of marque.

Once Spain demonstrated how profitable colonies in the New World could be, the French began to seek their own holdings by establishing Fort Caroline near what is now Jacksonville, Florida, in 1564. Although the settlement was destroyed by a Spanish attack from the larger colony at Saint Augustine, it presaged a flood of English, French, and Dutch traders and migrants into the New World. Spain, utterly unable to enforce its universal claim to the Americas, would fight a slowly losing battle for control. The Protestant Dutch and English defiantly opposed Catholic Spain's unenforceable title to all of the water and territory west of the line drawn by the Treaty of Tordesillas. The fact that the pope had validated the treaty became meaningless even to Catholic France, giving rise to the 16th-century phrase: "no peace beyond the line."

The "Golden Age" of the Pirates of the Caribbean

Gradually, as French and English power displaced Spanish authority in the Caribbean, freebooters, or pirates who were not in the service of any state, became a scourge of all civilized nations. The pirates were most successful from the 1650s until the 1720s, when buccaneering Anglo-French seafarers operated out of the relatively lawless British seaport of Port Royal in Jamaica and the French settlement at Tortuga. The Anglo-French pirates targeted Spanish colonies and shipping in the Caribbean and eastern Pacific, although no merchant vessel was entirely safe from attack.

During the Pirate Round of the 1690s, buccaneers conducted long-distance voyages from Bermuda and the Americas to capture shipping in the Indian Ocean and Red Sea. After the Treaty of Utrecht ended the War of the Spanish Succession, many of the idle Anglo-American privateers that had been attacking Spanish shipping in support of the Dutch turned toward piracy. The raiders terrorized the Caribbean, Florida, and the Eastern Seaboard, and sailed as far as West Africa and the Indian Ocean.

In response to the growth in piracy, Caribbean colonial governors sought stability and order in the oceans and so began to reject the policy of "no peace beyond the line." The peacetime issuance of letters of marque became rare. As the number of lucrative targets in the Caribbean declined, former English privateers became more creative in identifying targets.

In 1715, a group of English seafarers disrupted Spanish divers working to recover gold from a sunken treasure galleon off the coast of Florida. A sordid crew composed of Edward England, Henry Jennings, Charles Vane, and "Black Sam" Bellamy led the successful attack, but the governor of Jamaica later refused them entry into Kingston. The group holed up in Nassau, Bahamas, and settled for a time to spend the gold.

The pirates also reached beyond the Caribbean. The riches of the Indian Ocean became more attractive during the 18th century. The Indian economy at the time was enormous—larger than Europe's—and merchant ships stuffed with luxury goods such as silk and calico, which was a highly prized plain-woven textile that originated in Kerala, India, made tempting targets. Ships from Europe traded finished manufactured goods for slaves, which were then sold in the Caribbean in exchange for molasses and sugar, tobacco, and cocoa. Other raw materials, such as timber, cod, and rum, were shipped from North America to Europe in exchange for glass and metalware. As the shipping lanes connecting Africa, Europe, and the Caribbean became busier, there were greater opportunities for piracy.

Rise of the Steamship Navies and the Demise of Piracy

With the advent of powerful Anglo-American navies, piracy waned throughout the 19th century. After the Napoleonic Wars, the Royal Navy extricated itself from decades of conflict on the continent of Europe to emerge as the guarantor of *Pax Britannica*, or the "British Peace." In a process that began with the Treaty of Westphalia in 1648, by the early 19th century armies became more professional and more closely associated with the authority of the state. The organization, resources and skills, and firepower of national armed forces raised the risk of engaging in a life of piracy. Jean Lafitte, one of the last of the great pirates, operated in the Caribbean during the 1810s from hideaways along the U.S. Gulf Coast. Privateering was falling into desuetude.

Steamships entered service in the 1830s. By midcentury naval forces had completely converted from wind to coal power. The transition added additional technological barriers to entering maritime piracy, and ensured that most naval vessels outmatched the decrepit ships of the swashbucklers in terms of firepower, endurance, and speed at sea. There also was something in the air of the dawning of an age of modernism. As the 20th century lay around the corner and the world "shrank" in size and scope, there were fewer areas untouched by civilization. Law and order were the natural consequence of the presence and reach of the Royal Navy.

Frank Lesley's Popular Monthly, a prevalent magazine at the time, expressed wonderment that a steamship could circumnavigate the globe in 80 days—a trip that took Sir Francis Drake two years.[46] The passing of the age was lamented. One observer wrote:

> The romance of the sea was destroyed when the ocean steamship was invented, as it rung the knell of successful piracy. With the invention of the steamship, no more could the swift brigantine lie in wait among the nooks and bays of Cuba, or sweep the seas in search of her prey; sail as fast as she might, she could not outstrip the prosaic gunboat with its lungs of fire that bore it steadily onward through storm and through calm. Once the swift sailor was the sovereign of the seas, but with the coming of the steamer the domination of the white-winged craft was known no more. I repeat the question, who would be a pirate now?[47]

In the Americas, law enforcement, naval forces, and judicial systems stamped out piracy. During the early 1800s, U.S. federal courts were absorbed with prosecuting pirates. Privateering resurfaced briefly during wartime, particularly in the woolly Americas, where letters of marque were issued during the Mexican and Colombian wars of independence, as well as during the American Civil War. But piracy was fading as a feature of the seas, and even was becoming an unacceptable instrument of warfare. In Europe in 1856, the Treaty of Paris ended the Crimean War. An associated agreement, the Paris Declaration Respecting Maritime Law, signed on April 16, 1856, abolished the practice of issuing letters of marque to privateers during war. The confluence of naval technology, the maintenance of freedom of the seas by the Royal Navy, and the progress of international law all contributed to the demise of maritime piracy.

With the rise of steel warships powered by steam, the dominance of Western naval fleets in all of the world's oceans deterred large-scale maritime piracy. In most parts of the colonial world, armed robbery at sea was as ubiquitous as other crimes of theft, but the attacks were local affairs and rarely targeted large vessels on transcontinental voyages. After 1900, a series of conventional naval rivalries pitted the English against the Germans and the United States against the Japanese. The tension wrought from these contests erupted in World War I, simmered throughout the interwar period, and were rekindled during World War II. By the end of World War II, Anglo-American naval power was paramount, maintaining a relatively placid order of the oceans.

When the end of World War II gave way to obsession over superpower rivalry, the hegemonic dominance of the U.S. Navy assured freedom of the seas and the safety of maritime commerce. Furthermore, the powerful linkages between the superpowers and their client states in Asia, Africa, and Latin America helped to maintain regional order and supported maritime constabulary authority. But history raced ahead of the Cold War contest, and by the late 1980s, decolonization and globalization were forming the weak states and the shipping boom that would set conditions for a reemergence of piracy in the 1990s and 2000s. The epicenter of the new piracy in the 1990s and early 2000s was Southeast Asia, but the center shifted to the Horn of Africa after 2005.

Notes

1. Philip de Souza, *Piracy in the Graeco-Roman World* 2–3 (1999).
2. John L. Caskey, *Crisis in the Minoan-Mycenaean World*, 113 Proceedings of the American Philosophical Society 433–449, at 438 (December 15, 1969).
3. Caskey, *Crisis in the Minoan-Mycenaean World*, at 439.
4. Caskey, *Crisis in the Minoan-Mycenaean World*, at 443–444.
5. Edward Luttwak, *The Grand Strategy of the Roman Empire: From the First Century* A.D. *to the Third* 19, 69 (1979).
6. Philip de Souza, *Ancient Rome and the Pirates*, History Today 93 (July 2001).
7. de Souza, *Ancient Rome and the Pirates*, at 48–53.
8. H. Stuart Jones, A *Roman Law Concerning Piracy*, 16 Journal of Roman Studies 155, 158–159 (1926).
9. William Stearns Davis, *Readings in Ancient History: Rome and the West* 149–150 (Willis Mason West, Intro., 1913).
10. Andrew Pearson, *Piracy in Late Roman Britain: A Perspective from the Viking Age*, 37 Britannia 337–353 (November 2006).
11. Angus Konstam, *Piracy: The Complete History* 26 (2008).
12. Stephen Turnbull, *Pirates of the Far East: 811–1639* 46 (2007).
13. Robert Antony, *Like Froth Floating on the Sea: The World of Pirates and Seafarers in Late Imperial South China* 103 (2003).
14. Antony, *Like Froth Floating on the Sea*, at 104.
15. Ishii Susumu, The Decline of the Kamakura Bakufu, 128–174, *in* 3 *Cambridge History of Japan: Medieval Japan* 131–132 and 145–148 (Kozo Yamamura, ed., 1990).
16. Turnbull, *Pirates of the Far East*, at 14.
17. Kawazoe Shoji, Japan and East Asia, 396–446, *in* 3 *Cambridge History of Japan: Medieval Japan* 431 (Kozo Yamamura, ed., 1990).
18. Shoji, Japan and East Asia, at 396–446.
19. Turnbull, *Pirates of the Far East*, at 17.
20. Antony, *Like Froth Floating on the Sea*, at 15–16.
21. Maggie Koerth, Most Successful Pirate Was Beautiful and Tough, Mental Floss (CNN.com), August 28, 2007.
22. Antony, *Like Froth Floating on the Sea*, at 47–49, 51, 93, and 147.
23. Antony, *Like Froth Floating on the Sea*, at 52.
24. Adrian Tinniswood, *The $150m Question: How to Beat the Pirates; Corsairs Once Took a Million Europeans as Slaves. There are Lessons for Today*, The Times (London), March 13, 2010, at 8.
25. Tinniswood, *The $150m Question*.

26. Tinniswood, *The $150m Question*.

27. See generally, Robert C. Davis, Christian Slaves, *in Muslim Masters: White Slavery in the Mediterranean, the Barbary Coast and Italy, 1500–1800* (Rab Houston & Edward Muir, eds., 2003).

28. Robert C. Davis, *Holy War and Human Bondage: Tales of Christian-Muslim Slavery in the Early-Modern Mediterranean* 40 (2009).

29. Davis, *Holy War and Human Bondage*, at 11.

30. Davis, *Holy War and Human Bondage*, at 11–12.

31. Davis, *Holy War and Human Bondage*, at 41.

32. Merrill D. Peterson, *Thomas Jefferson and the New Nation: A Biography* 310–311 (1970).

33. Peterson, *Thomas Jefferson and the New Nation*, at 310–311.

34. James Parton, *Jefferson: American Minister in France*, Atlantic Monthly, October 1872, at 405.

35. Parton, *Jefferson: American Minister in France*, at 405.

36. Thomas Jefferson, Report to Congress on American Trade in the Mediterranean, December 28, 1790, reprinted in, *The Papers of Thomas Jefferson* 47 (Julian P. Boyd, Ruth W. Lester, & Lucius Wilmerding, Jr., eds., 1971).

37. Walter Russell Mead, *Special Providence* 106 (2002).

38. Letter from Samuel Smith to Richard Dale, May 20, 1801, reprinted in, *1 Naval Documents Related to the United States Wars with the Barbary Powers* 465, 467 (Claude A. Swanson, ed., 1939).

39. Francis Rennell Rodd, *General William Eaton: The Failure of an Idea* 13 (1932) and Gardner W. Allen, *Our Navy and the Barbary Corsairs* 95 (1905).

40. Robert F. Turner, *War and the Forgotten Executive Power Clause*, 34 Virginia Journal of International Law 903, 910–912 (1994).

41. Henry Adams, 2 *History of the United States of America during the First Administration of Thomas Jefferson* 137 (1889) and Donald Barr Chidsey, *The Wars in Barbary: Arab Piracy and the Birth of the United States Navy* 83–84 (1971).

42. Robert F. Turner, *State Responsibility and the War on Terror: The Legacy of Thomas Jefferson and the Barbary Pirates*, 4 Chicago Journal of International Law 121, 133 (Spring 2003).

43. Forrest McDonald, *The Presidency of Thomas Jefferson* 78 (1976).

44. John Bassett Moore, *Principles of American Diplomacy* 112 (2006) (2d rev. ed. 1918).

45. Konstam, *Piracy: The Complete History*, at 60.

46. Thomas W. Knox, A *Short Trip around the World*, 10 Frank Lesley's Popular Monthly 724, 726 (December 1880).

47. Knox, A *Short Trip around the World*, at 726.

CHAPTER 2

Contemporary Piracy in Southeast Asia and East Africa

No area has been entirely immune from armed robbery at sea and maritime piracy. In recent years, piracy hotspots have included the mouth of the Shatt al Arab waterway off of Iraq, Nigeria and the Gulf of Guinea, Bangladesh and the Bay of Bengal, and Jamaica and the surrounding waters of the Caribbean Sea. South America, including Brazil, have been victimized by maritime piracy. In South America and the Caribbean, there were 19 piracy incidents in 2008 and 36 in 2009.[1] In 2009, the areas of the world most affected by piracy were in the coastal waters of East Africa and the Far East, in particular the South China Sea, West Africa, South America and the Caribbean, and the Indian Ocean.

In West Africa, the number of piracy attacks went down slightly, from 50 to 46, over the same period. Even shipping in the North Pacific and the Caspian Sea was threatened by piracy. But over the past decades, the regions that saw the greatest threat of maritime piracy were the Horn of Africa and western Indian Ocean and Southeast Asia, extending from Vietnam through the South China Sea to the Philippines, and southward to include the Straits of Malacca and Singapore. These areas are discussed in detail because they have faced particular threat from piracy, and have led to the most concrete naval, diplomatic, and legal responses to the crime.

Sixty-nine piracy incidents occurred in the South China Sea in 2009; 27 incidents were reported in the Malacca Strait. In East Africa, the number of piracy attacks increased from 134 in 2008 to 222 in 2009. Two incidents were reported in the Arabian Sea in 2009, compared with only one reported in 2008. Worldwide, most of the reported attacks occurred in international waters, but this probably is due only to the high numbers of Somali pirates that prey on the international shipping lanes in the western Indian Ocean, the GOA, and the Arabian Sea. In other areas of the world, most maritime piracy

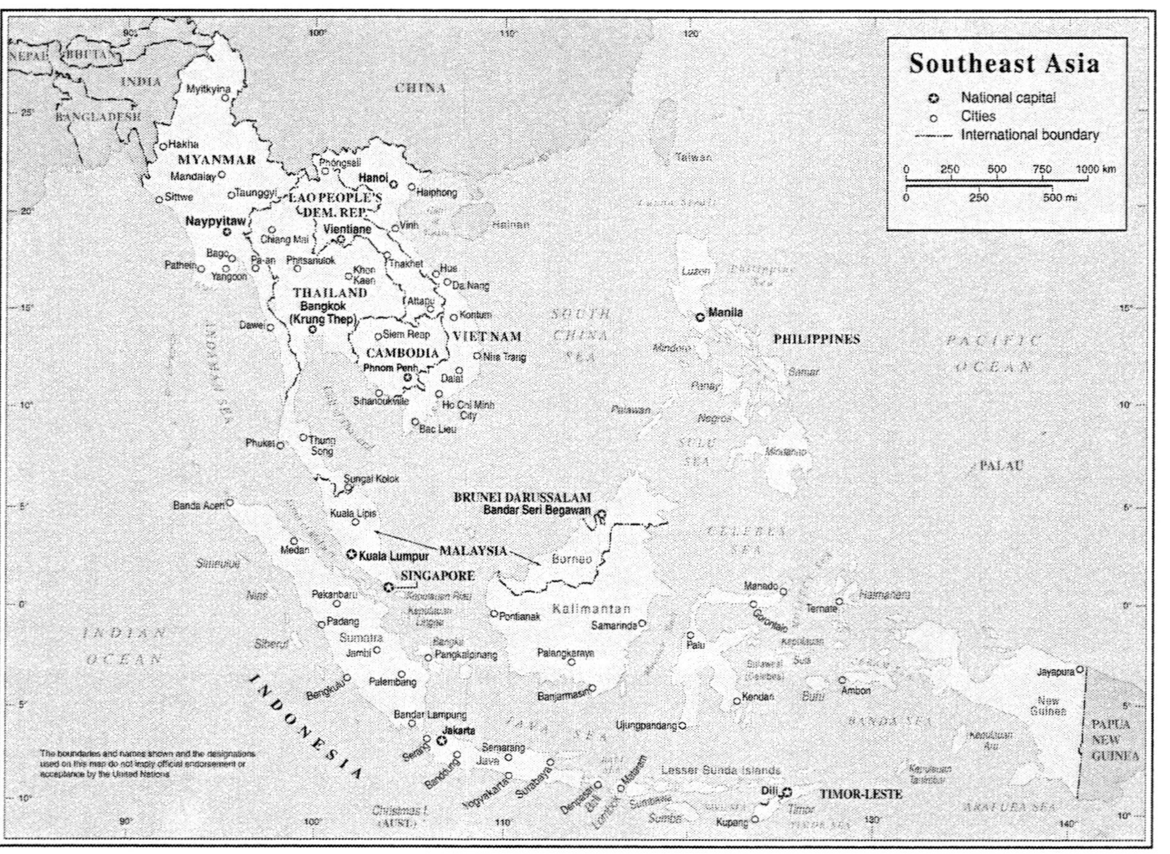

Map No. 4365, United Nations, May 2009

is reported within coastal state territorial waters, or while ships are at anchor or berthed.

Generally piracy and armed robbery involve violent attack or threat of attack by groups of 5 to 25 men carrying knives and guns. In 2009, 8 merchant ship crew were killed (6 in 2008), and 59 crew members were injured or physically assaulted by pirates (up from 42 in 2008). In 2009, 746 shipping crew members were taken hostage or kidnapped, which is about the same as in 2008 (774). Nine seafarers are still missing after being attacked by pirates in 2009, and 38 seafarers remain missing from attacks in 2008. Two vessels are unaccounted for after being attacked by pirates in 2009, and one vessel is still missing from an attack that occurred in 2008.[2]

Southeast Asia

Since the 1990s, Southeast Asia has been particularly hard hit by piracy. Asia features some of the most densely populated coastal areas in the world, as well as the foremost export-driven economies of Japan, South Korea, Hong Kong, Malaysia, Taiwan, Vietnam, Singapore, and, of course, now China. The World Bank, for example, reports that Vietnam's exports amount to about 80 percent of Gross Domestic Product (GDP); in the United States the figure is about 10 percent of GDP. In Japan, exports amount to 20 percent of the economy; in China the figure is 26 percent.[3] The Hong Kong Special Administrative Region of China, however, exports goods worth a phenomenal 212 percent of GDP. Similarly, Singapore's exports are 221 percent of GDP.

The huge volume of Asian exports relies on a massive infrastructure distribution system that includes vast land-based road and rail networks leading to sprawling dock and port facilities, which in turn are interconnected through tens of thousands of ships that ply the Indian Ocean and Pacific Ocean.

Incredibly, China dominates the world container shipping industry that forms the center of the world's trade in goods. More shipping containers are loaded and unloaded in China than travel to or from all other nations and territories of the world combined. The rest of the countries handle one-third of the container traffic managed solely by China. At least half of the container shipping in the world involves China, either as a departure, arrival, or transshipment port.[4] Although most media attention has focused on the rising economic prowess of China, Thailand, Malaysia, and Vietnam are also emerging export centers that are heavily reliant on shipping.

Amidst all of this shipping, Asian pirates never have far to look for opportunities to plunder vessels. The dense coastal populations of Southeast Asia, interspersed among thousands of islands, and the innumerable small fishing vessels, dhows, and coastal cabotage traders mean that Asian pirates easily can hide among legitimate shipping. Nearby shore side retreats are used for planning attacks and rest. The excellent banking and communications infrastructure facilitates the business of organized crime.

In contrast, Somali pirates are exposed to the possibility of interdiction as they seek prey throughout the western Indian Ocean. Far from shore, pirates off the coast of Africa are vulnerable to police action by the many naval patrols that operate in the region. The smaller distances traveled by Asian pirates also means that they can use smaller ships to launch attacks, which attract less attention from authorities and are easier to hide in coastal communities along the beach. Consequently, Southeast Asian pirates mark vessels transiting among the complex harbor works, roadsteads, and straits of the littoral states, only occasionally venturing beyond the territorial sea to strike at particularly susceptible—or promising—targets.

The Asian financial crisis of 1998 may have contributed to a rise in piracy in Southeast Asia, and the global "great recession" that engulfed the world economy in 2008 has also been a factor in drawing more seafarers into a life of maritime crime. At its roots, Asian piracy is an economic offense, but piracy also may have political overtones. Piracy attacks are one way that disenfranchised coastal populations are able to strike back at distant and indifferent central governments.[5] Piracy can provide the means to supply secessionist movements and resistance fighters with money and supporters, blurring the line between pirates and insurgents.[6] Furthermore, strong economic growth merely generates more trade, which means more ships that can be victims of piracy. The booming Asian economy also tempts organized criminal gangs to devise ways to cut into legitimate business.

Until the recent past, countering maritime piracy was a relatively low priority for most Southeast Asian nations. Greater threats, including the prospect of regional naval warfare, international drug trafficking, maritime terrorism and counterinsurgency, and policing illegal fishing and smuggling, preoccupied maritime security forces.[7]

Piracy also has been a local affair throughout much of the history of Southeast Asia. Most piracy actually occurs in port or at anchor—low-level armed robbery. Each coastal state is solely responsible for suppressing these crimes, which typically are aimed at coastal fishing vessels and small cabotage traders, and therefore do not involve large ships or large sums of money. A case in point is the Strait of Malacca. As one of the prime areas for marine piracy in Southeast Asia, the Straits of Malacca and Singapore constitute the major thoroughfare connecting the Indian Ocean with the Pacific Ocean. The straits are nestled along Malaysia, Singapore, and the Indonesian island of Sumatra, and the South China Sea, and have been a hotspot for maritime piracy.[8]

The International Maritime Bureau (IMB) reports that in 2010, the waters surrounding Bangladesh were also dangerous, with pirates targeting ships preparing to anchor near Chittagong. The island areas of Anambas, Natuna, off the shores of Indonesia in the South China Sea, and near Tioman, Pulau Aur, and the South China Sea coast of Malaysia, all have experienced an uptick in violent attacks by well-armed pirates. Piracy has also been reported south of the port of Vung Tau, Vietnam, in the South China Sea.

As trade increases for Vietnam, piracy has become a greater threat. Vietnam recently announced that the deep water port at Cam Ranh Bay was "open for business." Moscow withdrew from Cam Ranh Bay in 2002 just prior to completion of a 25-year lease granted by Hanoi in 1979. Much as the Philippines and Costa Rica attempted to extract greater rents for maintaining airport and seaport facilities at Clark and Subic for American forces, Vietnam sought to raise the rent charged to the Russians. But the price was too high, and the rent increase precipitated a Russian withdrawal.

The Kremlin now seeks to use Cam Ranh Bay as a staging area for combating maritime piracy in the Horn of Africa, rather than to maintain a larger geopolitical presence in Southeast Asia.[9] Although Moscow is in a better financial position to lease the port due to elevated energy prices, Vietnam has balked at reopening the port as a military base.[10] Instead, since the facility sits astride commercial sea lanes along the South China Sea, Vietnam hopes to make the port available to increased international merchant shipping. Furthermore, as a political motive, Hanoi seeks to limit China's influence in the region and diminish Beijing's spurious claims to over 80 percent of the South China Sea by establishing Cam Ranh Bay as a major shipping hub that hosts vessels from a variety of naval powers, including the United States.[11]

The ascendancy of China's economy, which grew nearly 500 percent during the 1990s, requires thousands of new ships to carry manufactured goods to Europe and North America.[12] In particular, the Straits of Malacca and Singapore constitute one of the most critical chokepoints on the planet. Each year more than 70,000 ships transit the straits, including virtually all of the oil used by China, Japan, and South Korea. Piracy in Southeast Asia peaked in the mid-2000s, when the "phantom ship" or "ghost ship" phenomenon began to fall off due to greater Chinese enforcement.[13]

The decline in piracy in the region also may be attributed to new commitments by states to expand national counterpiracy efforts, and to link these efforts more effectively to regional maritime security programs.[14] Multilateral assistance and capacity building has supplemented collaborative approaches to maritime security. It is not entirely clear, however, how much these efforts contributed to a reduction in Asian piracy. Some even suggest that the enormous Asian tsunami of December 2004 wiped out key pirate operating bases ashore, leading to a reduction in maritime crime.[15] But the downward progression in the incidence of piracy in Asia has been halted, and piracy is once again on the upswing in that part of the world.

Piracy in Asia increased threefold from 2009 to 2010, marking an unwelcome resurgence after a half-decade of decline.[16] Thirty percent of all piracy attacks worldwide still occur in Southeast Asia. After a decade of increased cooperation to suppress maritime piracy, it remains a pressing security issue in Southeast Asia, and especially in the Malacca Strait and waters around Indonesia. Nine attacks were recorded in the two-week span from August 16 to September 2, 2010. By comparison, in 2009, there were only seven maritime piracy incidents in the region for the whole year. During 2010 piracy attacks occurred around Indonesia's islands of Mangkai, Anambas, and Natuna. The IMB has appealed to Indonesia to increase antipiracy patrols, and has warned ships to strictly maintain a piracy watch.[17]

"Phantom Ships" in Asia

Maritime piracy in Asia differs from its Somali counterpart. The level of violence and the goals of the pirates are unique to each region. Rather than the hostage-for-ransom model popular among Somali pirates, the objective of Asia pirates typically is to seize vulnerable ships and cargo. Either the ship or the cargo (or both) is sold on the spot market. Oftentimes the pirated vessel is renamed and reregistered—a modern incarnation of the "phantom ship" or "ghost ship," a vessel that has been converted and lacks legal paperwork.[18] The crew and passengers are merely unwanted witnesses. Often executed in cold blood, their bodies are cast into the sea. The horrific attack on the *Cheung Son* epitomizes this model.

In 1998, the Hong Kong–flagged cargo ship *Cheung Son* was transiting off the coast of Kaohsiung, Taiwan, en route to Port Klang, Malaysia. The ship was intercepted and boarded by pirates who were masquerading as Chinese customs officers. The brigands were outfitted in official Chinese uniforms and carried firearms as they boarded the merchant ship. The owner of the vessel lost contact with the ship and its crew.

The pirates bludgeoned to death all 23 crew members of the *Cheung Son* and threw their weighted bodies into the South China Sea. The pirated vessel was sold in China for about $36,000 and the ship was resold for 10 times that amount to a Singaporean buyer. But later fishermen discovered the dead bodies of the crew. An informant's tip combined with adept police work led to a karaoke bar, where the pirates were celebrating their crime and new wealth. In all, more than 50 Chinese seafarers were arrested for the brutal murders on the *Cheung Son*. The gang was working for a shadowy kingpin of either Chinese or Indonesian origin. At trial, many of the pirates claimed they had been hired as contractors to conduct legitimate antismuggling operations. Only once they were at sea did they discover they had been tricked into attacking the *Cheung*

Son. Thirty-eight men were convicted of piracy, and 13 of them were executed in January 1999 for the heinous crime.[19]

The tragic case of the *Cheung Son* illustrates the problem of the emergence of ghost ships or phantom ships—one that was securely associated with Chinese gangs until only recently. Under Article 94 of the 1982 United Nations Convention on the Law of the Sea (UNCLOS), flag states retain duties of registration and regulation of international seagoing vessels. Asian pirates usurped the flag state's role by seizing a merchant ship, killing the crew and passengers, selling the cargo, and reregistering the ship under a different flag and new name.

Some flag states may unwittingly register a ship that criminals have converted with new papers and a manufactured new identity. In order to help states become more vigilant, the IMO assembly adopted a resolution in 2002 to help prevent the registration of phantom ships.[20] The international maritime community, and especially the ancillary financial and logistical sectors, spends considerable effort to obtain accurate information on newly registered vessels, including evidence of prior registration. Governments verify ship identity using the IMO Ship Identification Number and other records, to ensure that the ship does not fly the flag of two or more states simultaneously. States share information on such documentation, and provide registration information at time of sale or transfer to the flag state in which a ship previously has been registered.

Piracy in Asia had increased 40 percent from the year before the *Cheong Son* incident, providing a rallying point for expanding cooperation among the states in the region. Beginning in the late 1990s, pirates seized a number of other cargo ships besides the *Cheong Son*. Also in 1998, pirates stole the *Petro Ranger* and *Tenyu*, and in 1999, the *Alondra Rainbow*. In 2001, the *Global Mars* and *Arby Jaya* were hit. The IMB's Piracy Reporting Centre (PRC) in Kuala Lumpur reported 172 actual or attempted piracy attacks in Southeast Asian waters in 2003 and 165 attacks in 2004.[21] In 2004 there were 34 attacks in the Malacca Strait; in 2008 there were only two. Whereas there occurred 121 attacks in Indonesian waters in 2003, there were only 28 such attacks in 2008. Chapter 6 of this volume recounts the diplomatic initiatives that contributed to the decline of piracy in the region. The greatest incentive for states both in and beyond Asia to control Southeast Asian piracy is to ensure the safety and security of the Straits of Malacca and Singapore.

Straits of Malacca and Singapore

The Straits of Malacca and Singapore extend 520 nautical miles in length, linking the Indian Ocean to the Pacific Ocean. Extremely narrow passages and high traffic density are features throughout the waterways. Seventy thousand ships traverse the straits each year, and between 1999 and 2008, maritime traffic in the straits increased by 74 percent. The Japanese government expects the number of transits to rise to 114,000 ships per year within a decade.[22] Some of the largest and busiest ports in the world, including the ports of Klang, Singapore, Jakarta (Tanjong Priok), Hong Kong, Shanghai, Pusan, and Tokyo, feed large volumes of shipping traffic through the straits. Along with the Strait of Gibraltar and Strait of Hormuz, the Strait of Malacca is among the most important geographic infrastructures on the planet.

The vessels that transit the straits are particularly vulnerable to piracy and armed robbery at sea because they must navigate at greatly reduced speeds due to safety of navigation.[23] Since most of the piracy attacks that occur in the Straits of Malacca and Singapore are in the territorial seas of Indonesia, Malaysia, or Singapore, national responses of the littoral states to suppress piracy are particularly important to regional security.[24]

As the epicenter of piracy in Asia, Indonesian piracy poses a particularly difficult challenge. Composed of more than 17,500 islands and with 34,000 miles (54,718 kilometers) of coastline, the country offers generous natural protection for pirates who lurk near international shipping lanes. The Riau Archipelago island chain, for example, which lies on the south shore of the Phillip Channel just nine miles off the coast of Singapore, has been described as a "pirate paradise."[25] The island of Batam, the largest in the Riau group, is a known piracy enclave. The country is economically vibrant, but stubborn poverty persists. Social and economic conditions are ripe for instability. Terrorism and separatism threaten the nation's fragile democracy. At a regional counterpiracy conference in Tokyo in 2000, an Indonesian representative framed the dilemma: [Indonesia] has "so many islands, so many problems."[26]

Between 2000 and 2006, one-quarter of global piracy incidents (and two-thirds of those in Southeast Asia) occurred in the vast Indonesian archipelago.[27] Indonesia was overwhelmed with the task of maintaining maritime security throughout the vast archipelago, and a reduction in naval spending following the 1998 Asian financial crisis exacerbated the challenge. John F. Bradford, the top Western analyst of Indonesian maritime security policy, recounts that Indonesian leaders were preoccupied with more pressing matters that siphoned resources and attention away from counterpiracy activities.[28] Inaction abetted piracy throughout the archipelago.

In 2004, the U.S. Pacific Command unveiled a partnership program called the Regional Maritime Security Initiative (RMSI) as a way to strengthen security in the Straits of Malacca and Singapore. RMSI would have involved capacity building of the maritime forces along the straits, but statements made by the commander of U.S. Pacific Command, Admiral Thomas Fargo, were misinterpreted by Indonesia and Malaysia to foreshadow U.S. naval patrols in the straits. This interpretation was inaccurate, but coastal state sensitivities were aroused. Sensing that the U.S.-sponsored effort might prove an affront to coastal state sovereignty over the straits, which constitute territorial seas of Malaysia, Singapore, and Indonesia, the three nations combined efforts to establish coordinated naval patrols beginning in July 2004. Indonesia was especially concerned that the palpable lack of security in the straits might encourage other nations to conduct patrols in the straits, rather than simply enjoy the right of continuous and expeditious transit passage.

In 2004, Southeast Asia recorded the highest number of pirate attacks globally.[29] In response to the escalation in piracy, in July 2005 the Lloyds Market Association Joint War Committee (JWC) designated the Straits of Malacca and Singapore as a "war risk zone." The economic effect was immediate: carrier insurance premiums for transit through the Malacca Strait skyrocketed. The export-dependent economies of Singapore and Malaysia brought Indonesia on board with a program of complementary initiatives to enhance security in the waterway.

Indonesia had long been the laggard among the littoral states in developing effective maritime security. Determined to improve the country's image, in 2005, President Yudhoyono directed an increase in naval patrols throughout the Indonesian portions of the Malacca Strait. That same year, more than 20 Indonesian naval vessels were involved in a massive counterpiracy operation that resulted in the arrest of a large number of pirate gangs.

Although the littoral states were taking steps to reduce piracy, assistance from outside the region could supplement their efforts. Indonesia, Malaysia, and Singapore and the nations that routinely use the straits conducted three meetings from 2004 to 2007 under the IMO's Protection of Vital Shipping Lanes Initiative. The objective of the meetings, the first of which was held in Jakarta, Indonesia, on September 7–8, 2005, was to craft a framework for cooperation between the users of the straits and the littoral states of Indonesia, Singapore, and Malaysia. The resulting framework for cooperation, or Cooperative Mechanism, was the first time that littoral states and user states had combined efforts to manage the safety and environmental security of an international strait in accordance with the obligation to do so under Article 43 of UNCLOS.

The perspective of the littoral states was memorialized in the Fourth Tripartite Ministerial Meeting of the Littoral States, which was held just one month prior to the Jakarta meeting.[30] The three littoral states emphasized at both the Tripartite Meeting and the IMO meetings that the international straits were also coastal state territorial seas. Responsibility for security in the straits, therefore, fell within the exclusive purview of the coastal countries. The user states could have limited involvement in developing littoral state capacity to increase the ability of Indonesia, Malaysia, and Singapore to exchange information, and for the provision of training for local forces.

The 2005 Jakarta meeting adopted the Batam Joint Statement, and reiterated the importance of engaging the states that ring the western entrance to the straits—Thailand and India, in particular. The littoral states agreed to improve collaborative maritime domain awareness and conduct coordinated maritime patrols in the straits. The three littoral states signed a memorandum of understanding to implement a Marine Electronic Highway (MEH) demonstration project in the straits, which was built around a marine environmental management and protection systems (EMPS) and advanced marine navigation technologies.[31] The second meeting was held in Kuala Lumpur (KL), September 18–20, 2006. The KL meeting extended the discussions on the straits, and advanced an agenda of cooperation. The meeting considered a proposal for a new Cooperative Mechanism between the user states and the littoral states.[32]

Meanwhile, the littoral states began working more closely together. Surface ship patrols in the straits were augmented with an aviation surveillance program called Eye in the Sky (EiS). The surface patrols and EiS were linked in April 2006 to an information sharing network, which could vector real-time responses to reports of maritime piracy. The Indonesian navy conducted an exercise in March 2006 that simulated the retaking of a large passenger ferry being held by terrorists. Just months later, authorities captured a band of 16 pirates that had hijacked at least six vessels.

Pursuant to the 2005 Jakarta Meeting and the 2006 Kuala Lumpur Meeting, the 2007 Singapore Meeting convened to agree on a final framework for the Cooperative Mechanism.[33] The arrangement had three components: the Cooperation Forum, a Project Coordination Committee, and the Aids to Navigation Fund.[34] The user states pledged to continue capacity building projects. The United States, for example, delivered 10 surface search radars for installation along the eastern coast of Sumatra Island from Sabang at the northern tip of Aceh Province to Bengkalis, which is nearer Singapore in the southern stretch of the strait.[35]

In 2008, Thailand would join the initiative sponsored by the littoral states, which was renamed the Malacca Straits Patrols (MSP). Increased collaboration along the straits—among the three littoral states, and between the littoral states and more than 20 user states—contributed to a marked decline in piracy between 2003 and 2008, falling from 187 incidents per year to only 65 per year over that period.

Additional coordination in Asia is still unfolding. Asian states in general now think about defense in more regional terms. Whereas NATO has existed in Europe for decades, the ASEAN Defense Ministers Meeting (ADMM) met for the first time in 2006. The first meeting of ADMM Plus, the ADMM, plus ministers from the United States, China, Russia, Japan, India, South Korea, Australia, and New Zealand, was held in Hanoi on October 12, 2010. The 18 participating defense ministers command military and security resources comparable to that possessed by NATO, and they are beginning to consider how to manage shared, nontraditional security threats, such as disaster relief and humanitarian assistance, counterterrorism, and peacekeeping operations.[36] But maritime piracy is also a common threat.

The increased cooperation against piracy in Southeast Asia stands in contrast to the lack of regional capability in East Africa. Although the experience in Southeast Asia provides some impetus for greater regional approaches to piracy off the coast of Somalia, the two theaters are markedly different.[37]

East Africa—Somali Piracy

In 2009, 217 vessels were attacked in the waters off the Horn of Africa by Somali pirates, and of the 219 ships attacked in 2010. The figures are twice the rate of 2008. In 2010, Somali pirates successfully captured 49 ships, compared with 45 in 2009. The number of hostages held off the Somali coast in 2010 reached 1,181. At the end of 2009, Somali pirates held 12 vessels for ransom and 263 hostages. By February 2011, they held 685 seafarers hostage on board 30 hijacked ships.[38]

The pirates have also expanded the range of their attacks, striking as far as Mozambique, which is 2,500 miles from Somalia. By converting captured fishing vessels and mother ships, the pirates have been effective at using smaller seaworthy ships as mobile sea bases from which to launch high-speed skiffs. By targeting larger vessels in succession, pirates can hopscotch their way across the Indian Ocean until they capture a prized oil tanker or cargo ship that could bring them millions of dollars in ransom.[39]

For example, the Indian navy and coast guard interdicted three Thai fishing vessels that were being used as mother ships in the Indian Ocean. The *Prantlaya-11*, *12*, and *14*, along with their Thai crews, were hijacked in April 2010 and held by Somali pirates. *Prantalay-14* was used extensively as a mother ship to conduct piracy attacks and was sunk by Indian maritime forces on January 28, 2011. The remaining Thai fishing vessels were used as mother ships as well. On February 5, 2011, skiffs from the *Prantlaya-11* unsuccessfully attacked the MT *Chios*, a Greek-flagged crude oil tanker transiting from Singapore to Yemen in the area of the Lakshadweep and Minicoy Islands. While on a routine patrol off the Lakshadweep Islands, Indian Coast Guard Ship ICGS *Samar*, joined by the Indian Navy Ship INS *Tir*, was diverted to the distress call of the *Chios*, arriving on scene at daybreak on February 6, 2011. After trying to flee, the pirates on board *Prantlaya-11* surrendered under gunfire from the ICGS *Samar*. The ICGS *Samar* and INS *Tir* apprehended 28 Somali pirates and freed 24 Thai fishermen. In total, four fishing vessels from the *Prantalay* fleet were hijacked, and Indian police interned 43 pirates and 44 fishermen in Mumbai.

After Asia, Africa is the largest continent; it is also the second most populous continent. The land area is immense—covering one-fifth of the total surface of the earth and the coastline is 24,233 miles (39,000 kilometers) in length. The shoreline overlooks some of the most strategic waterways in the world.

Thirty-three thousand ships transit the Gulf of Aden (GOA) annually, for example. Six thousand five hundred oil tankers carrying 7 percent of the world's daily oil supply use the route.[40] The passage links trade between the East and West through the neighboring Strait of Bab el Mandeb and into the Suez Canal. Ironically, the spread of piracy throughout the Horn of Africa occurred just as the global economy began to collapse in slow motion during the 2008–2009 Great Recession.[41]

Somalia occupies the Horn of Africa, and Somali pirates have surged in recent years. While the incidence of maritime piracy is declining in most areas of the world in recent years due to cooperation among littoral states and the international community,[42] the threat has rapidly increased along the coast of East Africa.[43] Somali piracy became the epicenter for maritime crime, in part, due to economic desperation and a virtually lawless environment, all within close proximity of one of the globe's most lucrative trade routes.

The nation of Somalia is poor and dependent on agriculture, and livestock accounts for almost half of the GDP. Somalia emerged from British colonialism in 1960 as a protectorate and new nation. Mohamed Siad Barre seized power in a coup in 1969, imposing authoritarian rule, but also stability, on the nation for more than two decades. The government collapsed, however, in 1991 and the country descended into chaos. The nation was fractured into three regional states. The Republic of Somaliland declared independence in 1991. The regions of Bari, Nugaal, and northern Mudug formed the neighboring semiautonomous state of Puntland, which assumed local self-governance in 1998.

The UN conducted an ill-fated famine relief and peacekeeping mission in the country from 1993 to 1995. The operation involved 30,000 soldiers. Thousands of lives were saved through food aid, but the operation failed to provide political stability. The U.S. representative to the UN, Ambassador Madeleine K. Albright, remarked that the 1993 UN resolution authorizing the mission was "an unprecedented enterprise aimed at nothing less than the restoration of an entire country as a proud, functioning and viable member of the community of nations."[44] But the UN operation failed to bring peace.

Since 1991, Somalia has been wracked by hybrid warfare—a mixture of irregular clan and militia conflict combined with more conventionally capable forces, and the sporadic involvement of the nation's neighbors.[45] There has been no official control of Somalia's borders for two decades. Human trafficking and smuggling are as endemic to the Horn of Africa as maritime piracy—additional manifestations of the organized crime syndicates running amok in the collapsed nation. In the words of Sergey Lavrov, the Minister for Foreign Affairs of the Russian Federation, maritime piracy is just the "tip of the iceberg" of the problems facing Somalia.[46]

The civil war has continued to evolve through multiple phases, ruining the economy and destabilizing civil society. Violence hinders economic

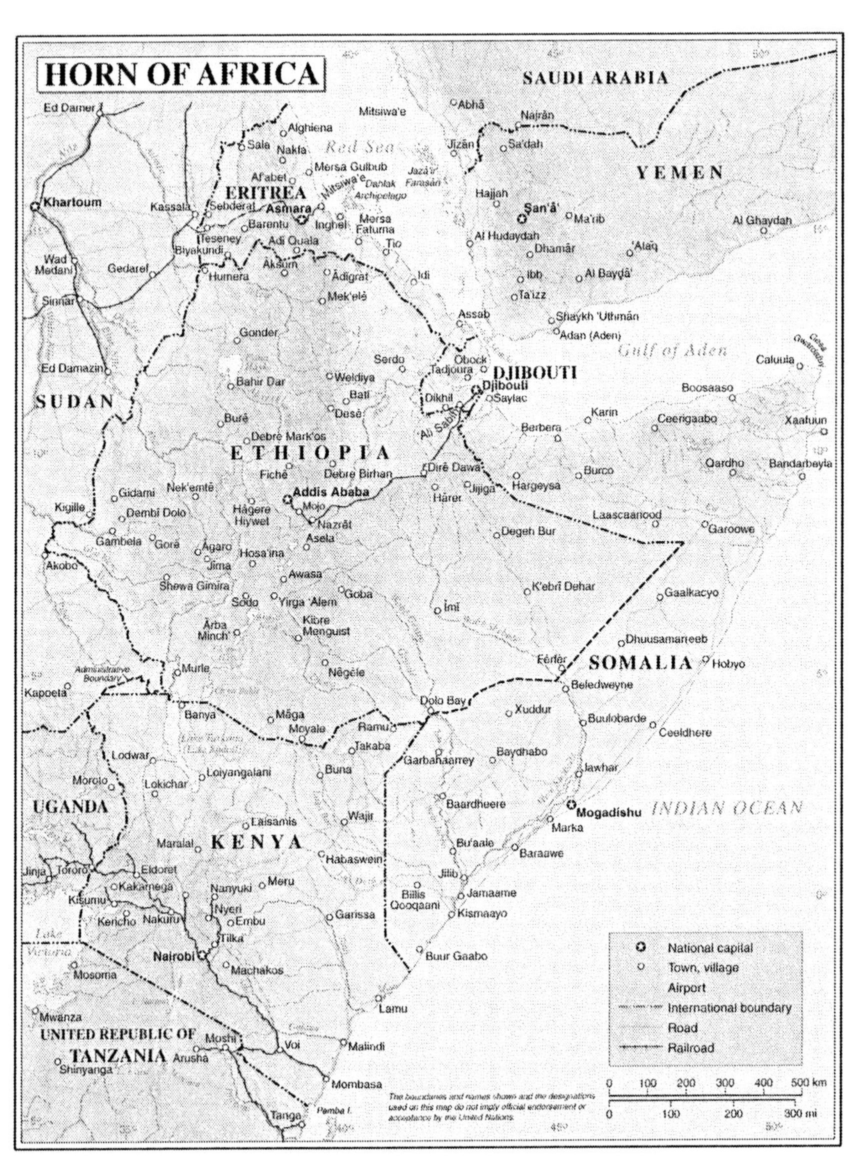

Map No. 4188 Rev. 1, United Nations, January 2004

development. Internal conflict surrounding the large port and trading hubs of Mogadishu, Kismayu, and other transportation nodes is perennial. The neighboring state of Kenya led negotiations in 2004 to create an interim Transitional Federal Government (TFG), which remains a weak authority with little real capability. Dr. J. Peter Pham, the dean of African security politics, recently described the TFG this way:

> Despite the doubling of the African Union Mission in Somalia (AMISOM) force protecting [the new prime minister] . . . and hundreds of millions of dollars in international assistance, the rather ironically named "Transitional Federal Government" (TFG) of Sheikh Sharif Sheikh Ahmed is not a whit closer to being the municipal government of its putative capital, much less the "federal government" of the Somali territories. Its many ministers, when they are not off on globetrotting tours to tell donors about all their great plans, are good only for whiling away their days camped out in the lobby of Mogadishu's Nassa Nablood II Hotel—effectively the only choice left to them since insurgents bombed the Shamo and the Muna—drinking tea and stiffing its owners for the bill.[47]

Pham reiterates that the TFG survives thanks only to the presence of 8,000 Ugandan and Burundian AMISOM troops. As governmental authority evaporated, clan and factional political elites rose to power amidst instability, Balkanizing the nation. The clan is the principal means of physical and social security, and the clan makes the most powerful claim on Somali self-identity. The clan also provides basic services. Pirates seek advantage in the breakdown of clan authority in Puntland. Some clan leaders in Puntland may be involved in the illegal trafficking of drugs and weapons. In comparison, the Somaliland authorities have been able to exert much better control over the youth, and have been relatively successful in demilitarizing civil society.

Somali pirates collect ransom money in exchange for hostages and vessels that are seized while in transit in the Gulf of Aden (GOA), the Somali Basin, and more recently, the western Indian Ocean. Piracy in Somalia has arisen within this milieu of impoverishment and clan dynamics, with competing religious and ideological groups vying for power. The underlying economic and political challenges include "crushing poverty, widespread unemployment, environmental hardship, a reduction of pastoralist and maritime resources due to drought and illegal fishing and a volatile security and political situation."[48] The confluence of these factors keeps the country on a downward arc and contributes to the persistence of piracy.

Warlord financiers use control of businesses, armaments, and resources to maintain power. A strong sense of clan fealty and an enduring duty to clan lineage dominate society. Al Shabaab and Hizbul Islam are Islamist Salafi movements in the country. Harakat al-Shabaab al-Mujahideen ("Movement of Warrior Youth," or al-Shabaab) has found confederation with Al Qaeda, and a number of the group's leaders have fought on behalf of the Taliban in Afghanistan.[49] The Ahlu Sunna wal Jama (ASWJ) comprises numerous Sufi branches of the Shafi'i school. As dangerous as the waters are around the Horn of Africa, Pham reminds us that pirates are "by no means the gravest threat to international security emanating from Somalia. That distinction probably belongs to the militant Islamists of [al-Shabaab]."[50] Piracy threatens dozens of vessels and hundreds of seafarers; al-Shabaab threatens to turn Somalia into Afghanistan. Al-Shabaab already rules over large swaths of Somali territory, and they operate freely even in areas they do not control.[51] Observers are becoming increasingly worried that the two Islamic extremist groups have begun to collaborate. The hijacking of the sailing vessel *Quest* and the murder of the four Americans on board the ship is worrisome in this regard.

On February 18, 2011, the S/V *Quest*, a 58-foot U.S. sailing vessel with four Americans on board, was captured by 19 Somali pirates. Sailed by owners Scott and Jean Adams, the yacht had been traveling off the coast of Oman in company with three other private sailing ships. I received an electronic mail from one of the ships alerting me of the capture of the *Quest* before it had been made public and asking for guidance on how to secure assistance. The desperate mariners already had contacted MSC HOA and MARLO, so naval forces had been dispatched and there was nothing else that could be done.

When U.S. naval forces arrived on the scene, the pirates sent two emissaries to negotiate for the release of the hostages. American officials became frustrated with the lack of progress and detained the two Somali pirates and requested that the Somalis send more serious negotiators to help resolve the crisis. By this time, the pirated yacht, stuffed with four hostages and more than 20 pirates was being shadowed by the guided missile destroyer USS *Sterett* (DDG 104), which was 600 yards off the stern of the *Quest*. The aircraft carrier USS *Enterprise* (CVN 65), the guided missile cruiser USS *Leyte Gulf* (CG 55), and the USS *Bulkeley* (DDG 84) were nearby. The massive flotilla, which represented more than 130,000 tons of sea power, was operating in support of Operation Enduring Freedom (Afghanistan) and Operation New Dawn (Iraq).

At 0100 on the morning of February 22, shots were fired aboard the yacht, and a U.S. Navy boarding party closed with the sailing vessel. During the non-permissive boarding 2 pirates were killed and 13 pirates were detained (along with the 2 pirates already in U.S. custody). But the U.S. forces also discovered that the four American hostages had been shot and were already dead or near death. At the time this volume went to press, it was unclear what had gone wrong, and theories abound. Some suggest that the pirates may have run out of khat, an amphetamine-like stimulant that is derived from a flowering plant native to the region. During the *Maersk Alabama* incident, tensions rose dramatically when the pirates ran out of khat, leading snipers aboard the USS

Bainbridge to shoot 3 pirates to ensure the safety of Captain Phillips. After the *Maersk Alabama* rescue, pirates had pledged to specifically target U.S. mariners.

Another theory suggests that Scott and Jean Adams, who were evangelical Christians carrying boxes of bibles aboard their yacht, were specifically targeted and murdered by Islamic-inspired pirates with connections to al-Shabaab. As the Al Qaeda affiliate in the Horn of Africa, al-Shabaab would view the Christians as polytheists, who should be executed. For several years, U.S. authorities have rejected the idea that the pirates and al-Shabaab were operating in league: only Jane's Information Group and the private security firm Osen-Hunter Security Group have suggested there is a connection between piracy and radical Islamic militants inside Somalia.

Despite the occasional violence between the two groups, it appears that al-Shabaab can set aside its religious aversion to piracy on occasion in order to demand a share of the profits. Al-Shabaab, for example, reportedly attacked pirates who were holding the New Zealand couple Bruno Pelizzari and Deborah Calitz hostage in the coastal town of Baraawe. The couple was seized from the sailing vessel *Schoizil* as it sailed off the coast of Tanzania. As a French warship intervened, the vessel ran aground in Somalia and although the couple was taken ashore, Peter Eldridge, the South African skipper, escaped and was rescued. Once on land, the pirates were ordered by al-Shabaab to drop their weapons. The pirates did so immediately, and the hostages were surrendered to the Islamists.

Adding credibility to the theory that the Islamists and pirates are cooperating, Reuters reported that al-Shabaab is awarded a "base take" of 20 percent of all ransom money by pirates operating from areas under the control of the organization. A pirate told Reuters, "We have no alternative other than agreeing to al-Shabaab demands." On February 22, 2011, Osen-Hunter Security Group shared its research with me that makes a strong case that the entry of al-Shabaab into piracy represents the most insidious game-changer yet. After al-Shabaab captured the piracy safe haven of Haradhere in April 2010, the Al Qaeda affiliate can be traced directly to the seizure of the M/V *Asphalt Venture* in September 2010. The murder of four American seafarers underscores the ineffectiveness of the maritime interdiction model of countering piracy. At the time that the *Quest* was hijacked, there were 34 warships patrolling the area under 15 different flags. Yet the massive coalition was unable to stop the murder of four civilians, which represented an unprecedented level of violence by Somali pirates. The Transitional Federal Government (TFG) accommodates a range of religious views, as do the regional, semiautonomous authorities that govern Puntland and Somaliland.[52] A nation of contrasts, the country has cellular wireless service in most major cities and it offers among the lowest international call rates in Africa. But the banking sector is underdeveloped, so money transfer and remittance services rely on the hawala system, which is notoriously difficult to monitor.

The total payoff for hijacking a single ship has skyrocketed from $50,000 in the early 2000s to as much as $7 million by 2011. Most of the money is siphoned off to organized crime kingpins living in Puntland—who, more recently, have seen fit to retire to elaborate luxury compounds in the exclusive neighborhoods of Mombassa, Kenya. Piracy "earnings" are difficult to track, but it is clear that the funds are being invested in other criminal business, such as mining and narcotics trafficking, as well as fueling a mini-construction boom along the coastline of Puntland.[53] One attack can yield $50,000 for a working-level pirate, and with few legitimate options, piracy and crime have flourished. The amount of money can be life changing. The money collected in ransom revenue each year now exceeds the entire budget of the Puntland government.[54] With the potential for generous payoff, there are plenty of recruits. The risks appear minimal and the rewards can be astonishing, particularly for a country where two-thirds of the population is unemployed.

The Somali diaspora, residing in Europe and North America, has a significant effect on shaping the politics and economics of the country. The clan identity is infused throughout the Somali diaspora. This identity imposes a strong and enduring obligation on the part of the first generation of the diaspora to remit as much money as possible to the clan and extended family members. Overseas Somalis cannot refuse to send remittances, as it would be tantamount to rejecting their self-identity. Remittances from overseas Somalis pump $1–$1.5 billion into the economy, making the Somali economy almost entirely dependent on the flow of remittances. Approximately 1.5 million Somalis—15 percent of the total population—live outside the country. External remittances eclipse the other major sources of Somali earnings, which are exports (about $100 million per year) and international foreign aid, which is thought to be about $100–$200 million per year. In comparison, in 2008 piracy ransom brought in $40–$100 million into the country. Many households are dependent on international remittances, which often are the difference between survival and destitution.

Pham suggests that professionals from the diaspora have returned to Somalia to operate businesses. Hotels and restaurants are able to operate in some of the most war-torn areas of the country only by hiring private-security militias for protection. Since Somalia is clan-based, personal attempts to build individual wealth are frowned on, whereas generous elders who spread wealth throughout the clan are highly regarded. Clans tend to congregate around elders and large personalities who can represent the interests of the people to outsiders—other clans, international donors, and political groups.

Somalis have expressed concern that little attention has been paid to the suffering and illegal dumping of hazardous waste and fish poaching that occurs throughout their exclusive economic zone (EEZ). At an IMO assembly meeting, the Somali delegate stated, "the Somali people were disappointed with the one-sided attitude of the international community, which had expressed little concern for their suffering; instead, there had been a lot of noise from the shipping world and international community about ships being endangered by acts of piracy and armed robbery in the waters off the Somali coast."[55] Somali officials have cited illegal, unreported, and unregulated (IUU) fishing and illegal dumping in the waters off the coast of Somalia as one of the causal factors in the rise of piracy.[56]

An IMO review suggests that IUU fishing does indeed take place in waters off the coast of Somalia, and there is evidence that "licenses" to fish in the waters may be obtained outside of official channels.[57] Prior to the demise of Siad Barre, piracy in the region was rare. In the 1990s, armed groups began to patrol the country's 200-mile exclusive economic zone as a self-appointed "coast guard," demanding the payment of "fines" for ships operating near the country. Although foreign fishing vessels have (and to a more limited extent continue) poached in Somalia's economic zone, fisheries protection was only one factor in the skyrocketing piracy of the mid 2000s.

Attacks increased throughout 2004–2005, and attracted the attention of the United States and other nations. The unsuccessful attack on the *Seabourn Spirit* luxury cruise liner in December 2005 was a harbinger of a steady escalation in piracy. The ship had 150 passengers on board. Approaching the vessel in high-speed skiffs, pirates shot at the ship with rocket-propelled grenades and automatic rifles.[58] Although the ship managed to escape by using a defensive sonic weapon called the Long Range Acoustic Device (LRAD), the attack underscored that virtually no vessel could transit the area safely.

When piracy first began to escalate in the region, pirates would conduct their attacks relatively close to land. Notices to mariners (NOTMARs) advised shipping to remain 200 nautical miles from Somalia in order to avoid the threat of maritime piracy. But even as ships moved farther offshore—well beyond 200 nautical miles—to avoid pirates, the attacks continued. Pirates went father out to sea in search of targets, and the number of attacks doubled from 2007 to 2008.[59] Now the IMB advises vessels not making scheduled calls to ports in Somalia to keep as far as possible from the Somali coast, preferably more than 600 nautical miles from the shoreline. In fact, some Somali piracy attacks now occur much closer to India or Madagascar than the Horn of Africa.

Somali pirates have become increasingly sophisticated in their methods and operations. They approach merchant ships in small, fast boats and are armed with Kalashnikov assault rifles, rocket-propelled grenades, global positioning devices, and walkie-talkies.[60] Somali gunmen in speedboats have seized and held for ransom seafarers and valuable or potentially dangerous cargo. The chemical tanker *Golden Nori,* for example, was seized in October 2007 and held for seven weeks, raising concern that the Japanese ship, laden with highly flammable benzene, could become a floating bomb.

In 2008 Somali pirates attacked 111 vessels in the GOA and western Indian Ocean.[61] Forty-two vessels were hijacked in the waters of the Horn of Africa and 815 crew members were held for ransom.[62] Some of the greatest trophies seized by pirates in 2008 include the M/V *Faina*, a Ukrainian-flagged vessel carrying 33 Russian armored tanks. The armored vehicles had certificates of delivery to Kenya for transfer to the democratic Sudan People's Liberation Army, an authorized regional force in Sudan. The supertanker, *Sirius Star*, belonging to the class of Very Large Crude Carriers (VLCC), was seized nearly 500 miles off the coast of Kenya. As long as an aircraft carrier, the tanker was carrying 25 crew members and a load of 2 million barrels of crude oil from Saudi Arabia bound for the United States, and worth more than $100 million.

The large coalition of warships operating in the GOA and the use of defensive measures by merchant vessels has encouraged pirates to seek prey farther from the Horn of Africa. The assaults occurred in the waters off the east and south coast of Somalia, including the Indian Ocean, GOA, southern Red Sea, Strait of Bab El Mandeb, off the east coast of Oman, and in the Arabian Sea.[63]

Overall, in 2009 there were 80 attacks off the east and south coast of Somalia, 116 attacks in the GOA, 15 attacks in the southern Red Sea, 4 attacks off Oman, and 1 reported in the Arabian Sea and 1 in the Indian Ocean.[64] In April and May 2009, 5 piracy attacks occurred within 200 miles of Port Victoria, Seychelles, and 2 of the assaults were successful. In June 2009, the ship *Charelle* was hijacked in Omani territorial waters nearly 800 nautical miles from Somalia. Forty-seven ships were hijacked and 867 crew members seized as hostages. Ten seafarers were injured and four killed; one crew member was missing.[65] The cost of Somali piracy is estimated to be $5 billion to $7 billion per year.

Typically, ransom negotiations are conducted in Dubai. London has also become a hub for firms that help ship owners deal with the legal aspects of paying the ransoms.[66] In early November 2010, Somali pirates reportedly extracted a $9.5 million ransom for the release of the *Samho Dream*, a South Korean supertanker, which was seized in April.[67] Reminiscent of the capture of the *Sirius Star* two years earlier, the *Samho Dream* carried 2 million barrels of crude oil valued at $170 million.[68] In late December 2010, Somali pirates were venturing farther south than ever before. The *NS Africa* and the *Majestic* were attacked in two separate incidents in the Mozambique Channel, which is about 950 nautical miles south of Dar es Salaam, Tanzania.[69] Prior to the attacks, the farthest south Somali pirates had operated was only about 80 nautical miles east of the Tanzania-Mozambique border.

The increasing reach of Somali pirates shows that they are clever and adaptive. They have attacked vessels at all times of day and night, but nighttime encounters are increasing. As the number of coalition warships operating in the region has increased, pirates operate in darkness to avoid detection. Interestingly, however, lunar illumination does not appear to be a factor in pirate activity, with attacks occurring throughout the lunar cycle. The criminal gangs are making greater use of mother ships and increasing their crew size in order to control more vessels. Pirates also are using a "stepping stone" strategy, in which they seize a small yacht, then a fishing boat and finally, a larger merchant ship. The pirates are also very adaptive to rules of engagement, and warning shots are becoming less effective in disrupting attacks. Weapons and other pirate paraphernalia are thrown overboard prior to boarding to destroy evidence needed in prosecution.

The escalating ransom payments to pirates and lack of enforcement of the 1992 UN arms embargo are fuelling the growth of piracy off the coast of Somalia.[70] Ultimately the only way to halt the attacks is to increase governance and the rule of law in Somalia, as the country lacks the capacity to patrol its own waters.[71] NATO commander General John Craddock stated flatly, "You don't stop piracy on the seas. You stop piracy on the land."[72] Piracy cannot be curbed without establishing minimum law and order in Puntland. Stability on land must be complemented by the disruption of the illicit revenues from maritime piracy, and implementation of vessel security measures to minimize the risks of new attacks on ships at sea.[73] Providing stability is difficult because Somalia's regional authorities have inadequate governance systems, human resources, delivery of public services, and are dependent on a decrepit physical infrastructure.[74]

In many ways, Somali piracy is a menace that is outpacing efforts by the international community to stem it.[75] Pirates are also taking greater risks and seeking higher ransoms because the cost-benefit calculus is favorable. Lynn Pascoe, the UN secretary-general for political affairs, testified before the Security Council in November 2010 that "as long as piracy is so lucrative, with ransom payments adding up to tens of millions if not hundreds of millions of dollars, and other economic incentives so bleak, the incentives are obvious."[76] Many of the ransom negotiations are conducted in Dubai; money is laundered in Dubai and as much as $100 million per year is laundered in Kenya.[77] Interpol's executive director for police services, Jean-Michel Louboutin, stated that same month that police investigators finally connected Somali piracy to support networks in Western Europe and East Africa.[78] By 2011, the full extent of the sophisticated financial and logistics network that supports Somali piracy came under more thorough scrutiny.[79]

Notes

1. IMO Doc. MSC.4/Circ.152, Reports on Acts of Piracy and Armed Robbery against Ships—Annual Report 2009, March 29, 2010, at 2.

2. IMO Doc. MSC.4/Circ.152, Reports on Acts of Piracy, at 2.

3. See, Exports of Goods and Services (% of GDP), The World Bank Data 2008, http://data.worldbank.org/indicator/NE.EXP.GNFS.ZS.

4. See, Container Ports Map 038 SASI Group (University of Sheffield) and Mark Newman (University of Michigan), 2006, www.worldmapper.org.

5. See generally, Peter Chalk, *Low Intensity Conflict in Southeast Asia: Piracy, Drug Trafficking and Political Terrorism*, 1 Conflict Studies 1–36 (1998).

6. See generally, Peter Chalk, *Contemporary Maritime Piracy in Southeast Asia*, 21 Studies in Conflict and Terrorism 87–112 (1998).

7. John F. Bradford, *Shifting the Tides against Piracy in Southeast Asian Waters*, 48(3) Asian Survey 473–491, at 478 (May/June 2008).

8. Simon Wilson, *The Boom in Piracy*, Money Week, December 11, 2009.

9. Emmanuel, Cam Ranh Bay, Now Open for Business, International Political Economy Zone, Newstex Web Blogs, November 18, 2010, http://ipezone.blogspot.com/2010/11/cam-ranh-bay-now-open-for-business.html.

10. Emmanuel, Cam Ranh Bay, Now Open for Business.

11. On March 14, 1988, for example, Chinese Marines invaded a handful of the Spratly islands owned by Vietnam, killing 64 Vietnamese. By balancing China against the United States, Vietnam hopes to thwart further Chinese aggression in the South China Sea, which Vietnam calls the East Vietnam Sea.

12. China's GDP was 1.854 trillion Yuan RMB in 1990. By 2000, China's GDP had grown to 8.946 trillion Yuan RMB. GDP growth, 1952–2008, May 4, 2008, http://Chinability.com/GDP.htm.

13. Gerard Graham Ong-Webb, Piracy in Maritime Asia: Current Trends, *in Violence at Sea: Piracy in the Age of Global Terrorism* 49–53 (Peter Lehr, ed., 2007).

14. Bradford, *Shifting the Tides against Piracy in Southeast Asian Waters*, at 474.

15. Bradford, *Shifting the Tides against Piracy in Southeast Asian Waters*, at 478. Bradford also recounts, however, that "the deployment of international military forces to the region to provide disaster relief likely further dissuaded surviving pirate crews from action in early 2005." The "tsunami theory" also does not account for the drop in Asian piracy attacks in areas beyond those affected by the tsunami.

16. *Ship Hijackings and Piracy at 5-year High: Watchdog*, Reuters, October 18, 2010.

17. Indonesia Defense and Security Report Q4 2010, CompaniesandMarkets.com, Newstex, October 28, 2010.

18. A "phantom ship" or "ghost ship" is a vessel that has been registered on the basis of false or inaccurate information. The term "ghost ship" was popularized by the short story "The Marie Celeste," written by Arthur Conan Doyle. The *Mary Celeste* was a brigantine merchant ship, which was discovered adrift in December 1872 in the Atlantic Ocean. The vessel had no passengers or crew and apparently had been abandoned, despite calm seas. The ship had been at sea only one month before it was found, and it had six months of food and water on board. There were no signs of struggle or theft.

19. Stefan Eklöf, *Pirates in Paradise: A Modern History of Southeast Asia's Maritime Marauders* 79–80 (2006).

20. IMO Doc. A 22/Res.923, Measures to Prevent the Registration of "Phantom" Ships, January 22, 2002.

21. International Maritime Bureau, International Chamber of Commerce, Piracy and Armed Robbery against Ships (July 2000–April 2008).

22. Sheldon W. Simon, Safety and Security in the Malacca Strait: The Limits of Collaboration, *in* Maritime Security in Southeast Asia: U.S., Japanese, Regional and Industry Strategies, NBR Special Report #24 at 3 (John Bradford, James Manicom, Sheldon W. Simon and Neil A. Quartaro, National Bureau of Asian Research, November 2010).

23. Joshua Ho, *Enhancing Safety, Security and Environmental Protection of the Straits of Malacca and Singapore: The Cooperative Mechanism*, 40 Ocean Development and International Law 233, 234 (April 2009).

24. Robert C. Beckman, *Combating Piracy and Armed Robbery against Ships in Southeast Asia: The Way Forward*, 33 Ocean Development and International Law 317, 328 (2002).

25. James A. Wombell, *The Long War against Piracy: Historical Trends* 134 (Occasional Paper 32, Combat Studies Institute Press, U.S. Army Combined Arms Center, Fort Leavenworth, Kansas, May 2010).

26. *Piracy Plagues Shipping*, Business Asia, May 5, 2000. The Tokyo conference eventually led to development of the Regional Agreement on Combating Piracy and Armed Robbery against Ships in Asia (ReCAAP).

27. Ian Storey, *Calming the Waters in Maritime Southeast Asia*, 29 Asia Pacific Bulletin 1 (East-West Center, February 18, 2009).

28. Bradford, *Shifting the Tides against Piracy in Southeast Asian Waters*, at 480.

29. In 2004, there were 8 incidents of piracy and armed robbery in the Singapore Strait, 37 in the Malacca Strait, and 93 in Indonesian waters. See, International Maritime Bureau, International Chamber of Commerce, Piracy and Armed Robbery against Ships, Annual Report, January 1–December 31, 2004.

30. IMO Doc. SGP1/INF.3, Annex 3, The Batam Joint Statement of the 4th Tripartite Ministerial Meeting of the Littoral States on the Straits of Malacca and Singapore, Batam, Indonesia, August 1–2, 2005.

31. IMO Doc. JKT1/INF.21, Marine Electronic Highway Demonstration Project, September 8, 2005.

32. IMO Doc. KUL.1/4, Kuala Lumpur Statement on Enhancement of Safety, Security and Environmental Protection in the Straits of Malacca and Singapore, September 20, 2006.

33. IMO Doc. SGP1/4, Singapore Statement on Enhancement of Safety, Security and Environmental Protection in the Straits of Malacca and Singapore, September 6, 2007. For additional detail on the Singapore meeting, including the scope and agenda, see, IMO Doc. C/ES.24.7, Protection of Vital Shipping Lanes: The Singapore Meeting: Note by the Secretary-General, September 9, 2007.

34. IMO Doc. C 100/7/Add.1, Annex: IMO Malacca and Singapore Straits Trust Fund, Protection of Vital Shipping Lanes, May 22, 2008.

35. IMO Doc. SGP 1/INF.12/1, The Cooperative Mechanism: Remarks by the United States, September 4, 2007. The United States also urged states in the region to become a party to the Convention for the Suppression of Unlawful Acts against the Safety of Maritime Navigation (SUA Convention) and its 2005 Protocols.

36. Ron Huisken, ADMM Plus Cooperates on Security and Defense Issues, East Asia Forum, East Asian Bureau of Economic Research (EABER), ANU College of Asia and the Pacific, October 19, 2010.

37. Martin N. Murphy, *Solving Somalia*, Proceedings of the U.S. Naval Institute, at 31–34 (July 2010).

38. IMO Doc. Circ. Ltr. No. 3164, Responding to the Scourge of Piracy, February 14, 2011.

39. *Somali Pirates Get Smarter, More Ambitious*, United Press International, February 2, 2011.

40. John W. Miller, *Piracy Spurs Threats to Shipping Costs*, Wall Street Journal, November 19, 2008.

41. Miller, *Piracy Spurs Threats to Shipping Costs*.

42. *Malacca Strait Shows Piracy Can Be Tackled*, Lloyd's List, June 13, 2007, at 3.

43. International Expert Group on Piracy off the Somali Coast, Piracy off the Somali Coast: Workshop commissioned by the Special Representative of the Secretary General of the UN to Somalia Ambassador Ahmedou Ould-Abdallah, Final Report: Assessment and recommendations, Nairobi, November 10–21, 2008. At 10. Andrew Linington of the National Union of Marine, Aviation and Shipping Transport (NUMAST) responded to a British House of Commons question (Number 47) regarding potential danger, "We have been extremely fortunate . . . that we have not had a major environmental disaster. We have had several cases of fully laden tankers going down the Malacca Straits, the second busiest shipping lanes in the world, with no-one at the controls because they are all being held at gunpoint." Transport Committee, House of Commons, Piracy Eighth Report of Session 2005–06 Report, together with formal minutes, oral and written evidence, July 6, 2006, at EV 20.

44. Paul Lewis, *UN Will Increase Troops in Somalia*, New York Times, March 27, 1993.

45. Martin N. Murphy, *Small Boats, Weak States, Dirty Money: Piracy and Maritime Terrorism in the Modern World* 102 (2009).

46. UN Doc. SC/9541, Security Council Authorizes States to Use Land-Based Operations in Somalia as Part of Fight against Piracy off Coast, Unanimously Adopting Resolution 1851, 6046th Meeting (PM), December 16, 2008.

47. J. Peter Pham, *Africa's Top Flash Points in 2011: Security Challenges and Strategic Opportunities*, World Defense Review, January 4, 2011.

48. UN Doc. S/2010/91, Report of the Monitoring Group on Somalia Pursuant to Security Council Resolution 1853 (2008), March 10, 2010, at 15.

49. UN Doc. S/2010/91, at 15.

50. J. Peter Pham, *Book Briefs (Book Review of Martin N. Murphy's Somalia, the New Barbary? Piracy and Islam in the Horn of Africa)*, 32 American Foreign Policy Interests 403 (2010).

51. J. Peter Pham, Somalia: Insurgency and Legitimacy in the Context of State Collapse, 277, 278, *in Victory Among People: Lessons from Countering Insurgency and Stabilising Fragile States* (David Richards and Greg Mills, eds., 2011).

52. UN Doc. S/2010/91, at 11.

53. International Experts Group on Piracy off the Coast of Somalia, Piracy off the Somali Coast, Workshop Commissioned by the Special Representative of the

Secretary-General of the UN to Somalia, Ambassador Ahmedou Ould-Abdallah, November 21, 2008, at 32 [Nairobi Report]. See also, Martin N. Murphy, *Small Boats, Weak States, Dirty Money*, at 110 and Jonathan Clayton, *Business Booms in Somali Pirate Village Eyl*, The Australian, November 19, 2008.

54. Nairobi Report, at 31.

55. IMO Doc. C/ES.25/12, Protection of Vital Shipping Lanes, Piracy and Armed Robbery against Ships in Waters off the Coast of Somalia, November 5, 2009.

56. Murphy, *Small Boats, Weak States, Dirty Money*, at 101.

57. UN Doc. S/2010/91, at 11.

58. *Cruise Ship Repels Somali Pirates*, BBC News, September 5, 2005. The *Seabourn Spirit* was a luxury liner for an affluent clientele, and the ship was replete with a casino, restaurants and lounges, and spacious private rooms selling for $3,000–$15,000 per journey.

59. Ellen Knickmeyer, *100 Hostages Held by Somali Pirates*, Washington Post, September 12, 2008, at A11.

60. David Montgomery, *Pillage People*, Washington Post, December 6, 2008, at C01.

61. ICC International Maritime Bureau, Piracy and Armed Robbery against Ships Annual Report January 1–December 31, 2008, at 21–22 and 40 (January 2009).

62. ICC International Maritime Bureau, Piracy and Armed Robbery against Ships (2009).

63. ICC International Maritime Bureau, Piracy and Armed Robbery against Ships.

64. ICC International Maritime Bureau, Piracy and Armed Robbery against Ships.

65. ICC International Maritime Bureau, Piracy and Armed Robbery against Ships.

66. Michel Moutot, *Somali Piracy Flourishes into Lucrative Business*, Agence France Presse, November 11, 2010.

67. *Pirates Release South Korean Supertanker*, Reuters, November 6, 2010.

68. *Pirates Release South Korean Supertanker.*

69. *Somali Pirates Venture Farther South*, Associated Press, December 29, 2010.

70. UN Doc. S/Res. 733, Imposition of Arms Embargo on Somalia, January 23, 1992 and UN Doc. S/2008/769, Report of the Monitoring Group on Somalia, November 20, 2008, at 55.

71. Christopher Browne, *Response to Somali Piracy Insufficient*, Fairplay, July 12, 2007, at 11 (citing expert at London-based Exclusive Analysis).

72. *EU Launches First Navy Mission, in Piracy-Infested Seas*, Agence France Presse, December 7, 2008.

73. UN Doc. S/2010/91, at 41.

74. UN Doc. S/2010/91, at 41.

75. *Somali Pirates Outpace Warship Coalition: UN*, Agence France Presse, November 9, 2010.

76. *Somali Pirates Outpace Warship Coalition.*

77. Moutot, *Somali Piracy Flourishes into Lucrative Business.*

78. Moutot, *Somali Piracy Flourishes into Lucrative Business.*

79. Moutot, *Somali Piracy Flourishes into Lucrative Business.*

CHAPTER 3

Maritime Sector Responses

Maritime shipping is a global industry, carrying more than 90 percent of international trade. Carriage by sea is also the most environmentally conscious method of moving large cargo, with a lower carbon footprint per ton of cargo per mile than any other mode. Consequently, vessel security is essential for expanding sustainable trade. The response to piracy in the western Indian Ocean and Southeast Asia has precipitated a renaissance in counterpiracy strategy, law, and diplomacy. The magnitude of the problem and the collective response has not been seen since nations cooperated in the fight against slavery during the 19th century. Governments and the worldwide shipping industry have developed and executed a variety of strategies to manage the threat.

The shipping industry has adopted numerous practices and safeguards to protect merchant ships against maritime piracy. After the ascendancy of piracy off the coast of Somalia, the variety of passive and active antipiracy countermeasures increased, and industry best management practices (BMP) and guidance to industry concerning preventive measures were promulgated by industry, states, and international organizations.

Best Management Practices

The International Chamber of Shipping (ICS), representing 11 shipping industry organizations,[1] has promulgated best management practice (BMP) to safeguard the industry from piracy. The most recent version is BMP3, which was adopted in June 2010.[2] The BMP consists of planning and operational practices for ship owners, operators, managers, and masters of vessels transiting the Gulf of Aden and the Somali Basin. Typical Somali piracy attack profiles are included in the BMP. Generally, successful attacks are characterized by five ship vulnerabilities. First, the ships have a low speed. Second, the vessels sit low in the water (low freeboard). Third, vessels that have inadequate planning are at greater vulnerability. Fourth, ships with a visibly low state of alert and evident lack of defensive measures are at greater risk, and, fifth, a slow response by the ship's crew increases the likelihood of a successful attack.

Companies should carefully plan their vessel transit. Prior to transit, ships are advised to contact United Kingdom Maritime Trade Operations (UKMTO), Maritime Safety Centre Horn of Africa (MSCHOA), and Maritime Liaison Office Bahrain (MARLO), all three of which connect the shipping industry to maritime security forces operating in the region. By providing advance notice of transit, warships are better positioned to provide deterrent cover, and respond quickly if a ship is attacked.

New York Declaration

In May 2009, the New York Declaration was opened for signature. The declaration commits states to maintain the BMP for merchant ships flying their flag. The declaration also provides that states will implement the International Ship and Port Facility Security (ISPS) Code. Just as the Fourth Plenary Session of the Contact Group on Piracy off the Coast of Somalia (CGPCS) was meeting in New York City on September 10, 2009, diplomats from the United States, Japan, the Republic of Cyprus, the Republic of Singapore, and the United Kingdom signed the New York Declaration. By July 2010, 10 countries had signed the declaration.

International Maritime Bureau

The International Maritime Bureau (IMB) is an industry consortium funded by the International Chamber of Commerce (ICC) and is also involved in advising merchant ships on tactics to avoid becoming a victim of piracy. In 1992, the IMB established a Piracy Reporting Centre in Kuala Lumpur, Malaysia. Funded by the merchant shipping industry, the 24-hour IMB Piracy Reporting Centre (PRC) serves as the shipping industry's clearinghouse for assisting ship masters in avoiding piracy attack, and in reporting actual or attempted attacks or even suspicious movements.

The PRC maintains an Internet website that provides location and other data on piracy attacks worldwide. The PRC issues daily status reports on piracy and armed robbery to ships via broadcasts on the Inmarsat-C SafetyNET service and makes reports to law enforcement. The PRC publishes quarterly and annual reports as well. Ship owners, masters, and crew whose ships have been attacked by pirates may seek assistance and advice from the IMB.

For a fee, the IMB also will investigate ship hijacking and maritime piracy on behalf of carriers or locate for insurance companies "phantom ships" that have been illegally reregistered. The IMB maintains a "live piracy map," which is an updated Internet map of the world displaying the locations of recent maritime piracy attacks.

The IMB also issues extensive guidance to the shipping industry. Crews should be briefed on the risks of piracy before transit, and vessels should conduct piracy response emergency drills to test communications procedures before entering into a high-risk area. The master of a vessel should adjust ship routines and watch standing schedules prior to entering higher-risk areas. Deck watches should work in pairs, both underway and in port. Watch standers should take rounds of the ship at irregular intervals to avoid a predictable schedule. Ships should eliminate exterior blind spots and lighten darker areas along the sides of the vessel. All crew should understand alarm procedures and muster stations, and this is particularly important for multinational crews. All of a ship's internal communications should be carried out in the working language of the ship, rather than in a mixture of tongues, which could prove confusing.

When transiting in higher-risk areas, ships should rig and pressurize fire hoses to prepare to repel boarders, and security and urgent messages should be ready to broadcast without delay if trouble arises. The telephone numbers of the flag state registry and the PRC should be kept on the bridge. If a ship is attacked by piracy, the master of the vessel should sound alarm and muster the crew, increase speed and execute evasive maneuvers to create a larger bow wave and stern wash to prevent small boats from approaching close to the ship. Interestingly, mariners are advised to steam away from land and head into the sea and swell—smaller pirate skiffs may have trouble boarding in heavier chop. If pirates board a ship successfully, the master and crew should keep calm and follow instructions, avoiding a physical confrontation.

The IMB is a private entity and represents the interests of the shipping industry; the counterpart organization that represents the interests of governments is the International Maritime Organization (IMO).

International Maritime Organization

The IMO is the United Nations' specialized agency for maritime matters. The organization serves as the principal venue for states to develop and implement rules to ensure safe, secure, and environmentally sound shipping throughout the world. In the early 20th century the *Titanic* disaster of 1912 galvanized attention toward improving the safety of international shipping. The first major treaty to address the problems associated with marine safety was the original 1914 Safety of Life at Sea Convention (SOLAS). The convention was put on the shelf, however, with the outbreak of World War I. A revised version of the convention was adopted in 1928 and entered into force in 1933. The original SOLAS was an outgrowth of the concern over the *Titanic* disaster, in which 1,500 lives were lost. The treaty was updated in 1948 and the new SOLAS convention entered into force in 1953. The most recent version, the 1974 SOLAS, as amended, entered into force in 1984, and it remains the most comprehensive treaty today to ensure safe and secure shipping.[3]

After World War II, states realized that they needed a standing international organization to continue to develop standardized rules for shipping. Diplomats met at a conference in Geneva in 1948 and adopted the Convention of the Inter-Governmental Maritime Consultative Organization (IMCO). The instrument entered into force in 1958. The purposes of the organization are captured by Article 1(a) of the IMO Convention, which states that the institution will "provide machinery for cooperation among Governments . . . relating to technical matters of all kinds affecting shipping engaged in international trade; . . . [and development of standards for] maritime safety, efficiency of navigation and prevention and control of marine pollution from ships." The IMCO met for the first time the following year. The name of the IMCO was changed to the International Maritime Organization (IMO) in 1982.

In the 1960s, the organization focused on new rules to manage international maritime traffic and regulate the carriage of dangerous goods at sea. During the 1970s, the IMO turned its attention toward reducing vessel source pollution. The comprehensive International Convention for the Prevention of Pollution from Ships, 1973, as modified by the Protocol of 1978 relating thereto (MARPOL 73/78), is the flagship treaty for marine environmental protection. The protocols to MARPOL 73/78 regulate marine oil pollution, chemicals aboard ship, packaged goods, plastics aboard ship, the discharge of vessel sewage and garbage, and diesel generator emissions. The organization also developed a worldwide search and rescue (SAR) system during the 1970s, creating the small International Mobile Satellite Organization (IMSO) to improve radio communications for ships. By the end of the 1990s, a more durable satellite-based Global Maritime Distress and Safety System (GMDSS) was fully operational. GMDSS releases an automatic message requesting assistance in any situation in which a vessel is in distress. During the 1990s, the IMO helped to develop several additional treaties that set international standards for ships and seafarers.[4]

Today the organization has 169 member states and three associate members, and its remit now includes not just maritime safety, but vessel source pollution discharge, maritime legal matters, protection of seafarers, technical cooperation, and maritime security. The organization also develops universally accepted standards of ship design, construction, equipping, and manning (CDEM) in order to facilitate global commerce. The IMO works extensively with nongovernmental organizations and the cargo and shipping industry.

Since the international organization is funded by member states in accordance with a formula based on the size of each nation's shipping registry, the states with the largest open registries—Panama and Liberia—pay a greater share of the budget than wealthier countries that have fewer registered vessels. Because of this funding formula and shared responsibility, the organization dispenses with much of the politics endemic to some other UN agencies.

The 300-member staff of the IMO Secretariat resides at the organization's headquarters, which is situated next to Lambeth Bridge along the Thames River in downtown London. The IMO operates a number of specialized committees and subcommittees, including the very large Marine Environmental Protection Committee (MEPC) and the Maritime Safety Committee (MSC), the latter of which also addresses matters relating to maritime security. Member governments and the shipping industry develop consensus solutions in committee that are then adopted by the Assembly.

The work of the IMO governs virtually every facet of international shipping. More than 50 treaties, and hundreds of codes and guidelines, have been completed. Once standardized rules are adopted, the member states are responsible for implementing them on ships flying their flags and in their international ports of call. Some nations have been rather lackadaisical in their enforcement of flag state rules, however, causing the nations at IMO to develop a Voluntary IMO Member State Audit Scheme to enhance implementation of international shipping standards.[5] The IMO also has an extensive capacity-building program, which identifies member states that are in need of training. Three advanced training and education institutions operate under the auspices of the IMO: the World Maritime University in Malmö, Sweden; the International Maritime Law Institute in Malta; and the International Maritime Academy, Trieste, Italy, which was established in 1988.

The SOLAS treaty once again underwent major revisions with the July 2004 adoption of the comprehensive ship-shore security regime called the International Ship and Port Facility Security (ISPS) Code, which was made mandatory for IMO member states. The ISPS Code requires flag states and port states to develop action plans to maintain a secure marine transportation system. Governments should provide guidance on the appropriate security level, special measures that ships should implement under Part A of the ISPS Code, and security measures that the coastal state has put in place.[6]

Part A of the ISPS Code outlines a systemic approach for flag states to evaluate and mitigate threats to merchant ships. In particular, flag states are obligated to develop action plans for emergency response in the event a ship flying their flag comes under attack from pirates. Ship security plans and emergency response protocols should be based on a risk assessment, including vessel freeboard, maximum speed of the ship, vessel location, type of ship and cargo on board, number of crew, level of security training of the crew, and existence of a secure or safe room on board the ship. Ideally, ships should not be routed through narrow seas or bottlenecks that may increase the risk of piracy attack. The reality of international shipping, however, is that it is dependent upon a few strategic straits, and two of them—the Strait of Bab el Mandeb on the Gulf of Aden (GOA) (leading to the Suez Canal) and the Straits of Malacca and Singapore—are essential arteries for global shipping. It is no accident that pirates congregate where large numbers of ships tend to be transiting.

Counterpiracy at IMO

Article 100 of the 1982 United Nations Convention on the Law of the Sea (UNCLOS) requires states to cooperate in the suppression of piracy. States may conduct operational naval patrols, share intelligence and law enforcement capabilities, and extradite and prosecute suspected pirates. Nations also should maintain robust internal communications among various law enforcement and diplomatic agencies, and between coastal states and flag states.

The IMO first addressed the problem of maritime piracy in 1983, the year after UNCLOS was adopted, when Sweden submitted a paper to the Maritime Safety Committee expressing alarm over the gathering threat of piracy.[7] Three years later, the organization approved more detailed guidance in Circular 443, which applied to passenger ships on international voyages of 24 hours or more, and the port facilities that service those vessels.[8] In November 1983, the IMO produced a draft text that served as the basis for Assembly Resolution A.545(13).[9] The resolution set forth measures to prevent acts of piracy and armed robbery against ships. "[G]overnments should take, as a matter of highest priority," the resolution declared, "all measures necessary to prevent and suppress acts of piracy and armed robbery."[10] The 1983 resolution also encouraged states to maintain close liaison with their neighbors to aid in catching and convicting pirates. States were further encouraged to increase the use of surveillance and detection to prevent piracy, and to coordinate patrols and develop cooperative agreements with other states.

The IMO issues monthly, quarterly, and annual reports on piracy and armed robbery against ships. Details of the names and types of ships attacked, date, time and position of the attack, any injuries or deaths suffered by the crew, or damage to the ship or cargo, and responses taken by the crew and coastal authorities are included in the reports. In November 2001, the IMO Assembly adopted a code of practice for investigating piracy and armed robbery against ships.[11] The resolution urged states to investigate piracy and report the results of their investigations to the IMO. Later, the Code of Practice was revised and updated in Assembly Resolution 1025(26) of January 18, 2010.[12]

The IMO Assembly also adopted a resolution to prevent the registration of "phantom ships," a fraudulent act whereby hijackers reregistered seized vessels under different names, often after having sold the cargo and killed the crew. The resolution invited governments to conduct the appropriate checks and to authenticate documents properly, in order to verify the identities of ships before vessel registration.[13]

On November 23, 2005, the IMO adopted Resolution A.979(24), reaffirming earlier resolutions relating to piracy and requesting the IMO Secretary-General to bring the matter of piracy off the coast of Somalia to the attention of the UN Security Council.[14] Two years later, in 2007, the IMO Assembly adopted A.1002(25), a comprehensive resolution on piracy and armed robbery against ships in waters off the coast of Somalia.[15] The 2007 resolution calls for action by IMO member states, the Somali Transitional Federal Government (TFG), and regional partners to address the problem of piracy off Somalia's coast. The resolution also strongly urges the IMO member states to increase their efforts to suppress piracy worldwide;[16] to develop their capacity to prosecute and extradite pirates through legislative and judicial reforms;[17] and to provide technical assistance to the states of East Africa to enhance regional capacity for repressing piracy.[18]

The IMO's 2007 resolution also requests the Somali TFG take action to prevent and suppress piracy originating from Somalia, and to deny the use of its coastline as a safe haven for pirates.[19] The IMO sought assurance from the TFG that vessels hijacked by pirates and taken into Somalia's territorial waters would be released promptly.[20] In addition, the IMO requested that the TFG advise the Security Council that it would consent to foreign warships conducting counterpiracy patrols in its waters, and to indicate its willingness to conclude international agreements to facilitate such operations, something the TFG consented to.[21] The major problem, however, is that the international community has an extremely weak—some would say nonexistent—partner in the TFG, so the IMO's efforts to suppress piracy at sea are not complemented by robust action ashore.

The earliest IMO efforts against piracy focused mostly on Southeast Asia. Then IMO Secretary-General William A. O'Neil developed a working group (WG) composed of experts from 10 member states to prepare a report on maritime piracy. Although the WG focused on outlining strategies for curtailing piracy in the Strait of Malacca, it also was instructed to prepare recommendations for suppressing piracy and armed robbery throughout the world. In fulfilling its mandate, the WG visited Indonesia, Malaysia, and Singapore in the spring of 1993, and prepared a report. The IMO has also released major circulars providing guidance on piracy repression to governments and industry, excerpts of which are reproduced in the appendix.

As a result of the 1993 report, two circulars, MSC/622 and MSC/623, were issued by the 62nd session of the MSC in May 1993.[22] The first document contained detailed recommendations to governments for preventing and suppressing piracy, and the second document focused on providing guidance to the maritime sector—ship owners, operators, shipmasters, and crews.[23] In 1999, Circulars MSC/622 and MSC 623 were revised, and then both were updated once again at the 86th session of the MSC in 2009.[24]

The first of these revisions, MSC/622/Rev.1, incorporated recommendations from regional seminars held in Brasilia, Brazil, and Singapore. The revision recommended states to work with seafarers and ship owners to craft action plans for preventing piracy and responding to piracy attacks. The document also set forth investigative protocols for use after a pirate attack.[25] Finally, the circular contained a draft regional agreement on cooperation for preventing and suppressing acts of piracy and armed robbery against ships. The draft agreement should be used as a model by states that want to work more closely together. It includes procedures for boarding and searching suspect vessels in each country, as well as provisions for criminal enforcement and choice of jurisdiction among coastal and flag states. In 2009, the IMO revoked MSC/Circ.622/Rev.1 and replaced it with MSC.1/Circ.1333, Recommendations to Governments for Preventing and Suppressing Piracy and Armed Robbery against Ships. Circular 1333 raises possible countermeasures that may be employed by Rescue Coordination Centers and maritime security forces, as well as illustrates a draft regional agreement on cooperation in preventing and suppressing acts of piracy and armed robbery against ships.[26]

States should share tactical information and conduct closer coordination. If states maintain a regional maritime security center, the facility can be used for coordinating responses to other maritime security threats, including drug trafficking, the interdiction of maritime terrorism and proliferation of weapons of mass destruction, and migrant interdiction. Since piracy is an opportunistic crime, perpetrators likely are involved in other offenses. Piracy and armed robbery at sea should not be viewed in isolation, and so other specialists in money laundering illegal arms transfers, drug smuggling, trafficking in people, and other crimes should form part of the counterpiracy team.

Coastal states are more effective when they coordinate maritime patrol activities, and IMO recommendations contain a model maritime security agreement in Appendix 6. Cooperative agreements enable naval and coast guard operations to suppress piracy and armed robbery in the national waters of a treaty partner only with the consent of the coastal state. The parties may, however, establish a law enforcement liaison officer or "ship rider" program between their law enforcement agencies. Liaison officers may authorize foreign warships on which they are embarked to conduct patrols in the national waters of the liaison officer. The embarked officer also may conduct or authorize search or seizure of property, detention of suspected pirates, or the use of force. In order to fulfill these responsibilities, coastal states and port states need adequate shore infrastructure, maritime domain awareness capability so they can discern threats, and a marine law enforcement presence.

A single national point of contact can receive and disseminate marine reports. Piracy attacks should be reported to the nearest maritime rescue coordination center (RCC). RCCs are established for search and rescue (SAR) response, but some nations have begun to use them as more comprehensive maritime security coordination nodes. In Asia, for example, the RCCs of some states serve as counterpiracy points of contact and pass information to law enforcement authorities. On receipt of radio reports of a pirate attack, the RCC should inform law enforcement or naval forces so that defensive action may be implemented and commercial ships in the area alerted. A template for ship message formats for such reports was included in Circular 1333. Reports may be used in diplomatic correspondence to approach flag states and provide information to the IMO and IMB.

The Directives for Maritime Rescue Coordination Centers (MRCCs) on Acts of Violence against Ships (MSC/Circ.1073) provides overall guidance for linking the regional search and rescue apparatus to ship security by providing MRCCs with a coordination role in some cases in which ships are attacked.[27] In particular, if the MRCC receives either an overt or covert ship security alert, it may take steps to facilitate communication with the assaulted ship and vector marine law enforcement forces to the scene.[28]

Flag states should institute emergency response procedures. Nations should maintain robust communication internally among their various law enforcement and diplomatic agencies, and between coastal states and flag states. Ideally, regional states should join together to share tactical information and conduct coordinated operational responses. This collaboration involves integrating communications, unifying the command structure, consolidating action plans, and comprehensive resource management. If states are able to develop an international mechanism such as a regional maritime security center, the facility can be used for addressing other maritime security threats, such as maritime drug trafficking and maritime terrorism.

In 2006, the British House of Commons Transport Committee examined maritime piracy and found that the crime is underreported and that potentially 25–50 percent of attacks are not disclosed.[29] Reports of piracy attacks can impose delays on vessels trying to leave port due to ensuing criminal investigations, so vessel masters may prefer not to report piracy attacks. "In some ports," moreover, "[vessel masters] are aware that reporting a crime will result in an unwelcome visit from corrupt police or other officials who will use the opportunity to extort cash."[30] British Department of Transport's John Grub asserted that disclosing attacks also carries consequences in terms of insurance liability.[31] In order to encourage masters to report incidents of piracy and armed robbery against ships, port states and coastal states should not unduly delay vessels or impose additional costs related to such reports. The cumulative effect of underreporting, however, is that it effectively complicates efforts to target pirates and their illegal enterprises. States should also clearly establish a division of labor inside government so that the legal authority for conducting law enforcement investigation is transparent. Lack of clarity during the period immediately following an incident impedes the investigation and can lead to loss of evidence.

The second major revised IMO circular, MSC/623.Rev. 3, suggested measures for the shipping industry to take in order to reduce vulnerability to piracy, such as employing enhanced lighting and detection mechanisms. The circular also provided additional steps that states can take during and after an attack, such as enhanced alarm procedures and reporting.[32] The revised MSC/623.Rev. 3 was replaced by new guidance to ship owners and ship operators in MSC.1/Circ.1334, which was adopted by IMO on June 23, 2009.[33] Circular 1334 provides the shipping industry with a menu of measures that may be taken on board vessels to prevent attacks or, if they do occur, to mitigate the danger to crew and ship.

Ship security plans should be formulated based on a risk assessment. Assessing risk involves a variety of factors, including vessel and cargo type and size, freeboard (the distance of the deck to the water), the maximum speed of the ship, the number of crew and their level of training, the ability to establish secure areas or a safe room sanctuary on board the ship to protect the crew, and installation of surveillance equipment that can help alert a ship under attack. In high-threat ports, states should minimize time at anchor. While underway, ships should be routed away from high-threat areas and avoid narrow seas and bottlenecks, but this measure is not always feasible. In the west, it is necessary for many carriers to use the Suez Canal, which channels vessels through the Red Sea and Gulf of Aden (GOA). In the east, the Straits of Malacca and Singapore are highly congested shipping corridors. Going around these bottlenecks via the Cape of Good Hope or south of Indonesia adds weeks of additional travel time.

Shipboard Security

Passive Defensive Measures

Mariners may choose from a menu of passive and defensive measures to deter or defeat pirates. Passive measures are not considered to constitute the use of force. The area to be transited, the time of year, the time of day, the type of ship, and the make-up of the crew are all important factors. Piracy off the coast of Somalia, for example, follows a variable annual pattern associated with the climate and weather conditions in the western Indian Ocean. The area is affected by a monsoon season throughout the summer months, in which winds and high waves drive traffic in the Indian Ocean toward the safety of the near shore. In September, as the summer monsoon season comes to an end, the rough seas dissipate and pirates are able to operate small skiffs more effectively. Predictably, piracy rises.

The Horn of Africa is also affected by a winter monsoon season beginning in December, and the number of attacks temporarily falls off. The two monsoon seasons increase sea states and generate high winds. Wave heights during the monsoon typically are greater than seven feet high. The monsoon season has less effect on the GOA, which is semi-enclosed; during the summer season in particular, as the winds blow from the southwest, there is less fluctuation in the weather in the GOA than in the western Indian Ocean. In sum, the weather in the Indian Ocean is calmest during the transition months of April–May and October–November, with both periods falling between the summer and winter monsoon seasons. During these times, the water is calmest, which is the best operating condition for pirates.

In any ocean, ships proceeding at speeds of 14 knots or less are at greater risk of piracy attack because they are easier to catch, and pose less of a challenge to board from a small skiff. Vessels that travel at 17 knots or greater are least susceptible to pirate attack because the pirate skiffs do not have sufficient time from the initial sighting to catch and climb on board the ships, and it is more difficult to board a faster vessel. Still, with a lower sea state, pirates are able to capture vessels proceeding as fast as 16 or 17 knots. But even ships traveling at 14 knots have successfully escaped boarding by maintaining course and speed, outrunning the pirates. Ships are tempted to operate at reduced speeds due to cost factors. Modern tankers and bulk carriers, for example, are designed to proceed at a service speed of between 14 and 16 knots, but the master of the vessel may reduce speed by as much as 25 percent to conserve fuel and reduce operating costs.

Razor wire may be secured tightly to the rails, which lowers the vibration made by the wire from the movement of the ship during the voyage. Some ships suspend 55-gallon drums from the side of the ship, and the swinging motion of the barrels makes boarding difficult. Finally, many vessels heading through the western Indian Ocean have hung large banners over the side of the ship, written in Somali, English, Arabic, or French, warning pirates that the ship is armed (even if it is not).

Once a vessel comes under attack, it may employ a number of active and passive measures to defeat a piracy attack. A ship being pursued by pirates may alter course, heading into wind and wave, which will leave a large wake that can impede small boat operations.

The United States permits ships flying its flag to use nondeadly force in defense of the vessel or in defense of property, or to prevent theft or intentional damage of property. Examples of nondeadly force include aggressive maneuvers to create a large wake that could swamp the pursuing pirate skiffs;

use of the sonic long-range acoustic device (LRAD), which is commercially available; aiming of fire hoses to deter boarding by pirates; use of disabling fire to halt skiffs; use of concertina wire or barbed wire around the deck rails in order to prevent boarding of the ship. Tasers, flash bangs, beanbag guns, and dazzling or blinding lights stop pirates. Warning shots are not considered a use of force by the United States, but instead constitute a warning signal.

Active Measures: Use of Force

Normally, the carriage of weapons and embarkation of armed personnel falls under the rules of the flag state. The flag state may authorize special teams of military or law enforcement officers to embark on board their commercial vessels. Doing so, however, raises some issue as to whether the master of the vessel or the head of the security team possesses the ultimate authority over the security of the ship. The issue becomes more complex if the merchant ship enters a foreign port. Generally, merchant ships that enter the port of another state are subject to the state's laws regulating international shipping. So while carriage of firearms on board the ship may be consistent with flag state law, entry into port with firearms could violate port state law.

Similarly, merchant ships and fishing vessels that enter the territorial sea of another state are, in some circumstances, subject to the laws of the coastal state while conducting innocent passage. The assertion of jurisdiction by a port state or a coastal state over foreign-flagged vessels can complicate plans by merchant shipping to carry firearms for self-defense. The carriage of firearms on board a merchant ship does not, by itself, make an otherwise innocent passage through the territorial sea of a coastal state noninnocent.

The global shipping community does not have a unified approach to whether merchant ships should be armed. In recent memory, however, there is not a single case of a ship with a contingent of well-armed security on board that has been successfully hijacked by pirates. Yet, legal challenges, flag state rules, and practical safety concerns have complicated the carriage of weapons on board commercial shipping. The question of whether to arm merchant marine seafarers or embark private armed security teams remains one of the most controversial aspects of counterpiracy law and policy. Invariably, some pirated vessels, such as benzene tanker *Golden Nori*, which was discussed in Chapter 2, carry highly flammable cargo or hazardous cargo, and thus may not be appropriate candidates for carriage of ship-borne armed security.

The IMO has found it particularly challenging to consider the possibility of a standardized firearms carriage policy for merchant ships, and it is unlikely that the UN Security Council could reach agreement on the issue. The IMO strongly discourages the carrying and use of firearms by seafarers, for personal protection or for the protection of their ship.[34] The use of firearms requires special training and aptitudes and the IMO considers the risk of accidental discharge to be great.[35] Consequently, the IMO clearly favors unarmed lookouts as a preferable means of shipboard security.[36] One of the more promising proposals envisions ship-borne firearms to be placed in a secure box during entry into foreign ports. The box would be double locked with one key retained by the master of the ship and the other turned over to the port authorities. Each flag state registry would have to implement such a provision through domestic legislation. Resistance to the concept of armed security on board ships, however, runs deep.

But for a variety of tactical reasons, the IMO recommends that flag states strongly discourage seafarers from carrying firearms for personal protection or for the protection of the vessel. The IMO also discourages emplacement of armed contract security on board merchant ships. First, the safe use of firearms requires special training, which in the past has not been part of seafarer training. Second, the IMO is concerned that use of private contract armed security personnel on board ships could lead to an escalation of violence in the event that armed force is used against pirates.[37] Currently, pirates expect that seafarers will use only passive measures to deter attack, and as a result there is some suggestion that they have minimized the level of violence during their attacks. But if merchant ships begin to use a high level of force to repel pirates, the resourceful attackers may use larger weapons.

On the other hand, reports in February 2011 that captured seafarers were being tortured by Somali pirates led to a softening in the resistance to armed security personnel on board commercial ships. There still is the concern that if crews use firearms, the pirates could become more violent. Captured mariners report that they are being thrown overboard, dragged suspended upside down behind ships, used as human shields, locked in freezers, or having plastic zip ties put on their genitals.[38] Royal Marines major general Buster Howes told the media, "If warships approached a pirate ship too closely, the pirates would drag hostages on deck and beat them until the warship went away."[39]

Pirates have also employed aggressive new tactics to defeat citadels—safe rooms on board the ship where the crew can lock themselves away in event of an attack. Citadels have foiled piracy attacks against 20 ships off the coast of Somalia. Since the pirates are unable to operate the ship, they often have given up and left if the crew managed to secure inside a citadel. Now, however, the pirates are using grenades, explosives, and rocket launchers to penetrate the safe room. On three occasions, the pirates set fire to the ship to smoke out the crew. During the last week of January 2011, the *Beluga Nomination* was seized by Somali pirates 800 miles off the Seychelles. The German-owned ship, which is flagged in Antigua and Barbados, and its crew of 12 were seized after a two-day stand off in which the crew had taken refuge in a citadel. One crew member was murdered when the pirates shot their way into the citadel before help could arrive.[40] These more aggressive pirate attacks led the International Chamber of Shipping, in frustration, to issue a media release on February 15, 2011, declaring that under normal circumstances, private armed security is not recommended on board commercial vessels. But after a sailor was executed by Somali pirates during the attack on the *Beluga Nomination*, the ICS acknowledged that the ship operator must be open to the option of armed security to deter attacks and defend crews.[41] Only days later, the murder of 4 Americans by Somali pirates on board the sailing vessel *Quest* reopened the issue of armed security on board merchant shipping in the waters off the Horn of Africa.

Unarmed security personnel are permitted to embark in South Africa, Sri Lanka, Egypt, Iraq, Malta, the United Arab Emirates, and Dubai. In such case, however, typically weapons must remain on board the ship, either in the master's cabin or the weapons locker. The firearms also must be disabled or security personnel must remain on board the ship. The UAE and Egypt permit merchant ships to transit with arms on board so long as the ship security officer tenders a special weapons declaration to the port authority.

Industry's resistance to the idea of armed security may involve some classic cost-shifting behavior on the part of the international shipping community, which seeks to externalize the costs of vessel protection onto the naval forces of the various countries. At the same time, the nations supplying military forces to protect the shipping lanes would see a reduction in costs and missions if merchant shipping had greater capacity for self-defense. Under Article 34 of SOLAS and Article 27(3) of UNCLOS, the master of a ship is in charge of vessel security. The vessel master retains control of authority over the vessel crew and embarked security. But neither a contract security force nor an embarked military team can operate subordinate to the master of the vessel.

The United States has authorized contract security personnel to be armed while on board U.S.-flagged ships. American citizens serving as contract security are required to meet qualifications and certifications required in Title 18, U.S. Code. Foreign nationals are required to meet the legal standards of all port states visited by the ship in addition to the Title 18 rules. Foreign persons must complete detailed training requirements set forth in 33 Code of Federal Regulations and hold a valid transportation worker identification credential (TWIC), and foreign nationals must be fluent in English and capable of effectively communicating.

Under U.S. maritime law, properly credentialed shipboard security personnel may exercise self-defense and even deadly force to repel an attack against the ship. Force may be used to protect the crew and to prevent damage or theft of a vessel or property in cases in which use of force by an attacker is imminent. "Imminent" is defined in U.S. law to mean that the action may occur at any moment—that is, a use of force by an attacker is either impending or menacingly near. There are three elements to an "imminent attack": (a) the attacker has the means to act, (b) the opportunity to act, and (c) the attacker commits an overt act to effect an attack. Combined, these three elements constitute the imminent danger formula derived from common law. Attackers manifest the means to act when they demonstrate an apparent ability to inflict death or great bodily harm.

The right of self-defense is triggered by a combination of circumstances by which the attacker could cause death or great bodily harm. An attacker manifests the apparent ability to cause great bodily harm or serious bodily injury if there is a threat of serious physical injury or grievous bodily harm, which includes unconsciousness, protracted and obvious disfigurement of the human body, or loss or impairment of a bodily member, organ, or mental faculty. In exercising self-defense and defense of others, force need not be met with equal or lesser force. All available means reasonably necessary for defense may be used to protect the crew from serious injury. Deadly force may be used in response to an imminent danger of death or serious bodily injury. There is no duty for seafarers to retreat from a pirate attack.

Contract ship security personnel must be vetted under 18 U.S.C. § 922(g). First, security forces must not have been convicted in any court of a crime of felony, or be a fugitive from justice or a drug user or addicted to illegal drugs. Second, personnel also cannot have been adjudged as mentally defective or committed to a mental institution. Third, the person may not be in the United States unlawfully; fourth, they cannot have received a dishonorable discharge from the U.S. armed forces; fifth, they cannot have been a U.S. citizen and renounced his citizenship; sixth, be subject to a restraining order number; or, seven, have been convicted of a misdemeanor of shipping firearms or ammunition.

Contract security also must have knowledge of current security threats and patterns, and be able to recognize dangerous substances and devices. Personnel must be able to recognize threatening behavior, attempts to circumvent security measures; be skilled in crowd management, communications and security equipment, emergency procedures, and contingency plans; and understand the vessel security plan (VSP). Merchant mariners carry on board a variety of firearms, including AK-47s, shotguns, .50 caliber semiautomatic rifles, sidearm firearms, night vision goggles, and body armor.

Notes

1. The following international nongovernmental organizations signed BMP3: Baltic and International Maritime Council (BIMCO), International Chamber of Shipping (ICS), International Group of P&I Clubs (IGP&I), International

Maritime Bureau (IMB), International Association of Dry Cargo Ship-owners (INTERCARGO), International Association of Independent Tanker Owners (INTERTANKO), International Shipping Federation (ISF), International Transport Workers' Federation (ITF), International Parcel Tankers Association (IPTA), the Joint Hull Committee (JHC), the Joint War Committee (JWC), the Oil Companies International Marine Forum (OCIMF), and the Society of International Gas Tanker and Terminal Operators (SIGTTO).

2. The shipping industry consortium that prepared BMP has requested that the International Maritime Organization distribute the document to member states and associated organizations. The IMO did so in IMO Doc. MSC.1/Circ.1337, Piracy and Armed Robbery against Ships off the Coast of Somalia: Best Management Practices to Deter Piracy off the Coast of Somalia and in the Arabian Sea Area developed by the industry, August 4, 2010. Version 1 of the BMP was disseminated by IMO in February 2009; version 2 was disseminated by IMO in IMO Doc. MSC.1/Circ.1335, Piracy and Armed Robbery against Ships off the Coast of Somalia: Best Management Practices to Deter Piracy off the Coast of Somalia and in the Arabian Sea Area developed by the industry, September 29, 2009.

3. 1184 UNTS 3, 32 UST 47. See also, G. P. Pamborides, *International Shipping Law: Legislation and Enforcement* 79–80 (1999) and Elli Louka, *International Environmental Law: Fairness, Effectiveness and World Order* 160 (2006).

4. These efforts included major amendments to the 1978 International Convention on Standards of Training, Certification and Watchkeeping (STCW) for Seafarers, which entered into force in 1997, and the development of the International Safety Management (ISM) Code, which entered into force in 1998. The ISM Code regulates passenger ships, oil and chemical tankers, bulk carriers, gas carriers, and cargo high-speed craft of 500 gross tonnage and greater.

5. IMO Doc. A.946(23), Voluntary IMO Member State Audit Scheme, November 27, 2003. The standards were developed in IMO Doc. A.974(24), Framework and Procedure for the Voluntary IMO Member State Audit Scheme, December 1, 2005.

6. IMO Doc. MSC.1/Circ.1333, June 26, 2009, Annex, ¶ 9, at 3.

7. IMO, Focus on IMO: Piracy and Armed Robbery at Sea, at 2, January 2000.

8. IMO Doc. MSC/Circ. 443, Measures to Prevent Unlawful Acts against Passengers and Crews on Board Ships, Maritime Safety Committee Circular, September 26, 1986. In 1991, the IMO requested governments to report all incidents of piracy promptly and in detail. See, IMO Doc A.683(17), Prevention and Suppression of Acts of Piracy and Armed Robbery against Ships, November 6, 1991.

9. IMO Doc. A.545(13), Measures to Prevent Acts of Piracy and Armed Robbery against Ships, November 17, 1983.

10. IMO Doc. A.738(18), Measures to Prevent and Suppress Piracy and Armed Robbery against Ships, November 4, 1993.

11. IMO Doc. A.922(22), Code of Practice for the Investigation of Crimes of Piracy and Armed Robbery against Ships, January 22, 2002.

12. IMO Doc. A.1025(26), Code of Practice for the Investigation of Crimes of Piracy and Armed Robbery against Ships, January 18, 2010 (revoking Assembly Resolution IMO Doc. A.922[22]).

13. IMO Doc. A.923(22), IMO, Measures to Prevent the Registration of Phantom Ships, November 29, 2001. See also *UN Convention on Conditions for Registration of Ships (1986)*, 26 International Legal Materials 1229 (1987). A successfully renamed ship would enable pirates to operate the stolen vessel under apparent authority and an air of legitimacy.

14. IMO Doc. A.979(24), Piracy and Armed Robbery against Ships in Waters off the Coast of Somalia, February 6, 2006.

15. IMO Doc. A.1002(25), Piracy and Armed Robbery against Ships in Waters off the Coast of Somalia, December 6, 2007.

16. IMO Doc. A.1002(25), ¶ 3.

17. IMO Doc. A.1002(25), ¶ 4.9.

18. IMO Doc. A.1002(25), ¶ 9.4.

19. IMO Doc. A.1002(25), ¶ 6.1.

20. IMO Doc. A.1002(25), ¶ 6.2.

21. IMO Doc. A.1002(25), ¶ 6.3–4.

22. IMO Doc. MSC/Circ. 622, Piracy and Armed Robbery against Ships: Recommendations to Governments for Preventing and Suppressing Piracy and Armed Robbery against Ships, May 1993 and IMO Doc. MSC/Circ. 623, Piracy and Armed Robbery against Ships: Guidance to Ship-owners and Ship Operators, Shipmasters and Crews on Preventing and Suppressing Acts of Piracy and Armed Robbery against Ships, May 1993.

23. IMO Doc. MSC/Circ. 622 and IMO Doc. MSC/Circ. 623.

24. The original documents were: IMO Doc. MSC/Circ. 622/Rev. 1, June 16, 1999; IMO Doc. MSC/Circ. 623/Rev. 1, June 16, 1999. Regional seminars held in Brazil and Singapore in 1998 provided input to both 1999 revisions. The 2009 revisions are provided in notes that follow and are excerpted in the appendix.

25. IMO Doc. MSC/Circ. 622/Rev. 1, ¶ 3–15, ¶ 16–20 (discussing protective measures and investigative protocols).

26. IMO Doc. MSC.1/Circ.1333, Recommendations to Governments for Preventing and Suppressing Piracy and Armed Robbery against Ships, June 26, 2009.

27. IMO Doc. MSC/Circ.1073, Directives for Maritime Rescue Coordination Centers (MRCCs) on Acts of Violence against Ships, June 10, 2003.

28. See also, IMO Doc. MSC/Circ. 1072, Guidance on Provision of Ship Security Alert Systems, June 26, 2003 and IMO Doc. MSC/Circ.1109/Rev. 1, False Security Alerts and Distress/Security Double Alerts, December 14, 2004.

29. Transport Committee, House of Commons (U.K.), Piracy: Eighth Report of Session 2005–06, H.C. 1026, at 12–14, July 6, 2006.

30. H.C. 1026, at 12–14.

31. H.C. 1026, at 12–14.

32. IMO Doc. MSC/Circ. 623/Rev. 1. This circular had been revised three times. See, IMO Doc. MSC/Circ. 623/Rev. 2 (June 20, 2001); IMO Doc. MSC/Circ. 623/Rev. 3 (May 29, 2002).

33. IMO Doc. MSC.1/Circ.1334, Guidance to Shipowners and Ship Operators, Shipmasters and Crews on Preventing and Suppressing Acts of Piracy and Armed Robbery against Ships, June 23, 2009.

34. IMO Doc. MSC.1/Circ.1333, June 26, 2009, Annex, ¶¶ 4–8, at 2.
35. IMO Doc. MSC.1/Circ.1333, June 26, 2009, at ¶ 5, at 2.
36. IMO Doc. MSC.1/Circ.1333, June 26, 2009, at ¶ 6, at 2.
37. IMO Doc. MSC.1/Circ.1333, June 26, 2009, at ¶ 5, at 2.
38. Daniel Howden, *Somali Pirates Are "Using Torture" as Defence Shield*, Independent (UK), February 3, 2011, and Andy Pierce, *Pirates "Torturing" Crew*, Tradewinds, February 2, 2011, www.tradewinds.no.
39. Howden, *Somali Pirates*.
40. Brian Rohan, *Somali Pirates Seize German Ship off Seychelles*, Reuters, January 25, 2011.
41. International Chamber of Shipping, Press Release, *Shipping Industry Changes Stance on Armed Guards*, February 15, 2011, http://www.marisec.org/pressreleases.htm.

CHAPTER 4

Naval Strategy and Policy

U.S. Naval Strategy and Policy

On February 8, 2011, the Chairman of the Joint Chiefs of Staff issued the 2011 National Military Strategy, which identified the threat of maritime piracy as a transnational security challenge.[1] The crime of piracy is also cited as an area of opportunity to expand cooperation with nations such as China. By including piracy as a threat on the order of other nontraditional or irregular security challenges, the new strategy amplified the Obama administration's concern for maritime security—an area of intense U.S. planning for more than a decade.

The terrorist attacks of September 11, 2001, spurred development of a presidential-level framework for developing maritime security inside the U.S. government. In 2004, a short policy statement called for development of a comprehensive national maritime strategy.[2] The result: the 2005 National Strategy for Maritime Security (NSMS), which is the overarching White House–level policy for maintaining security in the oceans. United States law permits warships to capture any vessel, including foreign-flagged ships, reasonably suspected of being used for piracy. Such vessels may be brought into a U.S. court and condemned.[3] After the 2005 attack on the *Seabourn Spirit*, the Pentagon began to work in earnest to develop a counterpiracy strategy and policy that would give effect to the law, and be consistent with national maritime strategy. The NSMS, which was signed by the president just as the *Seabourn Spirit* was attacked, only briefly mentions piracy. The Strategy states:

> The smuggling of people, drugs, weapons, and other contraband, as well as piracy and armed robbery against vessels, poses a threat to maritime

> security. Piracy and incidents of maritime crime tend to be concentrated in areas of heavy commercial activity, especially where there is significant political and economic instability, or in regions with little or no maritime law enforcement capacity.[4]

But national strategy against piracy lacked fidelity, and there was little specific guidance for operational commanders. Eight implementation plans provided greater detail to the NSMS, and they were appended to the Strategy as Annex A.[5] But none of the eight plans focused on maritime security or piracy specifically.

At the time of the *Seabourn Spirit* incident, the U.S. operational military commander for the Middle East and Arabian Gulf and Arabian Sea—commander, U.S. Central Command—was exploring ways that American forces could better deter maritime piracy off the Horn of Africa. The U.S. Central Command, located in Tampa, Florida, and the U.S. Fifth Fleet, forward located to Bahrain, took stock of the legal and diplomatic battle space for counterpiracy operations.

Somali pirates typically anchored captured ships near the shoreline, inside Somalia's 12-nautical mile territorial sea. Thus, obtaining legal authority to conduct counterpiracy operations inside Somalia's territorial sea might help naval forces in denying the area as a safe haven for pirates. The Transitional Federal Government (TFG) of Somalia had issued blanket authority for the United States to conduct naval operations inside the territorial sea for the purposes of suppressing maritime piracy operations. At the same time, however, the United States enjoyed a rather circumspect relationship with the TFG. The United States never severed diplomatic relations with Somalia after the 1991 peacekeeping mission, but it did not operate an embassy in the country.

The United States maintained a dialogue with the TFG, but also conducted diplomacy with other key stakeholders in the country. The overarching problem, however, was that if U.S. naval forces actually captured and detained pirates, there were few good options for ensuring that they would be prosecuted successfully. In early 2006, suspected pirates had remained on board U.S. warships for months while diplomats sought a friendly nation willing to prosecute the cases at trial. The detention of piracy suspects at sea imposes a hardship on warships. Usually, modern warships do not have a brig or detention facility on board the ship, as these have been phased out over the past decades. Moreover, since pirates are always captured in groups, the sheer number of suspects can overwhelm the logistical capability of a ship to provide secure billeting, food, and health care for more than a handful of suspects. While negotiations unfold to transfer the pirates to a nation for prosecution or on to the United States to stand trial in federal court, the Navy will arrange to keep the suspects on a noncombatant government vessel. As the U.S. Navy eagerly developed partnerships with Kenya and other nations to suppress maritime piracy, the importance of international cooperation in building maritime security became more apparent.

Cooperative Strategy for 21st-Century Sea Power

Because the U.S. Navy has the only sustained national presence and capability to challenge piracy in the Horn of Africa, the Department of Defense has played the leading role within the U.S. government, first in developing the policy and then in implementing it throughout the vast expanse of the western Indian Ocean. The U.S. Navy has been at the forefront of the effort, identifying piracy as an emerging strategic threat in 2006 in the Naval Operations Concept (NOC) signed by the Chief of Naval Operations and the Commandant of the Marine Corps.[6] The 2010 update to the NOC also discussed the threat of piracy.

The challenge of suppressing maritime piracy in Asia and Africa has encouraged a broad, informal coalition of states and international organizations to work together diplomatically and within naval coalitions. These partnerships and deployments manifest the first proof-of-concept of the U.S. Navy's "Thousand Ship Navy," which evolved into the U.S. Navy, U.S. Coast Guard, and U.S. Marine Corps operational vision, *A Cooperative Strategy for 21st Century Seapower*.[7] The strategy portends a new American approach to maritime order built upon multilateral collaboration. Traditional realists speculate that the strategy merely reflects an effort to enlist and co-opt other nations into perpetuating U.S. naval hegemony. In either event, the strategy has left a major and generally positive impression on many nations. With the United States often in the lead, the international community has responded. Somali piracy presages out-of-area deployments for European naval forces, Japan, and the emerging maritime powers of India and China. More than 20 nations have sent ships to the Horn of Africa to fight piracy.

The large number of warships has reduced the success rate of pirate attacks; however, they cannot patrol the entire area at risk, which measures more than two million square miles. The states situated in the Horn of Africa will have to be at the center of a long-term solution, and evolving international treaties and partnerships are the force multiplier to bring these states together and link them to overseas maritime powers and shipping states. The naval forces from distance states should serve as a temporary gap-filler until the capacity of regional nations can be developed. The African Union (AU), for example, is developing Africa's Integrated Maritime Strategy (AIMS) to address the full spectrum of threats and vulnerabilities, including illegal fishing; illegal dumping of hazardous wastes into the oceans;

trafficking in weapons, humans, and illegal drugs; illegal oil bunkering; and piracy and armed robbery at sea.[8]

Global Train and Equip: U.S. Capacity Building

For many years, the Department of Defense had rather muted interest in security assistance activities, as they were regarded neither as a military mission nor as an activity of more than marginal value to national security. In particular, training foreign military forces was not considered a task suitable for general military forces. Most training was conducted by Special Operations Forces, and often under State Department foreign assistance authority.

The Pentagon sought authority for geographic combatant commanders to expend money on capacity building in foreign countries to meet emerging threats. Rather than wait while threats gathered and manifested into a U.S. security challenge, eventually requiring a U.S. military response, the Pentagon proposed that funds could be shifted from the Department of Defense budget to directly fund foreign capabilities. The Global Train and Equip program was created under § 1206 of the U.S. National Defense Authorization Act (NDAA) of Fiscal Year (FY) 2006, and it is perhaps the best example of a country methodically assessing how partnerships can produce greater regional security. The program began as a counterterrorism initiative after the attacks of September 11, 2001, but it has evolved in fact into a general security program to head off threats before they emerge. Increased foreign capacity, including weapons and training, permits foreign military and security forces to take the lead in conducting maritime operations. Interestingly, the program requires that the Secretary of Defense certify that transferring funds to partner nations actually promotes U.S. military security more than spending the money for U.S. forces.

Since § 1206 was legislated, the United States has poured millions of dollars of maritime security aid into the coastal states of Asia, Africa, and Latin America through the Global Train and Equip program, which is part of § 1206 of the 2006 National Defense Authorization Act.[9] About one-third of the program focuses on strengthening maritime security in partner states and currently includes development of coastal surveillance infrastructure, patrol boats, and maritime interdiction capabilities.[10] The program extends authority of the Secretary of Defense, in conjunction with the Secretary of State, to train and equip foreign military and foreign maritime forces. From FY 2006 through FY 2009, § 1206 spent nearly $1 billion for U.S. bilateral programs in 24 countries. The initiative also provided funding to 13 multilateral programs, and a global human rights program.

More than 40 percent of the funds were obligated for three "top tier" countries to pursue a land-based counterterrorism strategy.[11] Another

20 percent of § 1206 funding during the period was allocated for bilateral programs in a handful of "upper middle tier" of nations, which are all coastal states, and include Indonesia, the Philippines, and Malaysia.[12] Much of the effort in Asia is focused on assisting the littoral states in maintaining order in the Celebes Sea (also known as the Sulawesi Sea), which provides a water border for all three countries and adjoins the Molucca Sea and Sulu Sea. The funds help to develop various coastal and maritime surveillance and detection systems, tactical marine communications equipment, and maritime interdiction packages. For the period from FY 2006 to FY 2010, for example, the Philippines received $73.5 million, Indonesia, $57.4 million, and Malaysia, $43.9 million.[13] These figures include all types of assistance, however, including in the case of the Philippine armed forces, a precision guided missile capability to assist the country's ongoing struggle against Jimaah Islamijah and the Abu Sayyaf Group (ASG).

The decision by Congress to grant the Pentagon authority under § 1206 has not been without controversy.[14] First, the program was resisted by some elements inside the military, and it was slow-rolled at the State Department, which feared it would undermine traditional Foreign Assistance Act responsibilities. But the State Department's process for developing traditional theater and engagement programs was antiquated, and unable to anticipate and head off emerging threats. Secretary of Defense Donald Rumsfeld and Secretary of State Condoleezza Rice, however, supported the § 1206 program. The military geographic combatant commanders also promoted the concept in their testimony to Congress.[15]

In the end, the Deputy Directorate for Global Security Affairs inside the Joint Staff made such a strong case for the legislation that it was adopted. The program represented a new approach to addressing acute threats in an environment of weak states and unstable and ungoverned areas. By using Pentagon authorization, the program is a budget-neutral way to mitigate risk and prevent small problems from growing into larger issues.

Under a modification in the FY 2007 John Warner NDAA, the § 1206 authority allowed the Secretary of Defense to use funds with the endorsement of the Secretary of State. Each year, the Pentagon seeks input from the combatant commanders as to critical shortfalls in the security posture of friends and allies in their AOR. The commanders recommend training or other security assistance that could address the shortfall under the program. The Joint Staff collects and validates the recommendations, and, in conjunction with the Deputy Assistant Secretary of Defense for Special Operations Capabilities and Counterterrorism in the Office of the Secretary of Defense, provides a proposed slate of programs for endorsement by the Under Secretary of State for Policy. Some proposals might be developed by U.S. embassy country teams and forwarded to the Bureau of Political-Military Affairs (PM) at the State Department for evaluation. In each case, however, the country's U.S. ambassador and the relevant geographic combatant commander each must concur in the suggestion. Finally, U.S. military support is contingent upon the individual programs being conducted in accordance with respect for human rights, fundamental freedoms, and on behalf of the legitimate civilian authority within the foreign country.[16]

U.S. Piracy Policy

Even a single successful piratical attack might affect important interests of numerous countries, including the flag state of the victimized ship, various states of nationality of the seafarers taken hostage, regional coastal states, and transshipment and destination states.[17] Since nearly 12 percent of the world's petroleum passes through the Gulf of Aden (GOA), for example, the increasing scope of attacks has the potential to create energy and economic shocks that could affect the EU economy and the economic exports of the oil-producing states of the Middle East. Furthermore, since over 80 percent of international maritime trade moving through the GOA is bound to or from Europe, the waterway is critically important for economic prosperity on the continent of Europe. Without a safe GOA, the Suez Canal is useless. Carriers would be forced to reroute vessels around the Cape of Good Hope. The longer route adds 2,700 miles to the voyage. The additional distance is not trivial, as it increases the operating costs of the vessel by reducing the delivery capacity of the fleet. Six round-trip voyages through the GOA become only five round-trip voyages around the Cape.[18]

The strategic imperative of piracy and freedom of navigation was gaining currency. Somali piracy was raised in the interagency community in 2006, and a brief was presented at the highest levels of the U.S. government in the spring of 2007.[19] The brief set in motion U.S. interagency efforts to encourage and develop greater international authority under a UN Security Council resolution for dealing with the problem of piracy off the coast of Somalia. The United States began working with international partners to draft a UN Security Council resolution that would attract multilateral support for a more robust response to the threat of Somali piracy. In late August 2007, Pentagon officials from the Office of the Secretary of Defense and the Office of the Chairman of the Joint Chiefs of Staff embarked on a three-pronged strategy. First, nations should adopt a UN Security Council resolution that would facilitate closer collaboration, particularly in the area of transfer of pirates to criminal courts in other nations. The United States and France cosponsored the resolution.

Second, a resolution sponsored by the International Maritime Organization (IMO) that addressed Somali piracy would begin to get the shipping industry more involved in dealing with the problem.[20] Third, the long-term solution was to develop greater maritime constabulary and governance capacity in Somalia, and eventually stabilize the nation. Eventually, UN Security Council Resolution 1851 of June 2, 2008, would bring a global focus to the challenge of piracy in the Horn of Africa. The resolution encouraged states to increase and coordinate their efforts to deter acts of piracy by working in conjunction with the Somali TFG, and it called on states to work through the IMO and other international organizations to develop capacity inside Somalia.

The U.S. effort to craft an antipiracy strategy culminated in a comprehensive policy signed by President George W. Bush in the summer of 2007.[21] The policy represents the most wide-ranging presidential articulation of U.S. guidance toward international maritime piracy since the time of the Barbary wars, and it was attached as Annex B to the 2005 National Strategy for Maritime Security.

The U.S. Piracy Policy establishes a framework for warships that encounter or intercept acts of maritime piracy and armed robbery at sea, as well as providing guidance for agencies charged with facilitating the prosecution of perpetrators and the repatriation of victims and witnesses. The new policy directed the Assistant to the President for National Security Affairs and the Assistant to the President for Homeland Security and Counterterrorism to share responsibility in counterpiracy strategy, and to issue further guidance on the subject.

There are seven tenets of the U.S. Piracy Policy: prevention, deterrence, vulnerability, accountability, protection of the sea lanes, freedom of navigation, and diplomacy, and they are discussed below.

Prevention

The U.S. piracy policy emphasizes strategies by states and the maritime sector to prevent piracy attacks and other criminal acts of violence targeted at U.S. vessels, persons, and interests.[22] One of the most ambitious prevention initiatives is the International Ship and Port Facility Security (ISPS) Code, a major amendment to the International Convention for the Safety of Life at Sea (SOLAS). The ISPS Code was negotiated in the wake of the terrorist attacks of September 11, 2001, and it was adopted in 2002. The ISPS Code is based on U.S. maritime security regulations and provides a comprehensive framework to tighten security throughout the world's commercial fleets and ports. Operators of ships and large-scale port facilities (those that handle ships of more than 500 gross registered tons) are required under the ISPS Code to develop, implement, and evaluate security plans.

The United States developed and enacted the Maritime Transportation Security Act of 2002 (MTSA), which served as the template for the ISPS

Code.[23] The U.S. Coast Guard has instituted a program to certify overseas ports of departure for vessels inbound into the United States, and destination ports that handle U.S. shipping. Because the ISPS Code requires countries to conduct a major overhaul of their port and vessel security infrastructure, systems, and processes, states were given two years to review and prepare their security programs before compliance became mandatory on July 1, 2004. Even now, however, some states struggle to attain full implementation of all aspects of the Code.

Deterrence

The United States seeks to deter acts of piracy, consistent with international law and the rights and responsibilities of port, coastal, and flag states.[24] Piracy is an opportunistic crime—one in which the benefits are calculated to outweigh the costs. Deterrence increases the potential costs of piracy in an effort to shift the decision calculus, making piracy less attractive.

The presence of competent port and coastal security forces, and offshore naval power can serve as a deterrent similar to a street cop walking through a neighborhood. Likewise, the United States and partner nations and international organizations have maintained a steady naval presence in the Horn of Africa, as well as provided capacity-building support to regional maritime security forces in Southeast Asia.

Piracy tends to surge when it is ignored and recede after it is addressed. Several international initiatives in the Straits of Malacca and Singapore appear to have helped to reduce the incidence of piracy. Presence missions with U.S. naval forces in the Horn of Africa, and Coast Guard forces in the Caribbean, remain important components of maritime security deterrence. These U.S. efforts are connected to international initiatives in a manner that amplifies their effect. Consistent with the "Thousand Ship Navy" concept, local and regional capabilities are particularly valuable in maintaining regional deterrence, and the United States is working to build capacity in regional maritime security forces.

Reduce Vulnerability in the Maritime Domain

The United States seeks to reduce the ability of criminals to exploit the vulnerability of the maritime domain, particularly when U.S. interests are directly affected. After 9/11, the imperative to reduce vulnerability through maritime domain awareness (MDA) has grown, with the United States releasing a national MDA Plan in October 2005. The complex nature of contemporary maritime threats places a premium on collection and dissemination of actionable information.[25] Achieving maritime security situational awareness depends on the ability to monitor activities so that trends can be identified and anomalies differentiated. Transparency aids operational decision makers in anticipating threats and developing tactics to counter them. Maritime situational awareness or maritime domain awareness (MDA) helps authorities locate and sort legitimate commercial or "white" shipping while more easily identifying anomalous vessels that might be engaged in piracy or other illegal activity.

In 1999, the International Maritime Bureau (IMB) introduced an Internet-based MDA system that ship owners and law enforcement use to track vessels.[26] The IMO has supported development of the Automatic Identification System (AIS), which is a VHF-bandwidth broadcast system that helps locate vessels at sea. AIS is used throughout the world, and especially in chokepoints around the globe, from the Strait of Gibraltar between Africa and Europe, to the entrance to Narragansett Bay in Rhode Island. Chapter V of SOLAS, Safety of Navigation, requires all ships displacing 300 gross tons or greater, or carrying 12 or more passengers on international voyages, to install AIS. The AIS signal is transmitted on a continuous basis, but when ships are transiting in the mid-ocean, the signal often does not reach shore-based security communications.

In the Mediterranean Sea and Gulf of Guinea, the commander of the U.S. Sixth Fleet is working with partner nations to promote an AIS-based system called the Maritime Safety and Security Information System (MSSIS). MSSIS makes AIS information available on an Internet-based exchange portal, which can be accessed by participating states. Intelligence collaboration could also improve maritime domain awareness. Developing greater intelligence capabilities for regional partners is a theme that resonates with Secretary of Defense Robert M. Gates, who declared that more effective intelligence is the "first thing" needed to energize the counterpiracy effort.[27]

AIS has made shipping safer. But the unsecure nature of the open broadcast VHF signal means that anyone with an off-the-shelf AIS receiver can use the circuit essentially as a targeting mechanism to locate ships for hijacking. The master of a vessel retains authority under SOLAS to switch off the AIS transmission if he or she believes that it places the vessel in danger. Ordinarily, ships are better off with AIS transmitting, since it provides locational data to nearby naval forces. The vulnerable nature of AIS has convinced naval forces and the shipping industry to recommend, however, that in high-risk areas, AIS should be turned off completely.[28]

The current advice to ships required to carry AIS is to transmit limited information while transiting the Gulf of Aden. The limited information should include only the ship's identity, position, course, speed, navigational status, and safety-related information. Most smaller vessels, such as yachts, carry only AIS class B transponders and therefore are not configurable by the mariner. By transmitting AIS information in the Gulf of Aden, most merchant ships can obtain help from patrolling warships more quickly. At the same time, navigation lights should be illuminated at dark or periods of low visibility. Completely turning off navigation lights during periods of low visibility due to the fear of piracy places the ship in danger of collision throughout the busy Internationally Recognized Transit Corridor. In the Somali Basin or Indian Ocean, however, there are fewer warships on patrol, and they are therefore not able to respond as quickly. The International Sailing Federation has recommended that yachts transiting outside of the Gulf of Aden turn off their AIS transponder unless there happen to be naval forces nearby.

In May 2006, an amendment to SOLAS Chapter V established a program for Long Range Identification and Tracking (LRIT) of ships of 300 gross tons or greater on international voyages, including passenger ships, cargo ships, high-speed craft, and mobile offshore drilling units. LRIT is a global, satellite-based vessel identification system that is more secure and more accurate than AIS. The LRIT system is still being developed, but it is expected to provide reliable and persistent global surveillance of maritime traffic. Ships can be detected, identified, and classified on a global basis while in transit.[29] In July 2010 the IMO adopted a resolution to ensure that LRIT would be available to track vessels in the high-risk waters of the Horn of Africa.[30]

Pursuant to IMO Assembly resolution A.1002(25) and through Maritime Safety Committee resolution MSC.298(87), the IMO established an LRIT information distribution facility (IDF) to pass shipping information to naval forces operating in the Gulf of Aden and the western Indian Ocean.[31] Already, EU NAVFOR and NATO are using the data to better counter piracy attacks, and the IMO has urged navies conducting antipiracy patrols to join the effort.

Hold Pirates Accountable

The U.S. Piracy Policy is an extension of 200 years of U.S. experience in prosecuting the crime of piracy in domestic criminal courts. Between 1815 and 1823, the United States was conducting so many piracy trials that they were among the most numerous types of cases reviewed by the U.S. Supreme Court.[32] Now, however, the most prevalent maritime crime cases in federal court tend to be related to international drug trafficking. The resurgence of piracy in the Horn of Africa has reintroduced the reality of criminal trials against maritime pirates. As of January 2011, there were four piracy prosecutions underway in U.S. federal court. All four trials resulted from piracy interdiction by the U.S. Navy in the Horn of Africa, and the cases are discussed in Chapter 7 of this volume.

The first modern case of a successful international piracy case arose from an interdiction of pirates attacking a merchant ship off the coast of Somalia in January 2006. The *Safina al Bisarat* was under attack by pirates; as it was escaping, the *Delta Ranger*, an Indian-flagged dhow, was overtaken by the pirates. The *Delta Ranger* was under assault by 10 well-armed Somali pirates. The attackers carried rocket-propelled grenades (RPGs), Kalashnikov AK-47 assault rifles, and smaller weapons. The USS *Winston S. Churchill* (DDG 81) was operating in the vicinity and was able to wrest control of the vessel and detain the armed Somalis.

After protracted international negotiations in which the United States attempted to find an appropriate venue for criminal trial, the pirates were transferred to Mombasa for prosecution. Because piracy is a crime of universal jurisdiction, the Kenyan court was able to assert jurisdiction over the defendants, and all of them were convicted in a multiple prosecution in a Kenyan court.[33] The pirates were sentenced to seven years in prison.[34] Ensuring that effective and meaningful legal sanctions exist against maritime piracy is critical. So far, nations have not been able to develop a critical mass of synergy among counterpiracy operations and criminal prosecution that would serve as a deterrent.

Preserve Freedom of the Seas

Before World War I, Rudyard Kipling observed, "For the bread that you eat and the biscuits you nibble, / the sweets that you suck and the joints that you carve, / They are brought to you daily by all us Big Steamers— / And if any one hinders our coming you'll starve!"[35] Freedom of navigation underpins global prosperity, peace, and security. Since states began conducting international trade in earnest, they have relied on freedom of the seas for their safety and prosperity. Preservation of freedom of the seas has been a central goal of American foreign policy since the founding of the country.[36]

Four hundred years ago, the Dutch legal scholar Hugo Grotius cogently set forth the commercial doctrine of freedom of the seas that would fuel a rapid expansion in transnational trade. "For do not the oceans," he wrote in the 17th century, "navigable in every direction with which God has encompassed all the earth, and the regular and occasional winds which blow now from one quarter and now from another, offer sufficient proof that Nature has given to all peoples a right of access to all other peoples?"[37] Contemporary literature and politics during the world wars also made reference to the impact of navigational freedoms on national welfare.

Grotius was writing during the period of the Dutch Revolt against Iberian rule of the early 1600s. While at war with the Spanish for independence, the Dutch were also engaged in competition with Spain and Portugal over the trade in luxury goods from the East Indies, including silks, spices, and porcelain. The original incident that led to Grotius's composition of his treatise on free seas was the Dutch prize seizure of a Portuguese carrack *Santa Catarina* in the Singapore Strait in 1603. The *Santa Catarina* was loaded with a rich cargo of goods that fetched three million guilders at auction in Amsterdam, a fabulous sum nearly equivalent to the revenue of the English government at the time. Grotius defended the seizure of the Portuguese vessels based on the laws of war and the law of the sea. The laws of war were derived from divine remit and entitled the Dutch Provinces to self-preservation, or what we refer to today as self-defense. He also argued that God had created the world in common for all humanity and that property could be acquired only through expenditure of labor and industry. Portugal claimed exclusive right to the trade of the East Indies by virtue of first discovery. Grotius challenged this view, however, by arguing that the lands already were in possession of their native rulers, albeit ones that were "partly idolators, partly Mahometans." The sea, ever fluid and changing, also could not be possessed by Portugal. Consequently, neither the Portuguese nor anyone else could claim to have exclusive right over the oceans surrounding the East Indies. The right of freedom of navigation could not be appropriated by a nation.[38] Throughout its history, the United States joined with the other maritime powers to resist maritime piracy and other disruptions to freedom of the seas. Freedom of the seas—the community right of all nations to travel freely and conduct traditional ocean activities throughout the global commons—is a core U.S. maritime interest, an heirloom passed from Amsterdam to London, and finally to Washington.

The threat that piracy poses to freedom of the seas is tangible, since the freedom to transit is meaningless unless the voyage can be made with confidence and safe from attack.[39] Piracy catalyzed President George Washington to build six frigates and launch the first American Navy against the Barbary pirates.[40] President Wilson made freedom of the seas a feature of his Fourteen Points in World War I, and Winston Churchill and Franklin Delano Roosevelt included freedom of the seas as one of the war aims set forth in the Atlantic Charter during World War II.

The rights of navigation and overflight associated with freedom of the seas have become an essential element of national security and economic prosperity; maritime mobility and maneuverability are paramount features of current U.S. foreign policy. Since 1979, the United States has instituted three measures as part of its Freedom of Navigation program to promote freedom of the seas and global mobility. First, the naval and air forces conduct operational assertions against excessive maritime claims. Second, the Pentagon conducts military-to-military engagement with counterpart armed forces throughout the world. Third, the U.S. Department of State conveys diplomatic demarches or protests of excessive maritime claims.[41]

Former U.S. Secretary of State Condoleezza Rice stated at the United Nations on December 16, 2008, that piracy was inimical to freedom of the seas. "The outbreak of piracy," she stated, "and the increasing threat to commerce, to security, and perhaps most importantly, to the principle of freedom of navigation of the seas is one that should concern every nation-state."[42] Counterpiracy operations complement the Freedom of Navigation program, demonstrating to international maritime criminal organizations that the United States considers open sea lanes to be an essential element of global stability.

Protect Sea Lines of Communication

The initial rise of the globalized economy began in mercantilist Europe. Over the past few decades, globalization has lifted billions out of poverty, and it can be credited in large part to the boom in interstate trade made possible by safe sea lines of communication (SLOC). Since more than 80 percent of the world's trade travels through the SLOCs, any closure, heightened violence, or increased criminal activity along them has grave implications. There is an interlocking and reinforcing quality to open SLOCs and economic prosperity, since freedom and safety in the maritime domain generate stability and affluent societies on land. Robust international trade also helps democracies socialize nondemocratic nations into an interdependent liberal world system.[43] The 2002 National Security Strategy of the United States declared "[a] strong world economy enhances our national security by advancing prosperity and freedom in the rest of the world."[44]

The vulnerability of the SLOCs through Southeast Asia and the Malacca Strait is made apparent by occasional piracy incidents in those waters. Piracy also threatens the SLOCs along East Africa, at the entrance to the Strait of Bab el Mandeb. But security of SLOCs and the entire marine transportation system is cast into doubt when Somali pirates can hijack a $200 million oil tanker that is the size of an aircraft carrier.[45]

Lead and Support International Efforts

The final key objective of the U.S. Piracy Policy is for the United States to continue to lead and support international efforts to repress piracy and other acts of violence against navigation. To achieve this objective, the United States must urge states to take decisive action, both unilaterally and collectively, against piracy. In addition to providing a framework for interagency coordination within the U.S. government, the U.S. Piracy Policy promotes development of international outreach and cooperation pursuant to the International Outreach and Coordination Strategy (IOCS), which is one of the eight supporting plans of the National Strategy for Maritime Security (NSMS).[46] The IOCS links the United States to other nations in a common project to suppress piracy and promote maritime security.

The closer cooperation in the Malacca Strait demonstrates the value of partnerships in securing strategic waterways.[47] Similarly, the United States and India are working more closely together to promote freedom of navigation and protect SLOCs in the Indian Ocean. When the two countries reached agreement on civilian nuclear cooperation in 2006, they also affirmed their commitment to address piracy and armed robbery at sea in the Indo-U.S. Framework for Maritime Security Cooperation.[48] The bilateral framework agreement calls for regular meetings on maritime security, although it has been underutilized since its completion. The framework, however, yet may serve as a basis for expanding U.S.-Indian cooperation against piracy and other transnational maritime threats in the Indian Ocean.

Somalia Partnership and Action Plan

With a rising tide of piracy attacks in the Horn of Africa in November 2008, including the high-profile seizures of the VLCC oil tanker *Sirius Star* and the roll-on/roll-off carrier *Faina*, the White House scrambled to demonstrate that the country had a plan for addressing the threat. In December 2008, the National Security Council (NSC) released a supplement to the U.S. Piracy Policy that focused specifically on the threat of Somali piracy, called *Countering Piracy off the Horn of Africa: Partnership and Action Plan*. The Action Plan implemented the National Strategy for Maritime Security and the president's Piracy Policy, for the Horn of Africa.

The NSC reiterated that piracy was a threat to the global economy, freedom of navigation, the country of Somalia, and its neighbors. The Action Plan focused on operational measures to disrupt and punish the crime, primarily within the GOA, but the results have been disappointing. From 2007 to 2009, the total number of ship hijackings reported to the IMB increased sharply. The shipping industry is paying more ransoms than ever.

The attacks in the Horn of Africa have spread from the Somali Basin and heavily patrolled GOA, which was the epicenter of piracy in 2008, to the Indian Ocean, which is a much larger area to protect. Since the Action Plan does not contain any measures of effectiveness, it is difficult to gauge whether naval assets that are tasked to disrupt piracy are being used efficiently. After more than two years, the 2008 Action Plan has not been revised. But since it was released, pirates in the Horn of Africa have adapted their tactics and broadened their financial and logistical support networks. The United States and its partners in the region may have to shift the focus of their effort. In particular, the international effort appears rather late in grasping the nature of the international financial networks that are supporting piracy. Another shortcoming of both U.S. and international efforts is the lack of an effective public diplomacy campaign to dissuade Somalis from entering into piracy gangs. More young Somali men than ever are entering into piracy—a clear signal that the benefits are perceived to be as high and the risks are perceived as low.

Executive Order 13536, Blocking Property

The United States has, however, begun to broaden the counterpiracy effort. Significantly, in April 2010, President Barack Obama issued an executive order to disrupt the financial networks that support piracy.[49] The president found that the "deterioration of the security situation in Somalia," combined with the acts of piracy and armed robbery at sea, "constitute an unusual and extraordinary threat to the national security and foreign policy of the United States." "I hereby declare a national emergency to deal with that threat."[50] The order blocked the transfer, payment, or export of any property under the authority of the United States that is associated with Al-Shabaab, certain named individual Somalis who are destabilizing the country, or other persons designated by the Secretary of the Treasury, in coordination with the Secretary of State. Any persons who are undermining the Djibouti Agreement of August 18, 2008, or who threaten the African Union Mission in Somalia (AMISOM) or the Transitional Federal Institutions, or who obstruct the delivery of humanitarian assistance to the country, are subject to having their financial transactions blocked. The order also applies to financial arrangements that are associated with the sale of arms to anyone inside Somalia. The executive order adds greater enforcement powers that complement the ongoing efforts at naval interdiction.

U.S. Piracy Strategy and Naval Operations

Rules of Engagement in Counterpiracy Operations

More than 20 nations have deployed ships to the Horn of Africa to conduct counterpiracy operations. Each nation operates under its own policy for the use of force, with some nations being more permissive than others. States apply international humanitarian law and in some cases human rights law through specific rules of engagement (ROE).

Rules of engagement are constituted from international law, domestic law, and policy considerations in order to refine and specify when force may be used, either in self-defense or in accomplishing a military mission. The United States has promulgated Standing Rules of Engagement for U.S. forces (SROE), which contain both classified and unclassified portions.

The U.S. experience with ROE emerged from confusion during the Vietnam War over when it was appropriate to employ certain methods or means of warfare. After the conflict, the Pentagon embarked upon a process to clarify and craft ROE. During the 1980s, the U.S. Navy led the process of ROE development. By the time of Operation Desert Storm in 1991, the United States had fully integrated legal, policy, and operational issues into a Standing ROE (SROE). The first SROE were published in 1994, and the current edition, which itself is under revision, was released in 2005.[51]

The SROE provide that U.S. armed forces may use force, including deadly force, in self-defense. Self-defense is warranted when U.S. forces experience a hostile act or a demonstration of hostile intent from another armed group or armed force. The SROE also contain more detailed rules concerning the force that may be used to accomplish certain missions, including supplemental measures and special instructions (SPINS) or fragmentary orders (FRAGOs) that may be made available in specific circumstances.

Commanders may use all available weapons and tactics unless restricted by higher authority. That is, the ROE are considered to be fundamentally permissive. In theory, supplemental measures are used to place limits on the use of force by a military commander. In reality, however, ROE often appear to authorize measures that are already permitted, usually because operational commanders seek the comfort of validation and permission from higher authority before using certain methods and means or the desire by higher echelons in the chain of command to exert a greater degree of control over the operations. Interestingly, although the United States has well-developed ROE, there is no standardized or controlling authority to delineate the circumstances in which supplemental rules, SPINS, or FRAGOs are used to disseminate additional guidance to operational forces.

The unclassified portion of the SROE contain general guidance concerning the use of force in counterpiracy operations: "US warships and aircraft have an obligation to repress piracy on or over international waters directed against any vessel or aircraft, whether US or foreign flagged. For ship and aircraft commanders repressing an act of piracy, the right and obligation of unit self-defense extend to the persons, vessels, or aircraft assisted. Every effort should be made to obtain the consent of the coastal state prior to continuation of the pursuit if a fleeing pirate vessel or aircraft proceeds into the territorial sea, archipelagic water or airspace of that country."[52]

Commander Maritime Forces: CTF 151 and MARLO

Naval forces operating in the Gulf of Aden and Somali Basin warn that the danger of piracy and consequent loss of life and property in the region is high. Yachts, in particular, are strongly advised to avoid the area. For the

United States and some coalition partners, the naval forces serving with Combined Task Force (CTF) 151 are at the forefront of counterpiracy operations. CTF 151 is associated with the U.S. naval presence in the Arabian Gulf. The three-star U.S. Navy admiral that serves as commander, U.S. Fifth Fleet in Bahrain also serves as commander, Maritime Forces (CMF), a multinational command to counter violent extremists and terrorist networks in the Arabian Gulf and Arabian Sea. CMF works with regional and coalition partners to improve the overall regional stability and strengthen maritime security. Numerous nations have provided forces or advisers to CMF.[53] CMF elements patrol more than 2.5 million square miles of ocean space, including the Gulf of Oman, the western Indian Ocean, the Arabian Sea, the Red Sea, and the Arabian Gulf. The area of operations (AOR) includes the Suez Canal, the Strait of Bab el Mandeb, the Gulf of Aden and the Strait of Hormuz.

Three international combined task forces (CTF) report to CMF. First, Combined Task Force 150 was established after the attacks of September 11, 2001, to support Operation Enduring Freedom. CTF 150 is a multinational task force that routinely operates in the area to deter maritime terrorism and promote the rule of law at sea. CTF 151 was created on January 12, 2009, to focus exclusively on counterpiracy operations. By September 2010, 11 countries had contributed forces to CTF 151. CTF 151 is dependent upon force participation from coalition partners and the cooperation of the merchant marine community. The shipping industry also should maintain communications with the United Kingdom's Maritime Trade Operations (UKMTO) and the U.S. Maritime Liaison Office (MARLO) to enhance their situational awareness. Finally, CMF includes CTF 152, which operates in the Arabian Gulf in partnership with the Gulf Cooperation Council (GCC) to deter threats. Although CTF 152 focuses for the most part on counterterrorism and conducts patrols to enhance security only in the Arabian Gulf, CTF 151 is a mission-specific organization that is not geographically constrained, so it may operate anywhere within U.S. Central Command AOR.

The Maritime Liaison Office (MARLO) is located in Bahrain and facilitates the exchange of maritime safety and security information between the CMF and U.S. naval forces, and the commercial shipping community.[54] The MARLO was stood up in 1987 during the Iran-Iraq "Tanker War" to bring together U.S. naval forces and commercial shipping, which were under attack by the belligerents to the conflict. After the U.S. Navy established a convoy system for merchant ships, MARLO served as a communications hub to share information about Arabian Gulf transits. MARLO still serves as an information sharing center, connecting U.S. naval forces and the regional maritime community. Ships of all nations are eligible to share information with MARLO, which operates a 24-hour watch. MARLO also serves as an emergency point of contact for mariners in distress. Furthermore, MARLO sends liaison officers throughout its 27-nation area of responsibility of the Gulf and East Africa to gauge port infrastructure and management and better understand the regional marine transportation system.

Maritime Operational Threat Response

The U.S. maritime security policy issued on December 21, 2004, required the development and implementation of a mechanism to ensure that tactical maritime incidents involving U.S. Coast Guard and Navy forces were coordinated within the U.S. government.[55] The ensuing Maritime Operational Threat Response (MOTR) plan provides a mechanism for coordinating interagency responses to maritime smuggling, piracy, and other incidents at sea.

The purpose of the strategic-level MOTR plan is to coordinate U.S. government responses to maritime incidents and threats that could affect the foreign relations or security of the country. As most challenges in the maritime domain affect multiple departments, including State, Justice, Defense, and Homeland Security, the MOTR plan importantly creates a process to ensure a whole of government response to maritime threats.[56] For example, if a foreign national is rescued from distress at sea by a U.S. Navy warship and then subsequently makes an asylum claim, the Departments of State and Homeland Security and potentially the Department of Justice could have roles in resolving the case. Similarly, if a U.S. Coast Guard cutter suspects a foreign-flagged vessel of transporting drugs, any U.S. response would be coordinated through MOTR, and contact with the flag state and prosecutorial issues would involve other departments.

The MOTR plan also designates responsibilities of lead and supporting agencies to enable the government to act quickly and decisively to counter maritime threats. The MOTR process, which facilitates the dissemination, discussion, and assessment of intelligence and the collection of evidence at sea for use in criminal trials, helps departments and agencies develop national solutions and courses of action.

Each year, more than 150 incidents require coordination through the MOTR plan process, and the process can occur by electronic communication, telephone conference, or video teleconference. The relevant agencies and departments of the government, such as the U.S. Coast Guard, U.S. Department of State, and U.S. Navy, have integrated the efforts of their individual command centers to ensure timely and coordinated U.S. responses to maritime threats, such as piracy. The successful U.S. government response to the piracy attack in 2009 on the U.S.-flagged M/V *Maersk Alabama* and the kidnapping of its master, Captain Richard Phillips, was coordinated through the MOTR process. An interagency office solely dedicated to managing the MOTR process, the Global MOTR Coordination Center (GMCC), was created in 2010, which is located in Washington, D.C.[57]

European Union: Operation Atalanta

United Nations Security Council Resolution 1846 of December 2, 2008, provides the international legal basis for the European Union (EU) to conduct an operational counterpiracy mission.[58] In November 2008, the EU Council provided tactical and strategic guidance for impending warship deployments for counterpiracy operations.[59] The operation was the first naval mission ever for the EU's Common Security and Defense Policy (CSDP). The CSDP uses military and civilian capabilities to prevent international conflict. Political control and strategic direction for the mission falls under the Political and Security Committee (PSC) of the Council of the EU. The EU Military Committee (EUMC) provides oversight for the operation.

The mandate issued by the EU grants warships from participating member states the authority to provide protection to vessels, patrol the Somali coastline and territorial waters, and to use force to deter or prevent acts of maritime piracy. The mission has robust ROE, including authority to approach and visit ships suspected of engaging in piracy, detention of suspected pirates and their craft, and use of deadly force to save innocent lives of seafarers under assault by pirates.

The EU established Naval Force (NAVFOR) Somalia—Operation Atalanta on November 10, 2008, to protect World Food Program (WFP) ships delivering humanitarian supplies into Somalia.[60] Operation Atalanta also was authorized to protect merchant vessels in the western Indian Ocean, with the use of force if necessary. EU naval forces have been deployed since December 2008, at a cost approaching €10 million per year. The EU force operates throughout an AOR that extends south of the Red Sea, and includes the GOA, the Somali Basin, and part of the western Indian Ocean and the water surrounding the Seychelles. This is an area equal in size to the Mediterranean Sea.

The EU maintains the Maritime Security Centre—Horn of Africa (MSCHOA) as a planning and coordination authority for EUNAVFOR in the GOA and the Somali Basin. The Centre safeguards freedom of navigation against piracy through close dialogue with shipping companies, vessel masters operating in the area, and other military forces. Manned by military and merchant mariner personnel from several nations, the Centre organizes group transits overnight, when attacks are less likely to occur. Naval forces steam at the head of the convoys as pickets to ensure the area is clear of pirates.

The EU effort includes deployment of naval vessels and surveillance aircraft.[61] Belgium, the United Kingdom, France, Germany, Greece, Italy, Luxembourg, Portugal, the Netherlands, Spain, and Sweden have made contributions to this effort.[62] Warships from the non-EU member states of Norway, Croatia, Montenegro, and Ukraine also have participated in the mission. During its first two years, the operation deployed 1,800 personnel and 20 vessels and aircraft. With a submarine, up to 10 frigates, and 3 patrol aircraft, Operation Atalanta is the largest counterpiracy mission in the region. These forces also concentrate during surges that focus operations to achieve specific effects within a window of time or specified area.

Although the EU force coordinates with other navies conducting counterpiracy missions, the primary focus is on protecting WFP ships. Frequently, WFP leases older vessels that are more vulnerable than newer ships because they are slower and smaller.[63] From its inception through the spring of 2010, Operation Atalanta escorted 110 ships, including 40 ships providing troop supplies for the African Union Mission in Somalia (AMISOM) in Mogadishu. The total amount of protected food aid amounted to 340,000 tons, which fed 1.6 million Somalis per day.[64]

The EU is also providing capacity-building support for Somalia. The Joint Strategy Paper for Somalia for 2008–2013, for example, allocates €215.8 million as part of the European Community's 10th European Development Fund (EDF). On April 7, 2010, the Council of the EU initiated a EU military training mission for Somali security forces (EUTM Somalia), and training started in May 2010.[65] Somali forces are being trained in Uganda, in conjunction with AMISOM. Working with the African Union (AU) and the UN, the EU cosponsored an international donor's conference in Brussels on April 22–23, 2009, at which $213 million was pledged to develop Somali security forces and to help stabilize the Somali Transitional Federal Government (TFG).

NATO: Operation Ocean Shield

The North Atlantic Treaty Organization (NATO) conducts Operation Ocean Shield to combat piracy off the Horn of Africa. The North Atlantic Council approved the operation in August 2009. Standing North Atlantic Treaty Organization Maritime Group Two executes the mission with vessels from eight member countries. Operation Ocean Shield follows earlier NATO efforts to protect WFP ships transiting high-risk waters.

Operation Ocean Shield builds on NATO's earlier counterpiracy experience in the Horn of Africa, Operation Allied Protector. Ocean Shield, however, is a broader approach to counterpiracy. Allied Protector was active from March to August 2009, and Ocean Shield took over responsibilities for NATO in September 2009. The new focus expands the mission from naval operations, to include capacity building for developing states in the region. The counterpiracy operation complements NATO's antiterrorism mission in the Mediterranean, named Operation Active Endeavour. Operation Ocean Shield is coordinated from Allied Maritime Command Headquarters in Northwood, United Kingdom. The NATO Shipping Centre provides a link between the organization's maritime forces and the commercial shipping industry. The Centre serves as the primary point of contact for NATO to coordinate with the private sector and other military actors, including MSCHOA and MARLO.

UK Maritime Trade Operations

The United Kingdom Maritime Trade Operations (UKMTO), located in Dubai, serves as an initial point of contact for vessels operating in the western Indian Ocean region.[66] The office maintains daily contact with participating merchant vessel masters transiting the area and also operates a Voluntary Reporting Scheme (VRS), under which merchant vessels make regular reports, providing their position/course/speed and estimated time of arrival (ETA) at their next port while transiting the region. The UKMTO tracks vessels and shares the information with CMF and EU headquarters, helping naval forces enjoy a common operating picture (COP). Because the office passes emergent and time-sensitive information affecting commercial traffic directly to ships, rather than via corporate headquarters, the office is key to ensuring quick response to any piracy incident.

Internationally Recommended Transit Corridor

In 2008, when the Gulf of Aden (GOA) became the world's hotspot for piracy attacks, the international coalition of warships began to set up escort convoys for merchant shipping through the area. The CMF, in cooperation with the EU and the UKMTO, promulgated the Internationally Recommended Transit Corridor (IRTC) through the Gulf of Aden, effective on February 1, 2009.[67] The IRTC provided increased flexibility for warships in the Maritime Security Patrol Area (MSPA). Vessels operating in the IRTC should avoid entering Yemeni Territorial Waters (YTW) because although all ships enjoy innocent passage in the territorial sea, non-Yemeni naval ships may not freely conduct counterpiracy patrols without the permission of Yemen. The new IRTC reduces the risk of collision and is farther from Yemeni fishing waters than the previous transit corridor in the GOA. The coordinates of the IRTC lanes are as follows:

Westbound lane	northern boundary: 12 00N 45 00E 14 30N 53 00E
	southern boundary: 11 55N 45 00E 14 25N 53 00E
Eastbound lane	northern boundary: 11 53N 45 00E 14 23N 53 00E
	southern boundary: 11 48N 45 00E 14 18N 5300E
	The course eastbound is 072°T and westbound 252°T

The IRTC has succeeded in deterring piracy in the area that it covers by enabling the limited number of warships in the region to concentrate their efforts. In 2010, only 7 of the 49 successful Somali piracy attacks occurred within the boundaries of the corridor.

Many of the ships passing through the GOA opt to join a Group Transit (GT) or convoy. When transiting in GT, vessels should maintain the speed of the group, and join a group that is operating at a speed less than the ship's maximum speed of advance (so there is some ability to increase speed, if attacked by pirates). If a ship does not join a GT, it should proceed at its maximum speed of advance throughout the IRTC, consistent with safety of navigation. International naval operations off the Horn of Africa have markedly reduced the success rate of pirate attacks in and near the IRTC. But the pirates have adapted. The resulting shift in piracy operating areas beyond the IRTC accounts for the growing number of successful attacks in other areas, especially the vast western Indian Ocean. Because the Indian Ocean is so large, there will not be adequate naval patrols or reconnaissance forces to effectively stem the spread of piracy. Shipping should continue to use the IRTC and employ best management practices (BMPs) to minimize the risk of pirate boarding.

Shared Awareness and Deconfliction

Each of the multilateral efforts—CMF/CTF-151, EU NAVFOR Somalia, and NATO—also coordinate with unaffiliated naval forces operating to suppress piracy in the area. Although it is too much to say that all of these efforts are efficiently orchestrated, there is a great deal of exchange and coordination that takes place.

In order to facilitate coordination, nations that have forces in the area established Shared Awareness and Deconfliction (SHADE) meetings. SHADE provides a forum for the several coalitions to make sound decisions on practical military coordination and deconfliction. Co-chaired by CMF and the EU, SHADE also has representatives from NATO, China, Russia, India, and other nations. Representatives from INTERPOL and the Oil Companies International Marine Forum (OCIMF) also participate. The MERCURY

(FEXWEB replacement) is the main means of disseminating unclassified tactical information among SHADE partners. SHADE-T and MERCURY technical teams have integrated their efforts. SHADE is also working to make naval operations more efficient by reducing the number of convoy assets required to patrol the IRTC.

Maritime Organization of West and Central Africa

As the international community considers the ideal of reducing distant state patrols in the Somali Basin and Horn of Africa, there is a need to consider regional models for maritime security. The regional model that may be most promising for the Somali coast is one that could be borrowed from the other side of the continent of Africa—the Gulf of Guinea.

The Maritime Organization of West and Central Africa (MOWCA) was created in 1975 but initially enjoyed an unremarkable record. Like the progressive city of Abidjan, Cote d'Ivoire, in which the organization is headquartered, however, MOWCA is experiencing a renaissance. The forum is helping the member states cooperatively manage all matters of maritime security—port and vessel security, maritime constabulary functions and safety of navigation, and environmental protection. The network has launched several programs to enhance collaboration in the international shipping transport sector. In 2006, MOWCA conducted a forum in Dakar, Senegal, in conjunction with the IMO for establishing an integrated coast guard network. The Dakar meeting led to a memorandum of understanding (MOU) in July 2008 to establish a Subregional Coast Guard Network for the West and Central African region. The comprehensive agreement establishes an institutional framework for close cooperation on suppression of piracy and armed robbery at sea, countering terrorism at sea, illegal, unreported, and unregulated (IUU) fishing, drug trafficking, fuel theft and smuggling, and pipeline security and maritime accident response. The agreement also provides guidelines for coastal surveillance, maintaining presence in the exclusive economic zones, and enforcement of international treaties, especially the Law of the Sea and IMO instruments. It is remarkable that of the 25 MOWCA states, five are land-locked, demonstrating that all states concerned with facilitating international trade and enhancing regional stability have a stake in maritime security.[68]

Caribbean Community

Another successful model for regional maritime security is the Caribbean Community (CARICOM), which is comprised of 15 nations and dependencies. The organization grew out of the Caribbean Free Trade Association, which evolved into a common market. The initial 1973 Treaty of Chaguaramas established CARICOM. The Treaty Establishing the Regional Security System of 1996 provided that members could exercise the right of hot pursuit for maritime law enforcement within the territorial seas and exclusive economic zones. The CARICOM agreement was revised in 2001 to create a single market and economy, including the Caribbean Court of Justice. In 2008, the member states signed the CARICOM Maritime and Airspace Security Cooperation Agreement. The treaty promotes cooperation against ship and aircraft piracy, hijacking, terrorism, and illegal drug trafficking. The CARICOM Arrest Warrant Treaty, which was also concluded in 2008, supplements the treaty.

Notes

1. The National Military Strategy of the United States of America 2011: Redefining America's Military Leadership, February 8, 2011, at 14–15.
2. National Security Presidential Directive 41 (NSPD-41), Maritime Security Policy, December 21, 2004.
3. 33 USC § 385 U.S. Code, Seizure and condemnation of vessels fitted out for piracy.
4. National Strategy for Maritime Security 5 (December 2005).
5. The eight plans are National Plan to Achieve Maritime Domain Awareness (identify threats in the maritime environment), Global Maritime Intelligence Integration Plan (to use existing capabilities to fuse all source intelligence regarding threats in the maritime domain), Maritime Operational Threat Response Plan (to coordinate U.S. government response to threats against the United States and its interests in the maritime domain); International Outreach and Coordination Strategy (to coordinate all maritime security initiatives undertaken with foreign governments and international organizations); Maritime Infrastructure Recovery Plan (recommends procedures and standards for the recovery of the maritime infrastructure following attack); Maritime Transportation System Security Plan (to improve the regulatory framework regarding the maritime domain); Maritime Commerce Security Plan (to secure the maritime supply chain); and Domestic Outreach Plan (to assist the implementation of national-level maritime security policy).
6. U.S. Navy and U.S. Marine Corps, Naval Operations Concept 2006 (2006). See also, U.S. Navy, U.S. Marine Corps and U.S. Coast Guard, Naval Operations Concept 2010: Implementing the Maritime Strategy 36–43 (2010).
7. James Kraska and Brian Wilson, *The Cooperative Strategy and the Pirates of the Gulf of Aden*, 154 The RUSI Journal 75, 76–77 (Royal United Services Institute, London, April 2009).
8. AU *Developing an Integrated Maritime Strategy for Africa*, Defence Web (South Africa), October 19, 2010.
9. The program was managed within the Deputy Directorate for Global Security Affairs, Strategic Plans & Policy, Joint Chiefs of Staff, to which the author was assigned from 2005 to 2008.

10. Nina M. Serafino, Security Assistance Reform: "Section 1206" Background and Issues for Congress 17 (Congressional Research Service, June 29, 2010).

11. These states include Yemen, Pakistan, and Lebanon. Serafino, Security Assistance Reform, at 8 (Congressional Research Service, June 29, 2010).

12. Serafino, Security Assistance Reform, at 7–8.

13. Serafino, Security Assistance Reform, at 7.

14. Serafino, Security Assistance Reform, at 1.

15. Serafino, Security Assistance Reform, at 3.

16. Serafino, Security Assistance Reform, at 9.

17. Countering Piracy off the Horn of Africa: Partnership and Action Plan 4 (National Security Council, The White House, December 2008).

18. Economic Impact of Piracy in the Gulf of Aden on Global Trade (Maritime Administration, Department of Transportation, undated manuscript). See also, *Piracy Could Add $400m to Owners' Insurance Cover Costs*, Lloyd's List, November 21, 2008.

19. While serving as the oceans policy adviser to the Director, Strategic Plans & Policy, Joint Chiefs of Staff, the author presented the brief to a White House–level interagency policy coordinating body on behalf of the armed forces. Pentagon officials also participated in negotiations with Arab and African states at a meeting in Tanzania in April 2008 that developed a draft regional agreement for counterpiracy, which was signed in Djibouti the following year. Pentagon officials also participated in negotiations with Arab and African states at a meeting in Tanzania in April 2008 that developed a draft regional agreement for counterpiracy, which was signed in Djibouti the following year. The Djibouti Code of Conduct is discussed in Chapter 6.

20. The IMO Assembly resolution that eventually was produced was IMO Doc. A.1002(25), Piracy and Armed Robbery against Ships in Waters Off the Coast of Somalia, December 6, 2007.

21. Memorandum on Maritime Security (Piracy) Policy, 43 Weekly Compilation of Presidential Documents 803, June 13, 2007, *reproduced in*, James Kraska, Developing Piracy Policy for the National Strategy for Maritime Security and the International Maritime Organization, *in Legal Challenges in Maritime Security* 331, 409–413 (Myron H. Nordquist, et al., eds., 2008). Navy judge advocates in the Office of the Under Secretary of Defense for Policy and Strategic Plans & Policy, Joint Chiefs of Staff, coordinated drafts through the National Security Council process.

22. Maritime Security (Piracy) Policy, at 411.

23. Maritime Transportation Security Act of 2002, Pub. L. No. 107–295, 116 Stat. 2064.

24. See, Maritime Security (Piracy) Policy.

25. U.S. Department of Homeland Security, National Strategy for Maritime Security: National Plan to Achieve Maritime Domain Awareness 1 (2005).

26. John Parker, *Tracking Ships Online*, Traffic World, June 19, 2000, at 45 (describing new tools for antipiracy efforts, including transponder and website tracked by satellite).

27. John Kruzel, *Defense Department Welcomes UN Resolution Aimed at Pirates*, American Forces Press Service, December 17, 2008.

28. IMO Doc. MSC.1/Circ.1337, Piracy and Armed Robbery against Ships off the Coast of Somalia: Best Management Practices to Deter Piracy off the Coast of Somalia and in the Arabian Sea Area developed by the industry, August 4, 2010, 7.5, at 15–16.

29. The LRIT system will operate by having vessels send reports of their positions periodically to cooperating national, regional, or international LRIT data centers. These data centers will then deliver data to SOLAS-contracted governments, which would be entitled to receive the data for official use only. Such an international data exchange will be a "router" for the data among data centers. In this networked system, data security is a paramount concern that will need to be closely monitored.

30. IMO Doc. Circular letter No. 3086, Availability of a Distribution Facility at IMO for the Provision of Flag State LRIT Information to Security Forces Operating in Waters of the Gulf of Aden and the Western Indian Ocean to Aid Their Work in the Repression of Piracy and Armed Robbery against Ships, July 22, 2010.

31. IMO Doc. Circ. Ltr. No. 3164, Responding to the Scourge of Piracy, February 14, 2011.

32. G. Edward White, *The Marshall Court and International Law: The Piracy Cases*, 83 American Journal of International Law 727 (1989).

33. Paul Raffaele, *The Pirate Hunters*, Smithsonian, August 2007.

34. Raffaele, *The Pirate Hunters*.

35. Letter from Rudyard Kipling to André Chevrillon, October 11, 1919, *in 4 Letters of Rudyard Kipling, 1911–1919*, at 580 (Thomas Pinney, ed., 1999).

36. James Kraska, *Maritime Power and the Law of the Sea: Expeditionary Operations in World Politics* 58–94 (2011).

37. Hugo Grotius, *Freedom of the Seas or The Right Which Belongs to the Dutch to Take Part in the East India Trade* 8 (Oxford Univ. Press: James Brown Scott ed., Ralph Van Deman Magoffin, trans. 1916 [1608]).

38. David Armitage, Introduction, *in* Hugo Grotius, *The Free Sea* 7–8 (Liberty Fund: David Armitage, ed. and intro., Richard Hakluyt, trans. 2004 [1609]).

39. John Bassett Moore, *Principles of American Diplomacy* 103 (2006) (2d rev. ed. 1918).

40. Michael B. Oren, *Power, Faith and Fantasy: America in the Middle East 1776 to the Present* 32 (2008).

41. More than 150 diplomatic protests have been filed and 500 operational assertions have been conducted against the excessive maritime and oceanic claims of more than 80 nations. The purpose of the Freedom of Navigation program is to encourage modification of, and to demonstrate nonacquiescence in, maritime claims that are inconsistent with customary international law, as reflected in the international law of the sea. The essential reference for excessive maritime claims and the U.S. response is J. Ashley Roach and Robert W. Smith, *United States Responses to Excessive Maritime Claims* (2d ed. 1996).

42. Condoleezza Rice, U.S. Secretary of State, Combating the Scourge of Piracy, December 16, 2008.

43. William J. Clinton, Remarks by the President in Address on China and the National Interest, Voice of America, October 24, 1997.

44. *The National Security Strategy of the United States of America* 17 (2002).

45. Andrew Marshall, *Why Hijack a Plane When You Can Seize a Supertanker?*, Reuters, November 28, 2008.

46. National Strategy for Maritime Security: International Outreach and Coordination Strategy 1 (2005).

47. UN Doc. A/54/PV.62, November 24, 1999, UN GAOR, 54th Sess., 62nd Plenary Meeting, at 13, 22.

48. A summary of this agreement is available at http://www.defenselink.mil/news/Mar2006/d200600302indo-usframeworkformaritimesecuritycooperation.pdf.

49. E.O. 13536, Blocking Property of Certain Persons Contributing to the Conflict in Somalia, April 12, 2010, 75 Federal Register 19869, April 15, 2010.

50. E.O. 13536, Blocking Property of Certain Persons Contributing to the Conflict in Somalia.

51. Chairman of the Joint Chiefs of Staff Instruction 3121.01B, Standing Rules of Engagement / Standing Rules for the Use of Force, June 13, 2005.

52. Enclosure A, Standing Rules of Engagement for US Forces, ¶ 4.d, CJCSI 3121.01B, June 13, 2005.

53. These include Australia, Bahrain, Belgium, Canada, Denmark, France, Germany, Greece, Italy, Japan, Kuwait, the Netherlands, New Zealand, Pakistan, Portugal, Singapore, South Korea, Spain, Turkey, United Kingdom, United Arab Emirates, and the United States. Jordan, Qatar, and Yemen are nonmembers that have a staff presence with CMF.

54. IMO Doc. MSC.1/Circ.1337, Piracy and Armed Robbery against Ships off the Coast of Somalia: Best Management Practices to Deter Piracy off the Coast of Somalia and in the Arabian Sea Area developed by the industry, August 4, 2010, at 11 and 66.

55. Maritime Security Policy, National Security Presidential Directive-41/Homeland Security Presidential Directive-13 (NSPD-41/HSPD-13), December 21, 2004.

56. The plan defines "maritime threats" as including "actionable knowledge of or acts of terrorism, piracy, and other criminal or other unlawful or hostile acts committed by terrorists, criminals, States, and State and non-state actors of proliferation concern." Furthermore, "Threats include but are not limited to drug smuggling, migrant smuggling, acts of violence in maritime navigation, and fisheries incursions." Maritime Operational Threat Response for the National Strategy for Maritime Security, October 2006. See also, Guidance for Maritime Operational Threat Response (MOTR)-Related Conferencing Coordination Activities Implementation, Department of Defense Instruction 3020.48, March 6, 2009.

57. CAPT Brian S. Wilson, who penned the foreword to this volume, is the Deputy Director of the GMCC.

58. EU President Jean-Maurice Ripert spoke positively about the resolution, since it gave the European Union "some legal basis" to commence much-needed international counterpiracy efforts. Stake out by Ambassador Jean-Maurice Ripert following the Adoption of Resolution 1846, December 2, 2008.

59. European Union (EU) Council Joint Action 2008/851/CFSP, 2008 Official Journal of the European Union (O.J.) (L 301) 33 (EU).

60. EU Council Joint Action 2008/851/CFSP.

61. See Jenny Booth, *Europe to Send Warships to Defeat Somali Pirates*, Times Online (U.K.), October 2, 2008 and Michael Evans, Rob Crilly, and David Charter, *Euro Task Force Declares War on Somali Pirates*, Times Online (U.K.), October 3, 2008.

62. EU Launches First Navy Mission, in *Piracy-Infested Seas*, Agence France Press, *reprinted in* Defense News, December 7, 2008.

63. European Union Committee, House of Lords, Combating Somalia's Piracy: The EU's Operation Atalanta, HL Paper 103, 12th Report of Session 2009–2010, April 14, 2010, at 13.

64. EU Council CSDP, EU Naval Operation against Piracy (EUNAVFOR Somalia—Operation ATALANTA), EUNAVFOR/17, April 2010.

65. See, www.consilium.europa.eu/eutm-somalia.

66. The UKMTO provides services for the area bound by the Suez Canal, 78° East and 10° South. This area encompasses the entire Arabian Sea, the Somali Basin, the Gulf of Aden, the Arabian Gulf, the Red Sea, and the western Indian Ocean (just beyond Cape Comorin, India). The area also includes the Maldives, Chagos, and Seychelles island groups. See Anti-Piracy Planning Chart Q6099, U.K. Hydrographic Office, April 24, 2009.

67. IMO Doc. SN.1/Circ.281, Information on Internationally Recognized Transit Corridor (IRTC) for Ships Transiting the Gulf of Aden, August 4, 2009.

68. MOWCA consists of the coastal states of Angola, Benin, Cameroon, Cape Verde, Republic of the Congo, Democratic Republic of the Congo, Cote d'Ivoire, Gabon, The Gambia, Ghana, Guinea, Guinea-Bissau, Equatorial Guinea, Liberia, Mauritania, Nigeria, Sao Tome and Principe, Senegal, Sierra Leone, and Togo, and the land-locked states of Burkina Faso, Central African Republic, Mali, Niger, and Chad.

CHAPTER 5

International Law

As Dutch and then English sea power displaced Spanish and Portuguese pre-eminence in the 17th century, Latin notions of the law of piracy, and of the law of nations, gave way to English interpretations. More liberal and modern, English approaches to law also proved to be flexible and adaptable.

Anglo-American Common Law

The common law grew to empower and facilitate commerce rather than freeze political and economic relationships to the benefit of the monarch. The contemporary law of maritime piracy has its origins in the English common law and the English understanding of international law.[1]

The British Experience

The classic English jurist Sir William Blackstone described the law of nations as "a system of rules, deducible by natural reason, and established by universal consent among the civilized inhabitants of the world . . . to insure the observance of justice and good faith . . . between two or more independent states."[2] He wrote that the crime of piracy or robbery and depredation upon the high seas was an offense against the universal laws of civilized society—what we refer to as "international law.[3] This finding is evident throughout Anglo-American case law, which regards pirates as *hostis humani generis*, a Latin term meaning "enemy of all mankind."[4]

> Piracy by the law of nations, in its jurisdictional aspects, is *sui generis*. Though statutes may provide for its punishment, it is an offence against the law of nations; and as the scene of the pirate's operations is the high

> seas, which it is not the right or the duty of any nation to police, he is denied the protection of the flag he may carry, and is treated as an outlaw, as the enemy of mankind—*hostis humani generis*—whom any nation may in the interest of all capture and punish.[5]

By describing piracy under the law of nations in its jurisdictional aspects, as *sui generis*, international law regards piracy as unique. Piracy is the original crime of universal jurisdiction.[6] All nations were endowed with authority to assert jurisdiction over pirates since the crime is so heinous and ships of all nations are at risk. Pirates "attack the rights of mankind, and menace the lives and property of all who resist their unlawful acts."[7] Having renounced all the norms and mores of human progress and enlightened government, pirates were considered by the common law to have reverted to a "savage state of nature." The criminal enterprise was held to be tantamount to a declaration of war against mankind.[8] In response, all nations were deemed to be free to declare war against piracy; indeed not only did every community enjoy the right of self-defense against piracy, but all civilized states had an affirmative obligation to suppress the crime.

One of the central features of the development of Anglo-American law against piracy is the displacement of the normal rule that a ship on the high seas is subject only to the jurisdiction of its own flag state, or state of vessel registry. Generally, the theory of exclusive flag state jurisdiction protects a vessel from being stopped or boarded by the warship of any other state. In cases of piracy, however, navy or law enforcement ships of any nation were deemed to have authority to assert jurisdiction over any pirate ship on the high seas. Since piracy was considered an exception to the general rule, by the 19th century it became particularly important for the crime of piracy to be more precisely defined in order to delineate the circumstances in which warships could board foreign-flagged vessels suspected of piracy. By crafting a basic checklist for approaching and visiting (boarding) ships suspected of piracy, English notions of international law sought to avoid any interference with vessels exercising legitimate freedom of the seas.[9]

The issue of jurisdiction in piracy cases also highlights a common error in the legal analysis of maritime piracy. Piracy is frequently called an "international crime," or an offense against the law of nations. Piracy is not an international crime. An international crime is one that may be prosecuted in an international criminal court or tribunal, such as the International Criminal Court at The Hague, the Netherlands. The crime of genocide is an international crime; all nations have laws proscribing the crime of genocide. Instead, piracy is a domestic or municipal crime of universal jurisdiction, meaning that international law recognizes that all nations may assert jurisdiction over such cases, but do so through domestic criminal law systems.

The terms "international crime" or "universal crime" would become appropriate to describe piracy only if the international community develops a functional international criminal tribunal with jurisdiction over the crime.[10] Barring prosecution of piracy in such an international court, however, the more operative question in any particular case of violence or armed robbery at sea is whether the criminal act constitutes piracy under a nation's municipal criminal law. The definition of piracy and the appropriate punishments for the crime are set forth in domestic laws, and these laws are not entirely updated or consistent among nations.[11] No nation has had more experience in prosecuting piracy than Britain, however, and much of the modern international law against maritime piracy originally emerged from the English common law system.[12]

Under English common law, the offense of piracy consists of robbery and depredation upon the high seas, which if committed upon land, would amount to a felony. Some related common law offenses also were considered piracy, including the commission by a natural-born subject of the British Crown of an act of hostility upon the high seas against subjects of His Majesty. Historically, piracy did not always involve the taking of property, however, and the lack of a subjective intent to rob or steal was not necessarily determinative. Gratuitous malice, or the goal of destroying another ship merely in revenge for real or supposed injuries, could also serve as the basis for piracy.[13] Early common law regarded piracy by a subject of the Crown to be a form of treason, a crime in violation of a subject's allegiance. Piracy committed by an alien was regarded as a felony.[14]

Originally, piracy was cognizable by British admiralty courts, which applied rules of civil law. This approach was deemed to be insufficient to protect the rights of the accused, however, and so a new court of common law jurisdiction was developed, which could impose the death penalty.[15] Any commander or master of a vessel or seafarer who betrayed the trust of his position and absconded with a ship or associated ordnance, ammunition, or goods, or who voluntarily delivered these items over to a pirate, or conspired to commit such acts, could be found guilty of piracy. Assault against or imprisonment of a commanding officer of a warship aimed at preventing the vessel from conducting naval warfare, or inspiring revolt or mutiny, was also punishable by death as a form of piracy. Trading with known pirates, or furnishing them with weapons and ammunition or other stores, or assisting in the outfit of their vessels or providing them with advice, also were held in English common law to constitute maritime piracy.

Britain also has an extensive legislative history, and Parliament adopted statutes to suppress piracy. Under the Statute of King William, persons convicted of piracy were declared to be felons. The convicted pirates were executed "without benefit of clergy." The Statute of King William also declared that naval commanders or seamen who were wounded defending a ship against a piracy attack, and the widows of seamen who were slain in a piracy attack, were entitled to a bounty (not to exceed one-fiftieth of the value of the cargo on board the ship). Furthermore, heroically wounded seamen injured defending against pirates were entitled to be cared for at Greenwich Hospital. On the other hand, cowardly ship commanders who shirked from defending a warship that fell into the hands of pirates forfeited all wages and could be imprisoned for six months.

Any discussion of piracy must distinguish between piracy as a crime of universal jurisdiction among nations, and the actual crime of statutory piracy that is found in the domestic legal systems. Generally, punishment of piracy in domestic law is made pursuant to specific legislation, and some municipal laws capture within the definition other illegal conduct related to piracy, such as ship hijacking or slave trading. In such cases, however, municipal laws of this kind are enforceable only within the ordinary limits of national jurisdiction.[16]

The American Experience

Law in the United States emerged from the English common law system, and the crime of piracy is no exception. The English tradition of recognizing pirates as *hostis humani generis* was carried over into the American legal system.[17] Ruling in 1718, for example, vice admiralty judge Trott presiding on the bench in Charlestown, South Carolina, ruled that robbery committed at sea constituted piracy.[18]

Article I, Section 8 of the U.S. Constitution of 1789 states "Congress shall have Power . . . to define and punish Piracies and Felonies committed on the High Seas and Offenses against the Law of Nations." Jurisdiction for cases in admiralty and maritime jurisdiction was extended to Federal courts by Article III, Section 2. By virtue of these constitutional provisions and subsequent legislation, laws in the United States against maritime piracy have been part of Federal law rather than state law. Since originally there were no common law crimes in Federal law, piracy was made an offense through enactment of legislation.[19]

Some nations may define piracy to include acts that do not fall within the classic definition of the crime in international law, or their domestic law against piracy may ignore certain aspects of international law in their rules against piracy. For example, in the early 19th century, a U.S. court ruled that although slave trafficking fit within the international law definition of piracy, it was not subject to prosecution in Georgia because the odious practice did not violate any U.S. statute in force at the time.[20] In the case of *The Antelope*, the court held that the slave trade did not constitute piracy unless it was so regarded by the flag state of the vessel involved. "[T]he legality of the capture of a vessel engaged in the slave trade depends on the law of the country to which the vessel belongs. If that law gives its sanction to the trade, restitution will be decreed; if that law prohibits it, the vessel and cargo will be condemned as good prize."[21]

A pirate is one who, without legal authority from the state (such as operating under a letter of marque and reprisal issued by the United States), attacks a ship with the intention to appropriate what belongs to it.[22] In a break from European practice, however, the United States treated privateers that operated under authority of a letter of marque and reprisal from another state as pirates.[23] The pirate is a sea brigand, and he has no right to any flag. Furthermore, a ship that navigates without a flag or, which on being summoned to do so does not show its flag, exposes itself to the suspicion of piracy.

The first legislation in the United States on the subject of piracy was the Crimes Act of April 30, 1790.[24] The 1790 legislation is sometimes regarded as having conferred on courts of the United States a jurisdiction far more extensive than that which they actually obtained. Section 8 of the Act provides:

> That if any person or persons shall commit upon the high seas, or in any river, haven, basin or bay, out of the jurisdiction of any particular state, murder or robbery, or any other offence which if committed within the body of a county, would by the laws of the United States be punishable with death; or if any captain or mariner of any ship or other vessel, shall piratically [*sic*] and feloniously run away with such ship or vessel, or any goods or merchandise to the value of fifty dollars, or yield up such ship or vessel voluntarily to any pirate; or if any seaman shall lay violent hands upon his commander, thereby to hinder and prevent his fighting in defense of his ship or goods committed to his trust, or shall make a revolt in the ship; every such offender shall be deemed, taken and adjudged to be a pirate and felon, and being thereof convicted, shall suffer death; and the trial of crimes committed on the high seas, or in any place out of the jurisdiction of any particular state, shall be in the district where the offender is apprehended, or into which he may first be brought.[25]

The early Supreme Court shaped the U.S. law of piracy. In the 1818 *United States v. Palmer* case, for example, the defendants were charged with having committed a robbery on the high seas against a vessel belonging to "persons unknown."[26] The Supreme Court heard two issues in the case. First, the Court grappled with the definition of piracy in the Crimes Act. Did Congress intend for actions that would constitute robbery on land but committed on the high seas be considered piracy?[27] The defendants argued that since the offense of robbery committed on land would not receive the death penalty, it would not be considered piracy when committed on the high seas. The Crimes Act contained the qualifying statement "would by the laws of the United States be punishable with death," and the defendants argued that under the laws of the United States, robbery did not warrant the death penalty. But the Court disagreed, stating that the "meaning of the term robbery," in the statute "must be understood in the sense in which it is recognized and defined at common law." Robbery committed on the high seas did constitute the act of piracy, and therefore was indeed punishable by death.

The second question certified from the lower circuit court of the United States for the District of Massachusetts was as follows: "whether the crime of robbery committed by persons who are not citizens of the United States on the high seas on board any ship or vessel, belonging exclusively to the subjects of any foreign state or sovereignty . . . be a robbery or piracy, within the true intent and meaning of the [law], and of which the circuit court . . . has cognizance to try and determine and punish the same?"[28]

In response to this question Chief Judge Marshall who delivered the opinion of the Supreme Court stated:

> The question, whether the statute extends farther than to American citizens, or to persons on board American vessels, or to offenses committed against citizens of the United States, is not without its difficulties. . . . [but] the words of this section are in terms of unlimited extent. The words "any person or persons," are broad enough to comprehend every human being. The general words must not be limited to cases within the jurisdiction of the state, but also to those objects to which the legislature intended to apply them.[29]

The Court decided that the words "any person" or "persons" must be limited by some degree, with the intent of the Congress determinative to the extent of the limitation. The Court found that:

> The court is of the opinion that the crime of robbery, committed by a person on the high seas, on board of any ship or vessel belonging exclusively to subjects of a foreign state, on persons within a vessel belonging exclusively to subjects of a foreign state, is not a piracy within the true intent and meaning of the act for the punishment of certain crimes against the United States.[30]

In sum, the Palmer case stands for two propositions: First, the Court clarified the definition of piracy as being the act of robbery, as recognized and defined by common law, committed on the high seas. But in the second issue, the Court held that piracy committed on the high seas against a foreign-flagged vessel not owned by an American was not considered piracy under the Act of 1790. To rectify the Court's interpretation in Palmer, Congress redefined the crime of piracy in Section 5 of the Act of 1790 through a new statute passed on March 3, 1819,[31] which stated:

> Piracy was the act of robbery, as recognized and defined by common law, committed on the high seas. However, the crime of robbery by a non-U.S. citizen committed on the high seas on board a vessel owned by subjects of a foreign state was not considered piracy under the Act of 1790, and as such, was not punishable in the courts of the United States.[32]

Section 1 of the 1819 statute authorized the president to deploy armed vessels to protect U.S. merchant shipping from pirates. Naval commanders also were authorized to retake a U.S.-flagged ship that had been seized by pirates. Section 4 of the 1819 statute provided that any captured pirate vessel retaken by the U.S. Navy and brought before an admiralty court of the United States could be condemned by the court and converted to a public vessel under the U.S. flag. This provision is an early analogue to the contemporary use of criminal asset forfeiture, which permits Federal law enforcement agencies to convert vehicles, aircraft, and boats that were seized as instrumentalities of certain felony crimes, such as international drug trafficking.

The United States also codified other aspects of English common law. Section 9 of the Act of 1790 stated that any citizen who committed an act of hostility against the United States, or against an American citizen, upon the high seas under color of a letter of marque or privateer commission issued by a foreign power, was regarded as a pirate. Seafarers who knowingly assisted pirates could be charged as accessories before the fact under § 10 of the Act of 1790. Sections 11 and 12 of the Act included the crime of accessory after the fact, such as knowingly receiving property stolen by pirates or helping to conceal pirates from law enforcement. Seafarers found guilty of §§ 11 and 12 could be punished by a fine and up to three years' imprisonment.

Further revisions to the U.S. law of piracy were adopted on March 3, 1835, and August 8, 1846, and also in 1847 and 1874, and several prominent cases followed in their wake. In the latter part of the 19th century, the *Virginius* case addressed the question of when a vessel takes on the status of a pirate ship.[33] In 1873 the *Virginius* was navigating under the American flag, but without a legal right to do so since its registration was defective. The ship was engaged in transporting arms and munitions for insurgents fighting in a Central American revolution.[34] The ship was not committing the classic crime of piracy, however, in that it was not conducting armed robbery at sea.

Spanish naval forces arrested the vessel as it was transiting on the high seas, and a number of crew were executed. The lawfulness of the executions was in doubt, however, since although the ship was carrying arms to be used in an insurgency, it was not a "pirate ship" within the meaning of the law. Instead, the Court suggested the ship should have been regarded as carrying belligerent articles of war and treated in accordance with the laws of naval warfare, which is a subset of international humanitarian law.

Federal courts in the United States have a rich history of interpreting and developing the law of piracy. For the most part, U.S. courts have adopted the international standard against piracy, ruling that by their crimes "pirates become the enemies of the human race and place themselves outside the law of peaceful people."[35] Courts also have upheld the custom and state practice of universal jurisdiction—the authority to assert jurisdiction over the crime of piracy even without some other legal connection (such as citizenship) between the court and the accused. One judge described this universality principle as "based on the assumption that some crimes are so universally condemned that the perpetrators are the enemies of all people," and "[t]herefore, any nation which has the custody of the perpetrators may punish them according to its law applicable to such offenses."[36]

Throughout the period from 1790 to 1909, the major change in the law of piracy in the United States was the January 15, 1897, statute that eliminated the death penalty as punishment for the crime.[37] Thereafter, piracy was punishable by confinement only, with a maximum punishment of life imprisonment. The 19th-century amendments to the law of piracy, with minor revisions, were carried into the 20th century by the enactment of the U.S. Criminal Code of 1909.[38]

U.S. Piracy Prosecutions

The contemporary law of piracy imports verbatim the definition of piracy from the 1909 statute into Title 18 U.S. Code § 1651. The current statute defines "piracy under law of nations," as the crime traditionally recognized as maritime piracy. "Whoever, on the high seas, commits the crime of piracy as defined by the law of nations, and is afterwards brought into or found in the United States, shall be imprisoned for life."[39] The statute is interesting because it imports the international law definition of piracy into U.S. law—creating a question of law for the district court in each case. The question in each case is whether the defendant committed an act of piracy, as that crime is recognized in international law, rather than any specific U.S. statutory definition of the crime. Congress codified its constitutional authority to "extradite or prosecute" offenders of maritime piracy in 18 U.S.C. § 2280. Section 2280(a)(1)(A) defines a pirate as an individual "who unlawfully and intentionally seizes or exercises control over a ship by force or threat thereof." The companion section, § 2280(a)(1)(B), prescribes "acts of violence against a person on board a ship" that are "likely to endanger the safe navigation of that ship." These provisions are by no means antiquated.

In the 2008 case *U.S. v. Lei Shi*, for example, a three-judge panel of the U.S. Court of Appeals for the 9th Circuit upheld the conviction and 36-year prison sentence of a Chinese cook convicted in Honolulu of forcibly seizing control of a foreign vessel in international waters and killing a Taiwanese captain and Chinese first mate.[40] Significantly, the court held that the normal nexus requirement between the accused and the jurisdiction in which he was tried, which is an ordinary feature of the landscape of due process under the Fifth Amendment, did not prevent prosecution in the case of piracy because pirates are stateless individuals who are universally condemned. Consequently, the U.S. position is that a pirate may be criminally prosecuted by any nation in which he appears in court, even though he has no connection to the jurisdiction or appears in the jurisdiction unwillingly.

Violence against maritime navigation beyond the defined limits of piracy is also a crime under U.S. criminal law.[41] Title 18 implements the 1988 Convention for the Suppression of Unlawful Acts against the Safety of Maritime Navigation (SUA).[42] Federal law further provides for the exercise of jurisdiction in accordance with international law, including jurisdiction over any vessel belonging in whole or in part to the United States or a U.S. citizen, or any corporation created by the laws of the United States, or any vessels registered in the United States, when it is located in international waters.[43] Additionally, the United States may assert jurisdiction over other categories of related offenses, such as those committed on board an aircraft in flight over the high seas or committed on waters within the admiralty or maritime jurisdiction of the United States, in addition to maritime offenses committed by or against a U.S. national.[44] It is also a Federal crime to commit an assault on the high seas.[45]

The United States has four ongoing prosecutions for Somali piracy. The first case, *U.S. v. Muse*, arose out of the seizure of the *Maersk Alabama* attack in early 2009. Abduwali Abdukhadir Muse pleaded guilty to two felony counts of hijacking maritime vessels, two felony counts of kidnapping, and two felony counts of hostage taking. Four Somali pirates hijacked the *Maersk Alabama* on April 8, 2009. The attack was the first seizure of an American-flagged vessel by maritime pirates in nearly 200 years. Four days later, U.S. Navy Seal snipers positioned on the fantail of the USS *Bainbridge* shot and killed three of the pirates who appeared to threaten the remaining civilian hostage, Captain Richard Phillips. Muse was on board the Navy ship engaged in talks and was the only surviving member of the group. Muse was indicted by a federal grand jury on May 19, 2009, and he pled guilty on May 18, 2010, in federal court. On February 16, 2011, Muse was sentenced to 33 years and nine months in federal prison. There is no parole in U.S. federal prison.

The second case, *U.S. v. Said, et al.*, involved six Somali defendants who were charged with the crime of piracy under the law of nations under 18 U.S.C. § 1651, and assault and firearms charges relating to an attack on the warship USS *Ashland* (LSD 48) on April 10, 2010. The case was brought in the Eastern District of Virginia. On August 17, 2010, the District Court dismissed the piracy count in the indictment, erroneously concluding that the law of nations did not include an attack that fell short of the seizure of the ship itself to be piracy. The U.S. government has appealed the ruling to the Fourth Circuit Court of Appeals, so a trial date is indefinitely postponed in the interim. Meanwhile, all of the defendants remain in custody and face additional felony charges. One of the Somalis pled guilty to three of the charges in the indictment and agreed to a 30-year sentence.

Third, in another case in the Eastern District of Virginia, *U.S. v. Hasan, et al.*, five Somali men were charged with the crime of piracy under the law of nations under 18 U.S.C. § 1651, and assault and firearms charges relating to an attack on the warship USS *Nichols* on April 1, 2010. The U.S. government prevailed on two pretrial motions—a motion to dismiss the piracy charge and a motion to suppress the defendants' incriminating statements. The court concluded that the law of nations springs from an evolving body of norms. The definition of piracy in 18 U.S.C. § 1651 may be determined by assessing the contemporary international consensus of the term at the time of the alleged offense. All five Somali men were convicted of piracy for the attack on the USS *Nichols*—the first successful piracy trial in the United States since the Civil War.[46]

Another of the *Ashland* pirates, Jama Idle Ibrahim, pled guilty in the District of Columbia on September 8, 2010, in a separate case, *U.S. v. Ibrahim*. Ibrahim pleaded guilty to conspiracy to commit piracy under the law of nations and conspiracy to use a firearm during and in relation to a crime of violence relating to his participation in an act of piracy against the Danish owned, Bahamas registered M/V CEC *Future* in November 2008. Ibrahim was sentenced to 25 years confinement for his role in the hijacking of the M/V CEC *Future*. Because the attack had no nexus to the United States, the case illustrates the long-arm reach of U.S. jurisdiction and substantive criminal law relating to the crime of piracy. Ibrahim also pled guilty to charges arising from participation in the *Ashland* attack, including 18 USC § 1659 (attack to plunder vessel), § 2291(a)(6) (act of violence against persons on vessel), and § 924(c)(1)(A)(iii) (use of firearm during crime of violence). In November 2010, Ibrahim was sentenced to 30 years in prison for his conduct in the attack on the *Ashland*.

1932 Harvard Research Draft

Developments in Anglo-American domestic law against piracy informed creation of the contemporary antipiracy provisions of international law. During the interwar period, a group of prominent West Coast legal scholars came together to codify the international law piracy. The group produced the 1932 Harvard Research Draft Convention on Piracy, a proposed treaty consisting of 19 articles. The Harvard Draft was crafted to capture and restate the existing international law on piracy as reflected in statutes, judicial opinions, and the writings of prominent scholars.[47] Article 3 of the Harvard Draft defined piracy as any act outside the territorial jurisdiction of a state and that was an "act of violence or depredation committed with intent to rob, rape, wound, enslave, imprison or kill a person with intent to steal or destroy property, for private ends." The document defined piracy in the common law as, "those acts of robbery and depredation upon the high seas, which, if committed upon land, would have amounted to felony."[48] A ship is a pirate ship under Article 4, if it was under "dominant control" of a person and used for the purposes described in Article 3.

The fundamental elements of the 1932 Draft Convention are that piracy under the law of nations is an illegal maritime act committed beyond coastal state territorial jurisdiction.[49] Piracy is an exception to the ordinary rules of jurisdiction in international law. Within the jurisdiction of the territorial sea, coastal states are responsible for prescribing and enforcing maritime criminal laws. Typically international law recognizes that states exercise exclusive, or at least primary, jurisdiction within their territorial seas. All nations also exercise jurisdiction on board their ships and aircraft registered to the state, wherever they happen to be located.

A state also may assert jurisdiction over certain of its persons or nationals abroad under the "nationality principle," in order to safeguard its citizens against threats. Since all nations may assert jurisdiction over persons suspected of piracy, the crime has a special status in jurisdiction beyond the familiar grounds of personal allegiance, territorial dominion, or flag state responsibility.[50]

Piracy is not a crime or offense under the law of nations, but rather international law affords special jurisdiction over the crime by any state.[51] This means piracy is not a universal crime, but rather a crime of universal jurisdiction. The purpose of codifying international law against piracy is not to unify the various national legal frameworks or even to develop uniform standards for punishing pirates, but rather to explore and define the basis of state jurisdiction over offenses committed by foreign nationals against vessels outside of the territory of the prosecuting state.[52] Furthermore, the special jurisdiction is expansive, encompassing judicial, executive, and legislative authority.[53]

Universal jurisdiction of all states to prevent piracy, and to seize and punish persons engaged in piracy, was incorporated into the Harvard Draft text. The document also suggested that only private vessels could commit piracy. Warships and other public vessels retained sovereign immunity, but if warships unlawfully committed unjustified acts of violence, the injured state could seek redress from the warship's flag state.[54] Furthermore, hot pursuit was permitted. After committing the crime of piracy, a ship did not erase its status as a pirate ship merely by fleeing to the high seas.

Article 10 of the 1932 draft included a provision imposing liability for any damage to a ship seized by law enforcement authorities that is neither a pirate ship nor a ship taken by piracy and possessed by pirates. Article 11 authorized the approach of a foreign-flagged ship, and stopping and questioning the vessel on reasonable suspicion that it was operating as a pirate ship. Article 14 stipulates that any state having custody of suspects may prosecute them at trial for piracy. Furthermore, the prosecuting state retains the authority to define the crime of piracy, and apply its procedural law at trial. The Harvard Draft also recognized states had an obligation to apply a minimum level of due process in such cases, requiring the state to provide defendants accused of piracy with a "fair trial before an impartial tribunal" and proceed with criminal charges without "unreasonable delay."

Furthermore, under principles of international humanitarian law reflected in the Harvard Draft, an accused was entitled to humane treatment during confinement awaiting trial. States also were not permitted to discriminate in the treatment of nationals from any state. Interestingly, under Article 15 of the Harvard Draft, a state could not prosecute an alien for an act of piracy for which he had been charged and convicted or acquitted in a prosecution in another state. Such cases really are not tantamount to double jeopardy, since different sovereign states ordinarily would not be debarred from prosecuting a defendant convicted of the same crime in another nation's jurisdiction. The Harvard Draft also included a dispute settlement provision in Article 19, in which state parties would refer disagreements to the Permanent Court of International Justice, the predecessor organization to the International Court of Justice.

The Harvard Draft represented both a continuation of Anglo-American approaches to the law of piracy, as well as a major advancement in restating and codifying the principles.

Post–World War II Development of the Law of Piracy

Because the earth's oceans are interconnected—forming one immense "world ocean"—states have sought to develop uniform standards for governance. In the modern world, the most conspicuous effort to fashion an international order was the Peace of Westphalia in 1648. The peace ended the Thirty Years War and ushered in recognition of the modern nation state.

In 1814–1815, the Congress of Vienna also established an international order with global impact, settling disagreements over international rivers and providing broad recognition for the abolition of slavery. The League of

Nations followed World War I, but the institution proved incapable of preventing World War II. In 1924, the Assembly of the League of Nations requested that the Council of the League form a committee of experts to codify specific areas of international law. The League Committee of Experts for the Progressive Codification of International Law selected piracy as one of the first offenses for consideration for codification. In 1926, the Committee released draft Provisions for the Suppression of Piracy. The draft provisions assumed that there was a single conception of what activities constitute the crime of piracy. There were eight provisions, which specified that piracy occurs only on the high seas and for private (i.e., nongovernmental) ends (Article 1); pirates lose the right to fly the flag of any nation (Article 2); warships cannot commit the crime of piracy (Article 3); during civil war, insurgents who are not recognized as belligerents may be treated as pirates (Article 4); every warship has the legal right to interdict a pirated vessel (Article 5); every warship has the right of approach and visit of a ship suspected of piracy (Article 6); the state of the warship capturing a pirate ship enjoys criminal jurisdiction over the piratical acts committed on board the ship (Article 7); and, the municipal or domestic law of the state of the capturing warship determines the rules governing the prize (Article 8).[55]

In the wake of World War II, the international community, led by the United States, adopted the Charter of the United Nations. The United Nations, in turn, created the principal governing organs—the UN General Assembly, the International Court of Justice (ICJ), and the UN Security Council, with the latter institution authorized to take enforcement action against threats to international peace and security.

In 1947, the UN General Assembly adopted a statute for creation of the International Law Commission (ILC), which was designed around 34 experts in the field of public international law who would lead codification and advancement of legal principles.[56] Article 15 of the ILC's statute states that the purpose of the ILC is "the more precise formulation and systematization of rules of international law in fields where there already has been extensive State practice, precedent and doctrine." The goal is to further the "progressive development of international law." In doing so, the ILC is involved in "the preparation of draft conventions on subjects which have not yet been regulated by international law or in regard to which the law has not yet been sufficiently developed in the practice of States."[57]

International Law Commission Draft Articles

With this charter in mind, the UN General Assembly adopted Resolution 899 (IX) on December 14, 1954, requesting that the International Law Commission consider the international rules that apply to the high seas and other areas of the oceans. The 8th session of the ILC met in 1956 and produced a draft treaty concerning the oceans. Articles 38–45 of the draft convention were devoted to antipiracy.[58] The 1956 antipiracy articles were drawn heavily from the 1932 Harvard Draft Convention, and form the basis for the modern international law of maritime piracy.

The ILC draft articles first set forth in Article 38 suggests that states have an obligation to cooperate in counter piracy.

Article 38

All States shall cooperate to the fullest possible extent in the repression of piracy on the high seas or in any place outside the jurisdiction of any State.

The ILC recognized the critical contribution of the research carried out at Harvard Law School under the leadership of Professor Joseph Bingham, which culminated in the draft convention of 19 articles in 1932.[59] Generally, the ILC endorsed the finding of the Harvard research team. ILC draft Article 38 makes clear that all nations are obligated to take measures to suppress piracy. If states pass up such an opportunity, they have failed to fulfill an affirmative duty in international law. The ILC recognized that in fulfilling this duty, states should be afforded a measure of flexibility and latitude in their approach.[60] The ILC also agreed that any state that had an opportunity to take measures against piracy, and yet neglected to do so, would be failing in a duty of international law.[61]

The definition of piracy was set forth in Article 39.

Article 39

Piracy consists in any of the following acts:

1. Any illegal act of violence, detention or any act of depredation, committed for private ends by the crew or the passengers of a private ship or a private aircraft, and directed:
   (a) On the high seas, against another ship or against persons or property on board such a ship;
   (b) Against a ship, persons or property in a place outside the jurisdiction of any State.
2. Any act of voluntary participation in the operation of a ship or of an aircraft with knowledge of facts making it a pirate ship or aircraft.
3. Any act of incitement or of intentional facilitation of an act described in sub-paragraph 1 or sub-paragraph 2 of this Article.

During the ILC negotiations, the Soviet Union and China criticized the view that the essence of maritime piracy was a crime "committed for private ends by the crew or the passengers of a private ship." At the time, Moscow and Beijing complained that nationalist Taiwanese naval forces operating in conjunction with the U.S. Navy to interdict supplies flowing to the Communist Chinese on the mainland were engaged in "piratical" conduct.[62] Despite the objections, however, the general definition of piracy coalesced around private conduct committed for private ends. Only private ships may commit piracy; warships and other government vessels are excluded from the definition. This tenet upheld the traditional rule that piracy was a private crime. In doing so, the Nyon Arrangement of September 14, 1937, which suggested that the sinking of merchant ships by submarines was a form of piracy, was rejected.[63]

From a legal perspective, the question of whether an attack by insurgent naval forces on merchant vessels constitutes an act of piracy is determined by whether governments recognize the acts as part of a lawful belligerency.[64] If an attack against commercial shipping is conducted pursuant to a lawful belligerency, then the ship is immunized from prosecution for piracy because the assault was for a public purpose.

On the other hand, if a naval force is operating outside of recognition of a lawful belligerency, then any violent acts are conducted for private ends and are not protected from prosecution for piracy. In the 1885 case of the *Ambrose Light*, for example, the U.S. Navy gunboat USS *Alliance* captured a brigantine cruising along the Colombian coast "in a suspicious manner." When approached by the man-of-war, the ship displayed Haitian colors, and then hoisted the Colombian flag.[65] Judge Brown, presiding over the case in the Federal District Court for the Southern District of New York, held that "recognition by at least some established government of a 'state of war', or of the belligerent rights of insurgents, is necessary to prevent their cruisers from being held legally piratical by the courts of other nations injuriously affected."[66] Consequently, the ship was released to the owners as a lawful belligerent vessel ferrying supplies from one port of Colombia to another.[67]

Criminal acts committed by the crew or passengers of a ship and that are directed against a ship or against persons or property on board the ship do not meet the classic definition of maritime piracy. Piracy ordinarily requires another ship, and this is the two-ship dilemma. In order for there to be piracy, both a pirate ship and another ship, the second being a victimized vessel, must be involved. The ILC also determined that the intention to rob is not an essential element of the definition of piracy, as the crime could be "prompted by feelings of hatred or revenge, and not merely by the desire for gain."[68]

Finally, piracy can be committed only on the high seas or in an area outside of the territorial jurisdiction of any state.[69] This rule follows the League of Nations subcommittee of 1926, which concluded, the concept of "piracy has as its field of operation that vast domain which is termed 'the high seas'."

The provision also reflects the Harvard Draft, which stated that the crime of piracy may be committed only, "in a place not within the territorial jurisdiction of any State." These statements reflect the dissenting opinion of Judge Moore in the *Lotus* judgment. Moore wrote, "the scene of the pirate's operations is the high seas, which it is not the right or duty of any nation to police."[70]

Article 40 of the ILC draft provides one exception to the two-ship dilemma posed by the classic definition of piracy. The Article states:

Article 40

The acts of piracy, as defined in Article 39, committed by a government ship or a government aircraft whose crew has mutinied and taken control of the ship or aircraft are assimilated to acts committed by a private vessel.

The sole exception to the rule that a warship or government ship cannot meet the criteria for becoming a pirate ship is the case in which the crew of a state ship (or aircraft) has mutinied and taken control of the vessel. In cases of mutiny, the ship or aircraft is assimilated to a private vessel. At that point, any criminal acts committed against the crew or passengers of another ship are considered maritime piracy. Once order has been restored and the mutiny suppressed, however, this exception ceases to apply.[71]

Article 41

A ship or aircraft is considered a pirate ship or aircraft if it is intended by the persons in dominant control to be used for the purpose of committing one of the acts referred to in Article 39. The same applies if the ship or aircraft has been used to commit any such act, so long as it remains under the control of the persons guilty of that act.

The mere lack of a flag or nation of registry for a vessel is not per se an act of maritime piracy. Ships that have either already committed piracy or intend to commit piracy may be considered as pirate ships so long as they remain under the control of the persons who have committed those acts. Furthermore, Article 42 specifies that the nation of registry or flag does not lose authority over a pirated vessel flying its flag.

Article 42

A ship or aircraft may retain its national character although it has become a pirate ship or aircraft. The retention or loss of national character is determined by the law of the State from which the national character was originally derived.

A ship does not lose its national character by committing an act of piracy unless the domestic laws of the state in which the ship is registered regard piracy as adequate grounds for loss of nationality.[72] The principle of exclusive flag state jurisdiction over the ship, however, is dissolved once a ship commits or intends to commit an act of maritime piracy. Once this occurs, all nations may lawfully assert jurisdiction over the vessel, including the flag state, and the relevant provision reflecting this rule was recorded as Article 43.

Article 43

On the high seas or in any other place outside the jurisdiction of any State, every State may seize a pirate ship or aircraft, or a ship taken by piracy and under the control of pirates. The nation also is authorized to arrest the responsible persons and seize the property on board. The courts of the State which carried out the seizure may decide upon the penalties to be imposed, and may also determine the action to be taken with regard to the ships, aircraft or property, subject to the rights of third parties acting in good faith.

A state that has seized a pirate ship, and associated vessels that have been captured by pirates, may subject the persons and property involved in civil and criminal litigation in court. Persons may be charged and convicted of piracy and vessels and personal property associated with the crime may be forfeited to the state. The ILC commentary states that the right "cannot be exercised at a place under the jurisdiction of another State."[73]

Article 44

Where the seizure of a ship or aircraft on suspicion of piracy has been effected without adequate grounds, the State making the seizure shall be liable to the State the nationality of which is possessed by the ship or aircraft, for any loss or damage caused by the seizure.

States may be penalized or civilly liable for seizing a ship for the crime of piracy without adequate grounds for doing so. If the seizure of an innocent vessel causes any loss or damage, such as economic harm due to delay in delivery of cargo, the owner, carrier, and shipper may be afforded damages.

Article 45

Only warships may capture a ship engaged in maritime piracy.

This provision reflects the final repudiation of privateering, which was abolished by the 1856 Declaration of Paris at the end of the Crimean War. Under the 1856 Declaration, states agreed to stop commissioning privateers.

The ILC went even further, suggesting that naval auxiliaries could not conduct counterpiracy interdiction because they did not "provide the same safeguards against abuse" that is inherent in a warship.[74] Article 45 also does not prohibit a merchant ship to seize a pirate vessel in self-defense by overpowering a group of pirates.

The 73 articles developed by the ILC in 1956 were referred by the UN General Assembly to the International Conference of Plenipotentiarics to Examine the Law of the Sea, which convened in Geneva in 1958.[75]

This First UN Conference on the Law of the Sea was conducted in 1958, and more than 80 states participated in the negotiations. The conference produced four treaties: the Convention on the Territorial Sea and the Contiguous Zone, the High Seas Convention, the Convention on the Limits of the Continental Shelf, and the Convention on Fishing and Conservation of the Living Resources of the High Seas. The instruments from the First UN Conference entered into force between 1962 and 1966. As of June 10, 2010, there were 63 states parties to the High Seas Convention, including the United States.[76] Article 15 of the High Seas Convention contains a general definition of piracy—one that was borrowed nearly verbatim by the superseding 1982 UN Convention on the Law of the Sea.[77] Because of the widespread acceptance of the definition of piracy and its reflection as a norm, the term is regarded as a tenet of customary international law and binding on all nations.[78]

1982 UN Convention on the Law of the Sea

The contemporary legal regime for countering piracy is reflected in the 1982 United Nations Convention on the Law of the Sea (UNCLOS).[79] When the Third UN Conference on the Law of the Sea adopted UNCLOS in 1982, Ambassador "Tommy" Koh of Singapore, while serving as the Conference President, declared that the treaty was a "constitution" for the world's oceans.

Since the inception of the present international system in 1945, the essential treaty framework for world order has been the UN Charter. The Charter governs affairs of war and peace among all states, and embodies the norms of the international community. After the UN Charter, the most comprehensive agreement in existence is UNCLOS. By October 2010, UNCLOS had more than 160 states parties, fulfilling Koh's hope that it become a "constitution" for the world's oceans. These nations represent the overwhelming majority of the 192 member states of the United Nations.

Moreover, since the agreement is an "umbrella" treaty, it provides the essential governing framework for a multitude of supporting treaties, codes, guidelines, and practices regulating international conduct at sea and in the air. UNCLOS prescribes rules for activity on, over, and under the seas, and many of its provisions amplify principles reflective of customary international law. Interlocking, complementary regimes set forth in UNCLOS delineate navigational rights and freedoms that may be exercised by nations that operate vessels, which are called "flag states." Nations geographically situated on the sea with a shoreline or beach are "coastal states," and they may assert sovereignty, or certain designated sovereign rights or jurisdiction, over ocean space adjacent to and parallel with their coastline. Coastal states also may elect to develop areas of their shoreline to accept international shipping commerce, thereby acquiring the status of a "port state," and these states inure associated legal obligations and duties of operating shipping and port facilities. Because UNCLOS apportions the rights and duties of flag, port, and coastal states, the entire architecture of oceans law represents a "package deal," in which states enjoy specific rights as well as fulfill enumerated and concomitant responsibilities. The compromises in UNCLOS are the bedrock of global oceans law and policy.

UNCLOS was the first—and remains the foremost—comprehensive multilateral instrument for realizing collaborative approaches to oceans governance. Attempts in 1930, 1958, and 1960 at developing a framework ended in either utter failure or achieved only modest gains. In contrast, UNCLOS was a breakthrough in resolving long-standing issues. The agreement replaced an abundance of conflicting maritime claims with functional and universally accepted limits on coastal state sovereignty and jurisdiction, albeit limits that are vaguely crafted and sometimes poorly defined. So while some state parties purport to enforce rules that evidence an unorthodox reading of the Convention, or even a violation of UNCLOS, for the most part the regimes in the treaty have served as a stabilizing influence.

Navigational Zones and Regimes

All of the supplemental or additional sources of oceans governance flow from the model set forth in UNCLOS. The point of departure for the law of the sea is the concept of the "baseline," since all of the various navigational regimes in UNCLOS are measured from this point. The baseline of a coastal state represents an imaginary line normally running along the low-water mark along the shoreline, as marked on the nation's official large-scale charts. In certain limited instances, coastal states may deviate from the requirement to draw a normal baseline along the low-water mark and instead draw straight baselines. Straight baselines may be used in locations where the coastline is deeply indented and cut into, or where there is a fringe of islands along the coast. Straight baselines must not depart from the general direction of the coast, and the sea areas they enclose must be closely linked to the land domain. States may misuse straight baselines in order to make a claim to exclusive authority over international water.

Lakes, rivers, some bays, harbors, some canals, and lagoons are examples of internal waters, which lie landward of the baseline. Coastal nations exercise the same jurisdiction and control over their internal waters and superjacent airspace as they do over their land territory. Because ports and harbors are located landward of the baseline, entering a port ordinarily involves the consent of the port state and navigation through internal waters. There is no right of innocent passage by foreign vessels into internal waters. Unless a ship or aircraft is in distress, it may not enter internal waters without the permission of the coastal state. In special circumstances, coastal states may be entitled to enclose limited parts of the oceans as "historic internal waters," but the test for doing so is notoriously difficult to meet. In order to qualify as historic internal waters, a coastal state must exercise authority over the area, it must have done so for a considerable period of time and, most important, the international community must have explicitly accepted the assertion of authority over the water by the coastal state.[80]

Archipelagic waters are a creation of UNCLOS. An archipelagic nation is a nation that is constituted wholly of one or more groups of islands. Such nations may draw straight archipelagic baselines joining the outermost points of their outermost islands, provided that the ratio of water to land within the baselines is between 1:1 and 9:1. Archipelagic baselines are also the baselines from which the archipelagic nation measures seaward the other zones of UNCLOS, including the territorial sea, contiguous zone, and exclusive economic zone (EEZ). The waters enclosed within the archipelagic baselines are called "archipelagic waters." Archipelagic waters have virtually the same legal character as internal waters, but with the caveat that the international right of transit passage and nonsuspendable innocent passage apply throughout. In order to channel international shipping and overflight, archipelagic nations may designate archipelagic sea lanes through their archipelagic waters suitable for continuous and expeditious passage of ships and aircraft.

All normal routes used for international navigation and overflight are to be included in designations of archipelagic sea lanes. If the archipelagic nation does not designate all routes normally used as sea lanes, the right of archipelagic sea lanes passage (ASLP) by foreign ships and aircraft may nonetheless be exercised by all nations. All ships and aircraft, including warships and military aircraft, enjoy the right of ASLP while transiting through, under, or over designated archipelagic sea lanes or all routes normally used for international navigation and overflight. The right of ASLP is substantially similar to the right of transit passage through international straits. Outside of the actual archipelagic sea lanes or routes normally used for international navigation, all ships, including warships, enjoy the more limited right of innocent passage, much as they do in the territorial sea.

Immediately seaward of the baseline is the territorial sea. The territorial sea is a belt of ocean that may extend a maximum of 12 nautical miles from the baseline of the coastal nation. The territorial sea is subject to the sovereignty of the coastal state. Ships of all nations, however, enjoy the right of innocent passage in the territorial sea, although aircraft are not entitled to assert a similar right to overfly the territorial sea. Innocent passage means continuous and expeditious travel for the purpose of transit in territorial sea, and may even include stopping and anchoring, but only insofar as is incidental to ordinary navigation, or as rendered necessary by force majeure or by distress. All civilian vessels and warships enjoy the right of innocent passage, which cannot be conditioned by consent of or notification to the coastal state. Generally, passage is innocent so long as it is not prejudicial to the peace, good order, or security of the coastal nation. UNCLOS contains an exhaustive list of activities deemed to be prejudicial to the peace, good order, or security of the coastal nation. These rules are set forth in Article 19(2) of UNCLOS, and include any threat or use of force against the sovereignty, territorial integrity, or political independence of the coastal state.

Coastal nations may enact certain reasonable and necessary restrictions on the right of innocent passage for purposes of resource conservation, environmental protection, and navigational safety. Such restrictions, however, may not have the practical effect of denying or impairing the right of innocent passage, they may not discriminate in form or in fact against the ships of any nation, and cannot prohibit transit rights of nuclear-powered warships. The coastal nation may designate sea lanes and traffic separation schemes, and even temporarily suspend innocent passage, in cases in which it is essential to do so for security. Beyond the territorial sea, coastal states are entitled to claim a contiguous zone, extending seaward from the baseline up to 24 nautical miles. Within the contiguous zone, the coastal state may exercise control necessary to prevent or punish infringement of its customs, fiscal, immigration, and sanitary (health) laws and regulations that occur within its territory or territorial sea. Ships and aircraft of all nations, however, enjoy high seas freedoms, including overflight, in the contiguous zone.

International straits are those areas of overlapping territorial seas that connect one area of the high seas or exclusive economic zone (EEZ) to another area of the high seas or EEZ, and that are used for international navigation. The waters are simultaneously territorial seas and constitute an international strait; because of the dual nature of the waterway, the regime of transit passage, rather than the rules of innocent passage, applies to foreign-flagged vessels and aircraft. Transit passage, which permits the continuous and expeditious transit of surface ships, submarines, and aircraft, exists throughout the entire strait (shoreline-to-shoreline) and not just the area overlapped by the territorial sea of the coastal nations. Unlike innocent passage, transit passage may not be suspended. Vessels and aircraft may transit in the "normal mode," meaning that submarines may travel under the water and aircraft may overfly the strait. While conducting transit passage, ships may conduct formation steaming and launch and recover aircraft and other military devices.

There are more than 125 international straits throughout the world. The Strait of Hormuz separating Iran and Oman is an example of an international strait with particular strategic importance. The passage is only 21 miles wide at its narrowest point.[81] During negotiations for UNCLOS, the issue of freedom of navigation through international straits was one of the most important for the maritime states, and the superpowers collaborated to ensure the regime of transit passage was adopted by the conference.

From a piracy perspective, the 200-nautical-mile exclusive economic zones (EEZ) of coastal states constitute the most important part of the oceans.[82] The EEZ is a resource-related zone adjacent to the territorial sea, but the close proximity of land and density of people, ships, and resources makes the EEZ an epicenter of piracy. Nearly all commercial fishing is in the EEZ, and worldwide, more than 1 billion people depend on fish as their primary protein source.[83] Because the EEZs cover the most important part of the oceans, the rules that apply in the zone constitute a big part of the law that matters most in world politics.[84]

The world's EEZs encompass 35.81 percent of the seas; 35.59 percent of the Atlantic and Arctic Oceans; 32.34 percent of the Indian Ocean; and, 36.29 percent of the Pacific Ocean. Seas that are enclosed or semi-enclosed by EEZs include the Baltic Sea, the Black Sea, the North Sea, the Red Sea, the Arabian Gulf, the East China Sea, the South China Sea, the Sea of Japan, the Java Sea, and the Celebes Sea. The Norwegian Sea, the Sea of Okhotsk, the Gulf of Mexico, the Arabian Sea, the Bay of Bengal, and the Sulu Seas are nearly totally enclosed by EEZs.[85]

Inside the EEZ, a coastal state may exercise certain sovereign rights and jurisdiction over resources, but not sovereignty, out to a distance of 200 nautical miles from the baseline.[86] Ships and aircraft of all nations, including warships and military aircraft, enjoy complete freedom of movement and operation on, over, and under the EEZ. Unlike the sovereignty over the territorial sea, the scope of sovereign rights and jurisdiction in the EEZ and competence of the coastal state to regulate affairs within the zone applies only to sovereign rights related to resources and jurisdiction in respect to most artificial installations, marine scientific research, and, to a more limited extent, marine environment protection.[87]

Proscription against Piracy

In 2010, Ukraine proposed on several occasions a draft convention against maritime piracy.[88] Provisions of the new instrument include criminal proceedings against pirates and the establishment of a judicial venue to hear piracy cases.[89] The reaction from other states has been cool, and the draft convention has not gained much support because it risks reopening long-settled questions of customary international law reflected in the United Nations Convention on the Law of the Sea (UNCLOS).[90] A new piracy convention also would be largely duplicative of existing treaties, and is therefore unnecessary.

UNCLOS contains provisions relating specifically to maritime security, which provide ample guidance for antipiracy activities. Article 99 pertains to trafficking in human slaves, Articles 100–107 address piracy, and Article 111 contains provisions for hot pursuit from the high seas into a coastal state's territorial sea. International maritime drug trafficking became more prevalent during the decade of negotiations for the treaty, and the Convention also provides for the control of the illicit traffic in narcotic drugs in Article 108. Article 110 incorporates the customary norm in international law that warships may approach commercial vessels in order to determine their nationality, and board them on suspicion of piracy.

The Third UN Conference on the Law of the Sea ultimately adopted without amendment the provisions concerning maritime piracy. Piracy affects the entire international community and therefore is a classic collective action problem that can be addressed through adoption and implementation of uniform rules. The provisions in UNCLOS represent both broad philosophy and specific mandate concerning piracy, and embody global norms. Consequently, Articles 100–107 now may be regarded as reflective of both conventional (treaty) law and customary international law. These articles contain five core components of the definition of piracy. First, piracy involves a geographic scope, which includes the high seas and waters beyond the territorial sea. Second, piracy entails a "private ends" element, meaning that the pirates are not licensed to act on behalf of a government, but instead are private individuals. Third, two ships must be involved in piracy. Mutiny is not piracy under UNCLOS. Fourth, the definition of a pirate ship or aircraft is specific. Fifth, piracy includes inchoate offenses, such as attempted piracy. Sixth, there is a distinction to be made between public vessels and private vessels; only public vessels may interdict piracy.[91]

Article 100—Duty to Cooperate in the Repression of Piracy

Unlike the 1932 Harvard Draft, UNCLOS contains a general duty for nations to cooperate in the repression of piracy. Article 100 of UNCLOS states that, "All States shall cooperate to the fullest possible extent in the repression of piracy on the high seas or in any other place outside the jurisdiction of any State." The provision obligates all states to cooperate in the repression of piracy, which is defined in Article 101 of UNCLOS. Article 101 is identical to Article 38 of the ILC 1956 draft articles on the law of the sea, which were carried over into Article 14 of the 1958 Convention on the High Seas. The duty to cooperate is also governed by the requirement of states to act in good faith under Article 300 of UNCLOS. Adoption of national legislation relating to piracy is a manifest precondition for states to fulfill the duty to cooperate. In the preamble of UN Security Council Resolution 1918 (2010), the Security Council noted that the domestic laws of a number of states, however, lack provisions criminalizing piracy or are deficient in criminal procedural rules needed to effectively prosecute pirates. Similarly, in December 2010, the UN General Assembly called on "states to take appropriate steps under their national law to facilitate the apprehension and prosecution of those who are alleged to have committed acts of piracy."[92]

The phrase "any other place outside the jurisdiction of any State" also was a feature of Article 39 of the 1956 draft articles, and was included in Article 101(a)(ii) as part of the definition of piracy. The commentary to the 1956 ILC draft articles determined that piracy could not be committed within the territory of a state, or the territorial sea of a coastal state. During the 8th, 9th, and 11th sessions of the Third UN Conference on the Law of the Sea in 1978, 1979, and 1982, Peru suggested that the words "or in any other place outside the jurisdiction of any State" be deleted and a new sentence added, which would have said: "In the exclusive economic zone States shall cooperate with the respective coastal State in the repression of piracy." The proposal was rejected each time.[93]

In sum, the law of the sea deems piracy to occur only beyond the territorial sea of a coastal state. In UNCLOS, the EEZ is considered to be subject to most of the functional rules applicable to the high seas through Article 58(2) of the convention. Furthermore, a coastal state does not have territorial jurisdiction in the exclusive economic zone, but rather may exercise jurisdiction only over a limited set of matters and competences related to fishing and other economic interests under Article 56(1)(b) of UNCLOS.

Article 101—Definition of Piracy

Article 101 of UNCLOS defines piracy under international law, and includes acts committed by individuals for private ends against a ship (or aircraft), and to the incitement of such criminal acts. This definition excludes violence against ships by navies or on behalf of a government as well as environmental "crimes." Article 101 adheres to the framework set forth in Article 39 of the ILC's 1956 draft report, which was integrated with only minor edits into Article 15 of the 1958 Convention on the High Seas. The 1958 treaty, for example, added references to acts committed by private aircraft. Article 101 of UNCLOS states:

Definition of Piracy

Piracy consists of any of the following acts:

(a) Any illegal acts of violence or detention, or any act of depredation, committed for private ends by the crew or the passengers of a private ship or private aircraft, and directed—

(i) On the high seas, against another ship or aircraft, or against persons or property on board such ship or aircraft;
(ii) Against a ship, aircraft, persons or property in a place outside the jurisdiction of any state;

(b) Any act of voluntary participation in the operation of a ship or of an aircraft with knowledge of the facts making it a pirate ship or aircraft;
(c) Any act of inciting or intentionally facilitating an act described in subparagraph (a) or (b).[94]

The 1932 Harvard Draft, which incorporated the concept of universal jurisdiction, defined piracy as occurring beyond the territorial sea. The ILC's definition was broadly inclusive to include robbery, rape, slavery, imprisonment, murder, and other crimes of "gratuitous malice" that were committed for private ends. This general formula was adopted in Article 15 of the 1958 High Seas Convention and subsequently carried over into Article 101 of UNCLOS. Piracy was defined as any illegal act of violence, detention, or depredation committed for private (rather than governmental) ends, and committed by crew or passengers of a private ship or aircraft against another ship, persons, or crew. For a violent act to meet the definition of piracy it must be committed outside of a state's territorial waters. Inside territorial waters, such crimes constitute armed robbery at sea and are the responsibility of the coastal state. "Armed robbery at sea" in territorial waters can, a few meters away, be considered "piracy." As the definition of piracy in UNCLOS is derived nearly verbatim from the 1958 Convention on the High Seas, it generally is considered to reflect customary international law and binding on all nations.

Subparagraph (a)(i) of Article 101 requires that for an attack on the high seas to constitute piracy, it must be perpetrated against "another" ship or aircraft. This provision follows the ILC's view in 1956 that internal mutiny or seizure of a vessel did not fall within the definition of piracy. But subparagraph (a)(ii) indicates that an attack directed against a "ship or aircraft in a place outside the jurisdiction of any state," may be within the definition of piracy. The key to deciphering the provision is whether subparagraphs (a)(i) and (a)(ii) are deemed to be separated by "and"—meaning that both elements are required to meet the definition, or the word "or"—meaning that an attack is considered piracy if it meets the criteria set out in (i) or (ii). If the latter approach is accepted, then acts that are considered "mutiny" under municipal law also may fall within the definition of maritime piracy.

The definition of piracy must be read in conjunction with other provisions of UNCLOS, and in particular Article 58(2), which applies the definition to the exclusive economic zone (EEZ) and not just the high seas, and Article 103. Article 101(a)(i) provides that acts "committed on the high seas" may constitute piracy, and Article 101(a)(ii) refers to acts committed "in a place outside the jurisdiction of any state." But Article 58(2) imports the provisions applying on the high seas found in Articles 88 to 115 into the EEZ, so long as they are not incompatible with the other provisions of the EEZ. Thus, piracy also may be committed in a nation's EEZ, and any state may assert jurisdiction over the crime if it is committed in waters that lie beyond the territorial sea.

The definition of piracy also requires that the crime be committed "for private ends." The Commentary to the 1956 Draft Articles, the ILC clarifies that "[t]he intention to rob (*animus furandi*) is not required. Acts of piracy may be prompted by feelings of hatred or revenge, and not merely by the desire for gain."[95] Piracy also includes the inchoate offenses of inciting any of the acts included in Article 101(a) or (b). Article 101(c) includes acts "inciting or intentionally facilitating" piracy. States should ensure that penal codes include inchoate crimes related to piracy, such as attempted piracy, conspiracy to commit piracy, and aiding and abetting piracy. These offenses round out the definition of piracy in UNCLOS and demarcate the boundaries of the crime in international law. Finally, in order to constitute the crime of piracy, an attack on a ship at sea must have been made from another ship (or aircraft).

For statistical purposes, the International Maritime Bureau (IMB) has adopted a broader approach by combining the terms "piracy" and "armed robbery at sea" into a single term, "piracy." For the IMB, "piracy" is "an act of boarding or attempting to board any ship with the apparent intent to commit theft or any other crime, and with the apparent intent or capability to use force in the furtherance of that act."[96] The Baltic and International Maritime Council (BIMCO), the world's largest ship owner's association, has suggested ocean shipping would be made more secure by including piracy in statistics collected for marine cargo theft, maritime drug smuggling and human trafficking, as well as maritime terrorism, creating a single omnibus category, "maritime crime." Furthermore, acts of piracy contained in Article 101, if committed by a warship or government ship or aircraft whose crew has mutinied, are assimilated to acts committed by a private ship or aircraft.[97]

Article 102—Piracy by a Warship

Under Article 101(a) piracy may be committed only by a private ship or aircraft. Article 102 of UNCLOS, however, states, "The acts of piracy, as defined in Article 101, committed by a warship, government ship or government aircraft, whose crew has mutinied and taken control of the ship or aircraft are assimilated to acts committed by a private ship or aircraft." Article 102 provides an exception to the general rule that a government ship or aircraft cannot be considered to have committed piracy. The language in Article 102 reflects that in Article 40 of the ILC 1956 draft articles, which was carried over into the 1958 Convention on the High Seas. The provision assimilates or incorporates acts of mutiny as piracy, irrespective of the requirement that piracy be committed by individuals, that the victim vessel be a private ship, and that the pirates be acting of their own accord and not in the service of a government (private ends). The practical effect of the rule is that if the crew of a warship mutinies and their acts are assimilated as piracy, the vessel loses its sovereign immunity. Warships of other nations may have the right of approach and visit against a warship that is reasonably suspected of engaging in piracy.

Article 103—Definition of a Pirate Ship or Aircraft

Article 103 amplifies the definitions in Articles 101 and 102:

> **Definition of a Pirate Ship or Aircraft**
>
> A ship or aircraft is considered a pirate ship or aircraft if it is intended by the persons in dominant control to be used for the purpose of committing one of the criminal acts referred to in Article 101. The same applies if the ship or aircraft has been used to commit any such act, so long as it remains under the control of the persons guilty of the act.

The definition of piracy set forth in Article 101(b) includes "any act of voluntary participation in the operation of a ship or of an aircraft with knowledge of facts making it a pirate ship or aircraft."

Article 104—Retention or Loss of Nationality of a Pirate Ship or Aircraft

Article 104 of UNCLOS specifies that a pirate ship may (or may not) lose its nationality by engaging in the illegal acts of maritime piracy, and that whether the ship retains or loses its nationality is determined by the domestic law of the state in which the pirate ship is registered. Article 104, in its entirety, provides that, "A ship or aircraft may retain its nationality although it has become a pirate ship or aircraft. The retention or loss of nationality is determined by the law of the State from which such nationality was derived." The provision tracks the language included in Article 42 of the ILC 1956 draft, which itself was included in the 1958 Convention on the High Seas as Article 18. The original provision was included in the 1956 ILC draft to dispel the belief that a ship always loses its national character or nationality by virtue of engaging in criminal acts of maritime piracy. Although a pirate ship is no longer subject solely to exclusive flag state jurisdiction—any nation may assert jurisdiction over the vessel—the ship retains the nationality of its original registry. A pirate ship, therefore, is not a ship to be regarded as without flag registry or nationality, unless it is made so under an operative provision of domestic law. This rule is also consistent with Article 91 of UNCLOS, which provides that every state party has the right and obligation to fix the condition for the grant of nationality to ships that fly its flag. Finally, the provisions of Article 104 do not change the rule in Article 92(2), which specifies that a ship that sails under more than one flag may be assimilated as a stateless vessel.

Article 105—Seizure of a Pirate Ship or Aircraft

Article 105 addresses the conditions for seizure of a pirate ship or aircraft. The generalized authority to assert universal jurisdiction over pirate ships or aircraft is preserved in Article 105, which states:

> **Seizure of a Pirate Ship or Aircraft**
>
> On the high seas, or in any other place outside the jurisdiction of any state, every state may seize a pirate ship or aircraft, or a ship or aircraft taken by piracy and under the control of pirates, and arrest the persons and seize the property on board. The courts of the State which carried out the seizure may decide upon the penalties to be imposed, and may also determine the action to be taken with regard to the ships, aircraft or property, subject to the rights of third parties acting in good faith.

The approach in Article 105 reflects the method contained in Article 43 of the Harvard Research Draft, which was integrated into Article 19 of the 1958 Convention on the High Seas. States may use any lawful means or method available to detect, pursue, and seize pirate ships and aircraft. The right of hot pursuit and the right of approach and visit may be employed in counterpiracy operations, and provisions governing these issues are contained in Articles 111 and 110 of UNCLOS. Pirate ships and aircraft, however, may not be seized in territorial seas, archipelagic waters, and internal waters, without the consent of the coastal state, even for criminal acts of piracy that were committed on the high seas. In areas that have national waters in close proximity to other nations, such as the maritime border between Malaysia and Indonesia, fleeing vessels can escape into the territorial sea of a neighboring state and avoid punishment if the adjoining state is unable to act. Furthermore, the authority of the state to seize pirate ships is balanced by Article 106, which makes states liable for capturing vessels without "adequate grounds."

Ordinarily, jurisdiction may be asserted over a ship at sea only by the flag state, or in special cases, by a port or coastal state. If the nationals of a state are taken as hostages on board a vessel that is flagged in another state, the state of nationality also might serve as a basis for jurisdiction over the pirated ship. In the case of piracy, however, there is no requirement for a jurisdictional link of flag or nationality between the state exercising jurisdiction and the suspected pirate ship. As an exception to the principle of exclusive flag state jurisdiction, nations may exercise universal jurisdiction over pirate ships regardless of the nationality of the ship, suspected offenders, or nationalities of the victim seafarers being held hostage.

In criminalizing piracy, states should develop national procedural and substantive laws with penalties commensurate with the severity of the offense. The enforcement measures in Article 105 are limited by the provisions of Article 106.

Article 106—Liability for Seizure without Adequate Grounds

Article 106 states:

> Where the seizure of a ship or aircraft on suspicion of piracy has been effected without adequate grounds, the State making the seizure shall be liable to the State the nationality of which is possessed by the ship or aircraft for any loss or damage caused by the seizure.

If a vessel or aircraft suspected of piracy is seized without legal justification, the state making the seizure is liable to the flag state of the vessel or aircraft. This means the liability creates a legal relationship for any loss or damage between the nation seizing the ship without adequate grounds and the nation in which the ship is registered; the penalty is not to the benefit of the owner of the vessel, the shipper, or the owner of any cargo on board the ship.

The provision in Article 106 concerning liability was borrowed verbatim from Article 44 of the ILC 1956 draft and reflected in Article 20 of the 1958 Convention on the High Seas. Article 111(8) also contains a provision for compensation for the unjustified exercise of the right of hot pursuit, which may include ships suspected of piracy.[98] Furthermore, seizure may be effected only by warships or state aircraft, or other ships or aircraft clearly marked and on nongovernment service. Article 107 of UNCLOS states: "A seizure on account of piracy may be carried out only by warships or military aircraft, or other ship or aircraft clearly marked and identifiable as being on government service and authorized to that effect."

Article 107—Ships and Aircraft Which Are Entitled to Seize on Account of Piracy

Article 107 specifies the ships and aircraft which are entitled to take action against piracy.

> **Ships and Aircraft Which Are Entitled to Seize on Account of Piracy**
>
> A seizure on account of piracy may be carried out only by warships or military aircraft, or other ship or aircraft clearly marked and identifiable as being on government service and authorized to that effect.

In practical terms, ships with sovereign immune status may be used to interdict piracy. All vessels owned or operated by a state and used, for the time being, only on government noncommercial service, are entitled to sovereign immunity. The 1958 Geneva Convention on the High Seas extends immunity to "ships owned or operated by a State and used only on government non-commercial service." The United States, for example, asserts full privileges of sovereign immunity for United States Ships (USS), United States Naval Ships (USNS), United States Coast Guard Cutter (USCGC) vessels, and other vessels owned by the United States, and U.S.-flagged bareboat and time-charter vessels. The United States also recognizes sovereign immunity for voyage charter vessels for the duration of government service.

States may choose to use a leased (chartered) vessel, such as a commercial ship that contains special maritime law enforcement or ship boarding forces, in the role of piracy interdiction, and in such case the chartered ship could lawfully engage in antipiracy operations. Ships that are cloaked in sovereign immunity are exempt from arrest or search by another state, whether in national or international waters. Such vessels are also immune from foreign taxation, exempt from any foreign state regulation requiring flying the flag of such a foreign state either in its ports or while passing through its territorial sea, and are entitled to exclusive control over persons on board such vessels with respect to acts performed on board.

The international law definition of the term "operated by" is found in the 1926 Brussels Convention for the Unification of Certain Rules Concerning the Immunity of State Vessels.[99] The treaty provides in part:

> Article 3. Exception: Vessels employed exclusively in governmental and non-commercial service—may not be arrested
>
> (1) The provisions of the two preceding articles are not applicable to warships, state yachts, Coast Guard vessels, hospital ships, auxiliary vessels, supply vessels and other vessels owned by a State or operated by it and employed exclusively, at the time when the lien

arises, in a governmental and non-commercial service, and such ships shall not be seized, arrested or detained under any legal process whatsoever nor under any legal process *in rem*.

(2) The same rules shall apply to cargoes belonging to a state and carried on board the vessels above referred to.

The Brussels Convention is still in force between several states and is, to date, the only attempt at an authoritative international restatement of the law of state vessel immunity.

On May 24, 1934, a protocol was added to the Brussels Convention, which further clarified the term "operated by" in Section I as follows:

> Doubt having been expressed as to the question whether, and to what extent, the words "operated by" in Article 3 of the Convention, apply or may be construed to apply to ships chartered by a state either on time or for a voyage, the following declaration is made for the purpose of dispelling such doubt:
>
> Ships chartered by a state either on a time basis or for a voyage, provided that they are used exclusively in a governmental and non-commercial service, as well as the cargoes which such ships carry, may not be seized, arrested or detained in any manner, but this immunity shall not affect all the other rights or remedies which the interested parties may have.

Sovereign immunity for vessels employed solely in noncommercial government service of a nation is also recognized in Article 32 of UNCLOS, which states:

> With such exceptions as are contained in subsection A [Articles 17–26] and in Articles 30 and 31, nothing in this Convention affects the immunities of warships and other government ships operated for non-commercial purposes.

Articles 95 and 96 of UNCLOS, relating to the high seas, provide that warships on the high seas have complete immunity from the jurisdiction of any state other than the flag state. Article 96 states that ships owned or operated by a state and used only on government noncommercial service shall, on the high seas, have complete immunity from the jurisdiction of any state other than the flag state. Finally, UNCLOS Article 236 addresses sovereign immunity for vessels owned or operated by a state as follows: "The provisions of this Convention regarding the protection and preservation of the marine environment do not apply to any warship, naval auxiliary, other vessels or aircraft owned or operated by a State and used, for the time being, only on government non-commercial service."

Article 110—Right of Visit

Similarly, Article 110(1)(a) and (5) indicates that the exercise of the right of visit on board a ship suspected of piracy must be undertaken by a warship or other government vessel authorized to take enforcement action. Article 110 also requires that warships must be clearly marked and identifiable as being on government service. Such ships may act against piracy through an exercise of the right of visit in order to verify the flag state of a suspicious ship or to investigate piracy. Article 110 sets forth requirements for visit and boarding of ships engaged in piracy. Warships of all nations enjoy the right of visit or boarding on the high seas, even without the consent of the flag state, for the purpose of disrupting maritime piracy. If suspicion is not dispelled after inspection of the ship's registration papers, a boarding party may inspect the ship further. There is, of course, no right of visit against warships and other ships on government, noncommercial service.

This peacetime right of approach and visit is separate from the belligerent right of visit and search of neutral vessels in time of war. Whereas the peacetime right of approach and visit permits warships to suppress piracy and other crimes of universal jurisdiction, such as slave trafficking, the right of visit and search in time of war is for the purpose of searching for contraband or to determine the enemy character of the ship or its cargo under the law of neutrality.[100]

Furthermore, pursuant to Articles 106 and 110, if suspicion proves unfounded, the state of a warship boarding a vessel flagged in another country may be liable in international law for compensation for any loss or damage that may have been sustained by the boarding or delay.

Article 111—Right of Hot Pursuit

Article 111 of UNCLOS concerning the right of hot pursuit is the final provision of the treaty that bears directly on counterpiracy operations. The Article establishes when hot pursuit may be undertaken by the coastal state, it restricts the right to military or law enforcement vessels and aircraft, sets forth the conditions under which hot pursuit may occur and the procedures that apply. A coastal state may lawfully pursue a ship from the territorial sea, archipelagic waters, or the contiguous zone onto the high seas when it has "good reason" to believe that the vessel violated the law of that state. If the pursuit begins within the contiguous zone, however, it may be conducted only for violations of the rules pertaining to the contiguous zone, such as customs-related offenses. Likewise, if a foreign ship violates the lawful regulations of the coastal state pertaining to the EEZ, such as fisheries laws, the coastal state may initiate pursuit of the vessel onto the high seas. Hot pursuit may not extend into the territorial sea of another state, however.

Hot pursuit was recognized as an uncontested right in international law during the 1930 Hague Conference for the Codification of International Law. Article 11 of the Report of the Second Committee set forth the right of a coastal state to initiate hot pursuit in the internal waters or the territorial sea of a foreign vessel that has violated the laws of the coastal state, and follow the ship onto the high seas, so long as the pursuit has not been interrupted.[101] This concept carried over into the Commentary to draft Article 47 of 1956 and ended up as Article 23 of the 1958 Convention on the High Seas, which was a product of UNCLOS I.[102] UNCLOS III incorporated the concept of hot pursuit. At the Fourth Session of the Conference in 1976, Peru proposed limiting hot pursuit inside the EEZ of a third state, but the idea was rejected.[103] The Conference did, however, adjust the language regarding hot pursuit to recognize new regimes in the Law of the Sea. Specifically, hot pursuit may be initiated in archipelagic waters or the contiguous zone or EEZ for violations of the coastal state's rights in those areas, and the right of pursuit extends throughout the EEZ and is permitted inside the EEZ of other states.

Notes

1. For a brief, authoritative restatement of the law of piracy, see, Ivan Shearer, Piracy, *in The Max Planck Encyclopedia of Public International Law* (R. Wolfrum, ed., updated, July 2010). A dense historical treatment of the development of the law of maritime piracy is Alfred P. Rubin, *The Law of Piracy* (2d ed. 1998).

2. Sir William Blackstone and John Lansing Wendell, IV *Commentaries on the Laws of England: In Four Books, with an Analysis of the Work* 66 (Harper & Brothers, 1850).

3. Blackstone, IV *Commentaries on the Laws of England*, at 65–69.

4. Judge John Bassett Moore, The Lotus, P.C.I.J. Series A, No. 10, at 70.

5. Moore, The Lotus, at 70.

6. See, Filartiga v. Pena Irala, 630 F. 2d 876 (2d Cir. 1980) and United States v. Yousef, 327 F. 3d 56 (2d Cir. 2003) (universal jurisdiction originated from the historical treatment of maritime piracy). See also, Eugene Kontorovich, *The "Define and Punish" Clause and the Limits of Universal Jurisdiction*, 103 Northwestern University Law Review 149, 151 (2009).

7. The Ambrose Light, 24 F. 408, 413 (S.D.N.Y. 1885).

8. Blackstone, IV *Commentaries on the Laws of England*, at 65–69.

9. The checklist for the rules governing approach and visit in the law of piracy have been incorporated in Article 110 of the 1982 United Nations Convention on the Law of the Sea (UNCLOS), and are discussed in this chapter, below.

10. Despite the status of piracy as a crime of universal jurisdiction, a careful study by Eugene Kontorovich found that of all clear cases of piracy punishable under universal jurisdiction, international prosecution occurred in no more than 1.47 percent. "This figure includes the unprecedented international response to the Somali piracy surge that began in 2008, which accounts for the vast majority of prosecutions."

Eugene Kontorovich and Steven Art, *An Empirical Examination of Universal Jurisdiction for Piracy* 104 American Journal of International Law 436 and 444 (July 2010).

11. J. Ashley Roach, *Suppressing Somali Piracy—Next Steps*, 14(39) ASIL Insight (American Society of International Law, December 1, 2010) and J. Ashley Roach, *Countering Piracy off Somalia: International Law and International Institutes*, 104 American Journal of International Law 397, 414–415 (July 2010).

12. Oscar Herrmann, *Pirates and Piracy* 4 (Press of Stettiner Brothers, 1902).

13. Joseph W. Bingham, *Reporter, Part IV: Piracy*, 26 American Journal of International Law Supp.: Research in International Law 739–885, at 793 (1932).

14. The Act of the Parliament of England (Treason Act), 25 Edward III St. 5, c. 2 (1351), *in* Edward Wavell Ridges, *Constitutional Law of England* 154 (2d ed., Stevens & Sons, 1915).

15. 28 Henry VIII. c. 15 (1536), *in* Geoffrey Rudolph Elton, *The Tudor Constitution: Documents and Commentary* 158 (1982).

16. See, e.g., The Antelope, 23 U.S. (10 Wheat.) 66 (1825).

17. J.L. Briely, *Law of Nations* 154 (Oxford University Press, 1928).

18. Joseph W. Bingham, *Reporter, Part IV: Piracy*, 26 American Journal of International Law Supp.: Research in International Law 739–885, at 769 (1932).

19. United States v. Hudson, 7 Cranch. 32 (1812) and United States v. Coolidge, 14 U.S. (1 Wheat.) 415 (1816).

20. The Antelope, 23 U.S. (10 Wheat.) 66 (1825).

21. The Antelope, 23 U.S. (10 Wheat.) 66, 118 (1825).

22. John Bassett Moore, 7 *A Digest of International Law* 953 (1906).

23. John Bassett Moore, *Principles of American Diplomacy* 34 (2006) (2d ed. 1918).

24. Act of April 30, 1790, § 8; 1 Stat. 112.

25. Act of April 30, 1790, § 8; 1 Stat. 112, 113–114.

26. United States v. Palmer, 16 U.S. (3 Wheat.) 610 (1818).

27. United States v. Palmer, at 627.

28. United States v. Palmer, at 627.

29. United States v. Palmer, at 630-1.

30. United States v. Palmer, at 633–634.

31. The provision was updated again by a provision passed by Congress on May 15, 1820. See, 3 Stat. 510 (1819) and 3 Stat. 600 (1820).

32. Act of March 3, 1819, § 5; 3 Stat. 510.

33. Charles Cheney Hyde, 1 *International Law Chiefly Interpreted by the United States* § 68, at 114–116 (Little, Brown, 1922).

34. George Tickner Curtis, *The Case of the "Virginius," Considered with Reference to the Law of Self-Defence*, 3 The Law Magazine and Review; A Monthly Review of Jurisprudence and International Law 609–617 (1874).

35. Mariana Flora, 11 Wheat. (U. S. 1826) at 39.

36. Demjanjuk v. Petrovsky 776 F.2d 571, 582 (1982).

37. 29 Stat. 487 (1897).

38. 4 Stat. 775 (1835), 9 Stat. 72 (1846), 9 Stat. 175 (1847), and 35 Stat. 1088 (1909).

39. Based on the Act of March 4, 1909, 35 Stat. 1145 (1909) and Act of June 25, 1948, 62 Stat. 774 (1948).

40. United States v. Lei Shi, 525 F.3d 709 (9th Cir. Haw. 2008).

41. Violence against maritime navigation, 18 U.S.C. §§ 2280, 2281 (2008). These provisions were implemented by the Convention for the Suppression of Unlawful Acts (SUA) against the Safety of Maritime Navigation (1988). SUA entered into force for the United States in March 1995.

42. Later, SUA was endorsed in UN Security Council in Resolution 1851.

43. Special maritime and territorial jurisdiction of the United States, 18 U.S.C. § 7 (2008).

44. Special maritime and territorial jurisdiction of the United States, 18 U.S.C. § 7(6), (7), and (9) (2008).

45. Assault on the high seas, 18 U.S.C. § 113 (2008).

46. Five Somalis Convicted in U.S. Court for Piracy, Reuters, November 25, 2010.

47. Harvard Research in International Law, *Draft Convention on Piracy, with Comments*, 26 American Journal of International Law Supp.: Research in International Law 749 (1932).

48. Joseph W. Bingham, *Reporter, Part IV: Piracy*, 26 American Journal of International Law Supp.: Research in International Law 739–885, at 751 (1932).

49. Joseph W. Bingham, *Reporter, Part IV: Piracy*, 26 American Journal of International Law Supp.: Research in International Law 739–885, at 749 (1932).

50. Joseph W. Bingham, *Reporter, Part IV: Piracy*, 26 American Journal of International Law Supp.: Research in International Law 739–885, at 757 (1932).

51. Joseph W. Bingham, *Reporter, Part IV: Piracy*, 26 American Journal of International Law Supp.: Research in International Law 739–885, at 760 (1932).

52. Joseph W. Bingham, *Reporter, Part IV: Piracy*, 26 American Journal of International Law Supp.: Research in International Law 739–885, at 760 (1932).

53. Joseph W. Bingham, *Reporter, Part IV: Piracy*, 26 American Journal of International Law Supp.: Research in International Law 739–885, at 762–763 (1932).

54. Lassa Oppenheim, 1 *International Law: Peace* § 273, 326–327 (Longmans, Green & Co. 1905).

55. Questionnaire No. 6, Committee of Experts for the Progressive Codification of International Law, Adopted by the Committee at Its Second Session, January 1926, 20 American Journal of International Law 222, 222–229 (July 1926) (Report presented by Sub-committee Rappaorteur M. Matsuda).

56. Statute of the International Law Commission, Adopted by the General Assembly in Resolution 174 (II) of November 21, 1947, as amended by Resolutions 485 (V) of December 12, 1950, 984 (X) of December 3, 1955, 985 (X) of December 3, 1955, and 36/39 of November 18, 1981.

57. Statute of the International Law Commission.

58. Report of the International Law Commission Covering the Work of Its Eighth Session, April 23–July 4, 1956. General Assembly Official Records: Eleventh Session, UN Doc. A/3159, Supplement No. 9, at 283.

59. International Law Commission, Report of the International Law Commission Covering the Work of Its Eighth Session, April 23–July 4, 1956, 2 Yearbook of the International Law Commission 282 (1956).

60. Report of the International Law Commission Covering the Work of Its Eighth Session, April 23–July 4, 1956. General Assembly Official Records: Eleventh Session, A/3159, Supplement No. 9, UN Doc. A/CN.4/104, at 282.

61. International Law Commission, Report of the International Law Commission Covering the Work of Its Eighth Session, April 23–July 4, 1956, 2 Yearbook of the International Law Commission 282 (1956).

62. D.H.N. Johnson, *Piracy in Modern International Law*, 43 Grotius Society Transactions 63–82, at 64 (1957).

63. International Agreement for Collective Measures against Piratical Attacks in the Mediterranean by Submarines, signed at Nyon on September 14, 1937.

64. Rose v. Himely, 4 Cranch. 241, and United States v. Palmer, 3 Wheat. 610.

65. *In Charge of a Prize Crew: Arrival of the Supposed Pirate Captured by the Alliance*, New York Times, June 2, 1885.

66. The Ambrose Light, 24 F. 408, 413 (S.D.N.Y. 1885).

67. *Ambrose Light Not a Privateer*, New York Times, July 3, 1885.

68. Report of the International Law Commission Covering the Work of Its Eighth Session, April 23–July 4, 1956. General Assembly Official Records: Eleventh Session, UN Doc. A/3159, at 282.

69. Report of the International Law Commission Covering the Work of Its Eighth Session, April 23–July 4, 1956. General Assembly Official Records: Eleventh Session, UN Doc. A/3159, at 282.

70. Judge Moore (dissenting), The Lotus, P.C.I.J. Series A, No. 10, at 70.

71. Report of the International Law Commission Covering the Work of Its Eighth Session, April 23–July 4, 1956. General Assembly Official Records: Eleventh Session, UN Doc. A/3159, at 283.

72. D.H.N. Johnson, *First Session: Piracy in Modern International Law*, 43 Transactions of the Grotius Society: Problems in Public and Private International Law, Transactions for the Year 1957 63–85, at 67.

73. Report of the International Law Commission Covering the Work of Its Eighth Session, April 23–July 4, 1956. General Assembly Official Records: Eleventh Session, UN Doc. A/3159, at 283.

74. Report of the International Law Commission Covering the Work of Its Eighth Session, April 23–July 4, 1956. General Assembly Official Records: Eleventh Session, UN Doc. A/3159, at 283.

75. Resolution 1105 XII adopted on February 21, 1957.

76. Convention on the High Seas, April 29, 1958, 13 U.S.T. 2312, 450 UNT.S. 92.

77. The only difference between the two definitions is Article 101 of UNCLOS removed a comma and added the word "or" between "violence" and "detention." Article 15 of the 1958 convention includes the phrase, "violence, detention or any act of depredation," whereas Article 101 of the 1982 convention adopted the phrase, "violence or detention, or any act of depredation."

78. Kiobel v. Royal Dutch Petroleum, 2010 WL 3611392, at 17–19 (2d Cir. September 17, 2010).

79. UN Convention on the Law of the Sea, Montego Bay, December 10, 1982, Article 101, 1833 UNT.S. 397.

80. Juridical Regime of Historic Waters, Including Historic Bays, UN Doc. A/CN. 4/143 at 56 (1962).

81. World Oil Transit Chokepoints—Strait of Hormuz (Energy Information Administration, January 2008).

82. See generally, James Kraska, *Maritime Power and the Law of the Sea* (2011).

83. Carrie V. Kappel, Benjamin S. Halpern, Rebecca G. Martone, Fiorenza Micheli, and Kimberly A. Selkoe, *In the Zone: Comprehensive Ocean Protection*, Issues in Science & Technology 33, at 33 (Spring 2009).

84. W. Michael Reisman, International Incidents: Introduction to a New Genre in the Study of International Law, *in International Incidents: The Law that Counts in World Politics* 4–6 (W. Michael Reisman and Andrew R. Willard, eds., 1988).

85. Boleslaw Adam Bocek, *Peacetime Military Activities in the Exclusive Economic Zone of Third Countries*, 19 Ocean Development and International Law 445, 447 (1988).

86. Articles 5–16 and 57, UNCLOS.

87. Article 56, ¶ 1, UNCLOS.

88. Baltic and International Maritime Council, Piracy: Outcome of CGPCS Working Group 2, November 4, 2010, https://www.bimco.org/Members/News/2010/2010/11/04_CGPCS_WG2.aspx. (Ukraine Presents in Copenhagen a Draft Convention to Combat Sea Piracy).

89. Baltic and International Maritime Council, Piracy: Outcome of CGPCS Working Group 2, November 4, 2010.

90. Baltic and International Maritime Council, Piracy: Outcome of CGPCS Working Group 2, November 4, 2010.

91. IMO Doc. LEG 98/8/3, February 18, 2011, Annex, Piracy: Elements of National Legislation Pursuant to the United Nations Convention on the Law of the Sea, 1982.

92. UN Doc. GA Res. 65/37, December 7, 2010, para. 86.

93. C.2/Informal Meeting/9 (1978 mimeograph), Article 100 (Peru), *reproduced in* V Third United Nations Conference on the Law of the Sea: Documents 346 (Renate Platzöder, comp. and ed., 1984), at 13 and 15; C.2/Informal Meeting/64 and Rev. 1 (1980 mimeograph), Article 100 (Peru), *reproduced in* V Third United Nations Conference on the Law of the Sea, at 66 and 69; and C.2/Informal Meeting/68 (1982 mimeograph), Article 100 (Peru), *reproduced in* V Third United Nations Conference on the Law of the Sea, at 73.

94. UN Convention on the Law of the Sea, Montego Bay, December 10, 1982, 1833 UNT.S. 397.

95. Report of the International Law Commission Covering the Work of Its Eighth Session, April 23–July 4, 1956. General Assembly Official Records: Eleventh Session, A/3159, Supplement No. 9, UN Doc. A/CN.4/104, at 282.

96. International Chamber of Commerce, International Maritime Bureau, Piracy and Armed Robbery against Ships, Annual Report 1 January–31 December 2006 2 (January 2007), at 2.

97. Article 102, UNCLOS.

98. 3 *United Nations Convention on the Law of the Sea: A Commentary* § 106.6(b) (Satya N. Nandan, C.B.E. and Shabtai Rosenne, eds., Center for Oceans Law & Policy, University of Virginia School of Law, 1995).

99. 176 LNTS 199; 3 Hudson, International Legislation 1837.

100. Louise Doswald-Beck, ed., *San Remo Manual on the Law Applicable to Armed Conflict at Sea* 31–32, ¶¶ 118–121 (1995).

101. Second Committee report, Article 11, Appendix I (Legal Status of the Territorial Rea), League of Nations Doc. C.230.M.117.1930.V, I Acts of the Conference for the Codification of International Law, at 123, 130, *reproduced in* 3 *United Nations Convention on the Law of the Sea: A Commentary* 466, 473 (Satya N. Nandan, C.B.E. and Shabtai Rosenne, eds., Center for Oceans Law & Policy, University of Virginia School of Law, 1995).

102. Report of the International Law Commission Covering the Work of Its Eighth Session (A/3159), Article 47 Commentary, ¶ (1), 2 *Yearbook of the International Law Commission 1956*, at 253 and 285.

103. 3 *United Nations Convention on the Law of the Sea: A Commentary* ¶ 111.6, at 255 (Satya N. Nandan, C.B.E. and Shabtai Rosenne, eds., Center for Oceans Law & Policy, University of Virginia School of Law, 1995).

CHAPTER 6

Diplomacy

Nations pursue counterpiracy collaboration and diplomacy within the broad framework of the norms, regimes, and rules of international law and international institutions. This chapter focuses on multilateral and bilateral diplomatic partnerships that facilitate closer cooperation to combat contemporary maritime piracy.

After World War I, a subcommittee of the League of Nations sought to capture the governing legal criteria of maritime piracy. In particular, the subcommittee wanted to sever piracy in the law of nations from its association with unrestricted submarine warfare, which had emerged during the world war and was dubiously included in the 1922 Washington Naval Treaty. The Committee of Experts to the League's efforts concluded that "[s]tates have occasionally, by treaty or in their internal law, established a piracy by analogy which has no claim to be universally recognized and must not be confused with true piracy."[1] The subcommittee declared also that there was not an "urgent" need for a new treaty on piracy, and that the issue of piracy might be "temporarily left on one side" as more pressing issues were addressed.[2]

Against this backdrop, in 1930–1931 a collection of law professors from schools located for the most part in the West was recruited by the Harvard Research Program to examine the law of maritime piracy. The most salient question tackled by the Group was the significance of piracy in international law. Although the Harvard Group developed a draft convention that never was adopted, the work became influential in municipal court proceedings and scholarship.[3] Under the leadership of Joseph W. Bingham of Stanford University, the Group developed a draft antipiracy convention, which was known as the Harvard Draft.

The Harvard Draft incorporated the concepts of universal jurisdiction, defined piracy as occurring beyond the territorial sea (at the time deemed to be a width of three nautical miles), and was broadly inclusive of the acts that constitute piracy, including armed robbery, rape, slavery, imprisonment, murder, and other crimes of "gratuitous malice" committed for private ends. Later, this general formula was refined by the International Law Commission and would be adopted in Article 15 of the 1958 High Seas Convention as well as in Article 101 of the 1982 United Nations Convention on the Law of the Sea (UNCLOS).[4] In these treaties, piracy was regarded as an illegal act of violence or depredation committed for private ends (i.e., not under governmental authority) on the high seas against another ship. For nearly 30 years, the law and diplomacy of piracy remained relatively placid, until a resurgence of maritime piracy off the Horn of Africa initiated another round of legal and diplomatic development. The epicenter of this effort was the adoption of a flurry of UN Security Council resolutions beginning in 2008, and the associated work of the International Maritime Organization (IMO) during the same period.

As much progress occurred in the development of the international law of counterpiracy in the 100 days at the end of 2008 and January 2009, as had occurred in the previous 100 years. First, in the summer of 2008, the UN Security Council finally became active in the fight against piracy with the adoption of Resolution 1816. Notably, the resolution was crafted under Chapter 7 of the UN Charter, authorizing coalition warships from the international community to enter Somali territorial waters to suppress piracy. By denying Somali pirates the safe haven of the 12-nautical-mile territorial sea, the Security Council hoped to tip the scales in favor of the international naval forces patrolling offshore. Just months later, in October 2008, the UN Security Council adopted Resolution 1838, which confirmed the formula for defining piracy that was contained in the 1982 Law of the Sea Convention. The resolution called on states to deploy naval forces to the Horn of Africa to deter Somali piracy.

On December 2, 2008, the Security Council adopted Resolution 1846, which strongly endorsed the application of the 1988 Convention for the Suppression of Unlawful Acts against the Safety of Maritime Navigation (SUA 88) to the problem of piracy off the coast of Somalia. The SUA 88 Convention originally was developed in the wake of the attack on the *Achille Lauro* cruise ship hijacking. Two weeks later, the Security Council adopted Resolution 1851, which authorized coalition naval forces to conduct military operations against pirate safe havens on the shore in Somalia. Significantly, UN Security Council Resolution 1851 also recommended creation of an international Contact Group on Piracy off the Coast of Somalia. Since its creation, the Contact Group has joined the IMO in becoming a major institution for development of counterpiracy law and policy.

Most active diplomatic initiatives are focused on disrupting piracy off the Horn of Africa. These efforts, which first emerged in 2007–2008, include concerted action by the UN Security Council, creation of the Contact Group on Piracy off the Coast of Somalia (CGPCS), the New York Declaration, and the Djibouti Code of Conduct. The activities foster unprecedented counterpiracy collaboration at the global level, but they follow earlier initiatives by the nations of East Asia to address piracy in the Straits of Malacca and Singapore.

In Asia, the 16-nation Regional Agreement on Combating Piracy and Armed Robbery against Ships in Asia (ReCAAP), for example, was adopted in 2004 and entered into force in 2006. The ReCAAP agreement was the first time in history that nations came together in a binding multilateral treaty to repress maritime piracy. The major accomplishment of the ReCAAP treaty, however, was largely overshadowed by the rise of piracy in the waters off the Horn of Africa—the GOA, the Arabian Sea, and the western Indian Ocean. The rapid rise in piracy off the coast of Somalia generated global action, first at the International Maritime Organization (IMO), and then at the United Nations.

Regional Agreement on Combating Piracy and Armed Robbery against Ships in Asia

In 2000, a group of Asian nations met in Tokyo to begin discussions on how to share information and disrupt piracy, which was becoming a favored tool of well-organized but shadowy Asian crime syndicates.[5] Beginning in 2002, the Association of Southeast Asian Nations (ASEAN), plus six additional regional states, began to negotiate in earnest to adopt a counterpiracy agreement proposed by Prime Minister Koizumi Junichiro of Japan in 2001. Under the leadership of Japan, on November 11, 2004, 16 nations signed the text of the Regional Agreement on Combating Piracy and Armed Robbery against Ships in Asia (ReCAAP), the first treaty dedicated solely to combating piracy.[6] The treaty entered into force on November 29, 2006. In 2007, the number of reported incidents of marine piracy in the region decreased more than any previous year.

There are three pillars to ReCAAP: information sharing, capacity building, and cooperative arrangements. The members operate under the principles of sovereignty and transparency. The treaty provided the mechanism for creating an Information Sharing Centre (ISC) in Singapore to share piracy-related information among member states. This ambitious endeavor has better equipped states to communicate and respond. The Information Sharing

Centre's Executive Director, Yoshiaki Ito, praised the organization because it enables parties to attain greater operational coordination and efficiency.[7] In part, this is accomplished through information sharing, but the pact also focuses on capacity-building initiatives and establishing cooperative arrangements with interested parties.[8]

Each state party to ReCAAP assigned a point of contact for handling real-time maritime security cooperation with neighboring states. The responsibilities of each ReCAAP focal point member includes authority for managing and coordinating all incidents of piracy and armed robbery against ships within its jurisdiction. The focal point is also the lead within the government for acting as a conduit for the exchange of information, facilitating national country law enforcement investigations, and for coordinating counterpiracy surveillance.[9] The focal point manages piracy and armed robbery incidents within the states' territorial waters, coordinates surveillance and enforcement with neighboring states, acts as the representative to the ISC, and facilitates national maritime law enforcement. Nations may designate any one of a variety of agencies to fill the role, including naval forces, coast guards, maritime shipping registries, shipping agencies, fisheries enforcement, port authorities, maritime and national police forces, and customs services. India, Sri Lanka, Japan, and the Philippines, for example, have designated their coast guards as the national point of contact. Thailand and Myanmar have designated their navies and Vietnam and Brunei have designated the Marine Police, whereas Indonesia designated the Maritime and Port Authority. The focal points are connected through the Information-Sharing Network. The members collate and analyze statistics on piracy incidents.

The ReCAAP program is an effective regional approach that could serve as a model for the Horn of Africa. ReCAAP requires member states to designate representatives to act as conduits for decisions and to pass information to other countries, which is a capacity lacking in most African states.

A multilayered regional approach has led to a dramatic decline in the incidence of maritime piracy in the Straits of Malacca and Singapore. On November 29, 2006, an Information Sharing Centre (ISC) was established in Singapore.[10] The ISC institutionalizes regional cooperation in combating piracy and armed robbery against ships. It is a permanent body with full-time staff. According to the Centre's Executive Director, Yoshiaki Ito, the Centre has improved communication among member states, enabling them to attain greater operational coordination and efficiency.[11] The ISC facilitates communications, information exchange, and operational cooperation among the participating governments to improve their counterpiracy capability.[12] The Centre also collects and prepares statistics and analysis of the piracy and sea robbery in Asia. The ReCAAP Agreement also contains capacity-building initiatives and additional cooperative arrangements.[13]

In October 2005, the significance of the ReCAAP Agreement was recognized by the ASEAN Regional Forum (ARF) Inter-sessional Support Group Meeting on Confidence Building and Preventive Diplomacy, and the September 2006 IMO Meeting on the Straits of Malacca and Singapore held in Kuala Lumpur. The Plenary of the 60th session of the UN General Assembly welcomed the progress in regional cooperation brought about by the ReCAAP Agreement.[14]

In November 2007, IMO Resolution A.1002(25) also called upon these regional states to conclude an international agreement to prevent, deter, and suppress piracy.[15] Seeking to replicate the success of ReCAAP, the IMO sponsored meetings from 2005–2008 in Yemen (Sana'a Seminar),[16] Oman (the Oman Workshop),[17] and Tanzania (Dar es Salaam),[18] to open up the possibility of regional agreements among states to implement antipiracy measures in the western Indian Ocean. At a final meeting in Djibouti in January 2009, a group of East African states agreed to cooperate in the prosecution and repatriation of captured Somali pirates. They also agreed to create the concept of a Regional Maritime Information Centre or System, which Security Council Resolution 1851 recommended.[19]

Cooperative Mechanism

The IMO was involved in yet another regional initiative that serves as important precedent for increasing maritime cooperation in the Horn of Africa. In 2005 more than 25 user states and the littoral states of Malaysia, Indonesia, and Singapore met in Jakarta to develop a framework for improving maritime safety, security, and environmental protection in the Straits of Malacca and Singapore.[20] The "Jakarta Initiative" began a series of meetings that resulted in increased cooperation between the littoral states, the distant water states that were regular users of the straits, and the international shipping industry.[21] The meetings have been effective in facilitating an increase in maritime patrols by the straits states and toward focusing user states on assisting with capacity building. The negotiations were continued in Kuala Lumpur in 2006[22] and in Singapore in 2007.[23] At the Singapore meeting, states signed the "Cooperative Mechanism," an agreement that provides for user states to help littoral states develop maritime security capacity for the management of the straits. The Cooperative Mechanism marked the first time that littoral and maritime states have worked together to ensure the safety and security of an international strait, as envisaged in Article 43 of the Law of the Sea.

The Singapore meeting also recognized the contributions of the straits states in the development of Malacca Strait security initiatives. The Cooperative Mechanism focuses on safety of navigation and environmental protection in the Straits, and consists of three main components:

- Co-operation Forum, which is an avenue for user states and stakeholders to meet and engage the littoral states of the Straits of Malacca and Singapore;
- Project Coordination Committee, which is the platform for coordinating the implementation of Straits Projects; and
- Aids to Navigation Fund, which receives financial contributions for renewal and maintenance of aids to navigation in the Straits.[24]

The UN Security Council

The epidemic of Somali piracy spurred unprecedented international diplomacy to address the threat to international merchant shipping. Consequently, great progress was made in counterpiracy diplomacy in the100-day period running from the end of 2008 through January. First, in the summer of 2008, two years after Somali piracy became a manifest hazard to maritime traffic in the waters surrounding the Horn of Africa, the UN Security Council finally became active in the fight against piracy. The Security Council adopted Resolution 1816 under Chapter 7 of the UN Charter. The resolution authorized the international community to enter Somali territorial waters to suppress piracy. Although the country of Somalia had claimed a 200-nautical-mile territorial sea dating back to the regime of dictator Mohamed Siad Barre, in more contemporary times both Somalia and the international community observed a 12-nm territorial sea, as permitted under the United Nations Convention on the Law of the Sea (UNCLOS).

The territorial sea was an important feature of the topography of Somali piracy because the pirate gangs would hijack unsuspecting ships transiting in international waters and then sail and anchor the vessels in Somalia's territorial sea. Since the territorial sea constitutes Somali sovereign air and sea space, foreign naval forces generally were not entitled to enter the area without Somali permission. The fractious and chaotic state of government in the country, however, made securing consent from Mogadishu virtually impossible. The pirates were able to use the jurisdictional 12-nm seam to create a safe haven in which to hide while they conducted ransom negotiations, unmolested by foreign naval patrols. By authorizing foreign warships entry into the Somali territorial sea, the Security Council sought to deny pirates a secure rear base of operations.

Security Council Resolution 1816 called for greater logistics cooperation, particularly in the disposition and prosecution of suspected pirates. The resolution also called for increased efforts to build capacity in the Horn of Africa by helping the nations of the region develop coast guard forces, a stronger judicial system, and greater capacity for governance.

In October, the UN Security Council adopted Resolution 1838, which confirmed that the Law of the Sea convention was the essential rules set for addressing piracy. Also, the resolution called on states to deploy naval forces into the area. At the same time, the UN undertook a study to identify the root causes of piracy off the coast of Somalia.

The Nairobi Report, which was issued in November 2008, found that a lack of effective governance and public services created a situation of anarchy in Somalia, and an environment in which piracy thrived. On December 2, 2008, the UN Security Council adopted Resolution 1846. Resolution 1846 strongly endorsed the application of the 1988 Convention for the Suppression of Unlawful Acts against the Safety of Maritime Navigation (SUA 88) to the problem of piracy off the coast of Somalia. SUA 88 commits nations to cooperate in the extradition and prosecution of pirates in cases of ship hijacking. Originally developed in the wake of the hijacking of the *Achille Lauro* cruise ship by four Palestinian terrorists, the treaty was found to have relevance for piracy involving ship hijacking as well. The SUA Convention now has more than 150 state parties, but many of these nations lack implementing legislation or governmental machinery that would enable them to meet their obligations.

The Nairobi Report

In the fall of 2008, UN experts gathered in Kenya for 11 days to consider new legal and political approaches to combating piracy.[25] The meeting was commissioned by Ambassador Ahmedou Ould-Abdallah, the Special Representative of the Secretary-General of the United Nations to Somalia. The ambassador gathered experts from diplomacy, private industry, the military, humanitarian aid organizations, and peacekeeping operations, to produce a study on the social, legal, and policy issues associated with Somali piracy. The result of this effort was the Nairobi Report, which provides context, background, and analysis on the problem of maritime piracy in the Horn of Africa. Weeks after its release, the report influenced several operative paragraphs of UN Security Council Resolution 1851.

Somalia's descending trajectory has evolved to the level of a global imperative. For nearly 20 years, Somalia has been a failed state, a virtual "black hole in the international community, divorced from the world economy, regional and global institutions, and the rule of law."[26] Similarly, eminent Harvard political scientist Robert Rotberg described Somalia as occupying a category all its own. It is not merely a failed state, but a "collapsed state," "that rare and extreme version of a failed state," that is a "mere geographic expression."[27] So long as the problems of Somalia were confined within its borders, however, global attention tended to focus elsewhere.[28]

The Nairobi Report calls the rise of piracy part of the "costs of doing nothing on land." Stability on land must be complemented with the disruption of the illicit revenues from maritime piracy, and implementation of vessel security measures to reduce the success of attacks on ships at sea.[29] But even though the best solutions begin on land, there are serious impediments to stabilizing Somalia. The three semiautonomous Somali governments all have inadequate governance systems, limited human resources, abysmal public services, and are handicapped by a decrepit infrastructure.[30] The underlying economic and political challenges include "[p]overty, lack of employment, environmental hardship, pitifully low incomes, reduction of pastoralist and maritime resources due to drought and illegal fishing, and a volatile security and political situation."[31] The confluence of these difficulties has kept the country on a downward arc, contributing to the rise and continuance of piracy in Somalia. Furthermore, the absence of border control over the past two decades has enabled human trafficking and smuggling. These crimes are as endemic on land as maritime piracy is at sea. Like maritime piracy, trafficking and smuggling are manifestations of the power of organized crime syndicates to operate freely.[32]

The report also suggests that increased surveillance of the Somali coastline using manned and unmanned airborne reconnaissance would be beneficial.[33] Establishment of a shore monitoring system using local communities as lookouts for suspicious boats could also prove helpful.[34] But while some technical systems can enhance maritime domain awareness, they may raise security concerns of their own. A ship outfitted with an Automatic Identification System (AIS) transmitter, for example, is able to display to similarly equipped vessels or shore receivers tactical vessel data, such as vessel size, heading, and speed. Unfortunately, that information is broadcast via open VHF bandwidth, and therefore is available to anyone, including pirates.

The Nairobi Report recognized that the international community needs effective methods of disrupting the payment of ransom. The issue involves not just the shipping industry but governments as well. When ship owners and governments pay ransoms they place other seafarers and vessels at greater future risk. Nevertheless, it can be impossible to ignore calls from the ship owners, family members of seafarers, the general public, and the media. Somali pirates regularly force captured crew members to telephone family members at home to inform loved ones that they are about to be killed or tortured. Families bring pressure on companies and governments, often through the media, in order to bring political influence to bear against governments to do whatever is necessary to ensure the safety of the hostages.[35] "The decision not to pay a ransom demand . . . is almost always a decision that is too big for ship owners and even governments to take on their own."[36]

The report recommends two possible actions with respect to ransoms. First, an education program could be pursued at international and national levels to inform the media and the wider public about the greater long-term risks inherent in surrendering to the demands of hijackers and kidnappers. Second, formal or informal international agreements can help to discourage or even ban the payment of ransoms. Although such a ban could not be enforced, it would provide some justification for individual ship owners and governments to withstand media or public pressure to pay.[37]

The Nairobi Report also includes ship rider agreements among its recommendations, which would allow regional law enforcement personnel to embark on board foreign warships patrolling the area.[38] The Nairobi Report specifically suggests that shipping nations and regional coastal states should collaborate so that ship rider law enforcement powers may be used to board, search, detain, arrest, and transfer ashore Somali pirates. The concept of partner nation ship riders that serve on board foreign warships is not new; such agreements already are in place to facilitate counternarcotics naval interdiction in the Caribbean and eastern Pacific, and to support cooperation in fisheries enforcement in the western Pacific. The UN Security Council in Resolution 1851 eventually adopted this specific recommendation as a potential tool against Somali piracy. Resolution 1851 invited states and regional organizations to conclude special agreements or arrangements with countries willing to take custody of pirates, which necessarily requires allowing law enforcement officials to embark onto vessels. The involvement of regional countries is particularly important because often they are ideally situated to conduct investigations and carry out trial prosecutions of detained persons. The Security Council adopted ship rider authorizations only so long as ship riders obtain advance consent from the TFG for the exercise of third-state jurisdiction in Somali territorial waters.[39]

Finally, the Nairobi Report addresses the challenging operational situation that arises when warships capture pirates. The retention of suspected pirates on warships at sea for indefinite periods significantly impairs the ability of the ships to carry out other missions.[40] Because of the problems that arise from such situations, the report identifies and focuses on the long-standing need for states to make permanent arrangements for the transfer of persons taken under control by naval forces from sea to land.[41] The United States has long sought such a solution, after the U.S. Navy had to retain a number of captured pirates on board U.S. warships in 2006 due to the difficulty of obtaining agreement with a nearby coastal state to accept transfer of those pirates ashore. The recommendation for states to facilitate transfer of suspected pirates was embraced by Security Council Resolution 1851.[42]

Since states may decline to have their warships used to transport pirates for any extended periods of time, the Nairobi Report recommends efforts to enhance existing legal structures within neighboring states, particularly Kenya, to prosecute, convict, and imprison pirates after they are transferred to shore.[43] Except for Somalia, all the other regional states have well functioning courts of law, prosecutors, judges, and legislation. Most of these countries also are parties to some or all of relevant international legal instruments, which could be leveraged to broaden cooperation. Taken together, there is sufficient jurisdiction.

Another recommendation from the Nairobi Report to consider is the creation of a dedicated intelligence system directed at penetrating the piracy organizations. The intelligence network should be established under the umbrella of an existing organization enjoying experienced law enforcement or military capability.[44] Developing greater intelligence capabilities for regional partners is a theme that resonates with Robert M. Gates, the U.S. Secretary of Defense—who has declared that more effective intelligence is the "first thing" needed to more effectively focus the counterpiracy effort.[45]

Security Council Resolution 1816

The United States and other nations sought adoption of Security Council Resolution 1816 in order to obtain greater international cooperation against Somali piracy, and to provide authority for entry into Somalia's territorial sea to fight piracy.[46] Pirates eluded capture by boarding parties from warships operating in international waters by fleeing into Somalia's 12-nautical-mile territorial sea. Resolution 1816, which was adopted under Chapter VII of the UN Charter, closes that sanctuary by authorizing entry into Somali's territorial waters.

The resolution, which since its adoption has been extended through passage of follow-on resolutions, also sought to build greater international assistance for disposition and logistics of persons who entered custody during counterpiracy operations, including victims, witnesses, and suspected pirates. The resolution specified that flag, port, and coastal states, states of the nationality of victims and perpetrators of piracy, and other states with jurisdiction under domestic or international law, should cooperate to resolve jurisdictional questions. All nations also should cooperate in the investigation and prosecution of suspected pirates.[47]

The provision concerning jurisdiction was an especially important authority for the Pentagon, which had experience with captured pirates that were detained on board warships for months at a time. The assistance of other states is an essential component, since interdictions resulting in the capture of suspects who must remain on warships for extended periods of time can have a chilling effect on naval piracy suppression missions. To address this problem, the resolution called on states to cooperate in the choice of jurisdiction issues, investigation, and prosecution of persons responsible for acts of piracy off the coast of Somalia. Additionally, states also should render assistance by providing disposition and logistics assistance support with respect to persons under their jurisdiction and control.[48]

While Resolution 1816 does not compel any state to take suspected pirates or other persons in custody from a warship, it provides a valuable umbrella of political legitimacy for providing logistics to aid disposition and repatriation of persons. The resolution also encourages states to increase and coordinate their efforts to deter acts of piracy in conjunction with the Transitional Federal Government of Somalia (TFG), the notionally recognized transitional ruling authority inside the fractured state. Since adoption of Resolution 1816, the UN Security Council repeatedly recognized the authority of the TFG as the governing body in Somalia. The resolution further called on states, the IMO, and other international organizations to build a partnership to ensure regional coastal and maritime security. The TFG is struggling to maintain the semblance of a functioning government. It has no maritime law enforcement capability, and the resolution makes clear that states should support the nascent effort by Somalia to patrol its near shore environment.

Security Council Resolution 1838

Next, the Security Council adopted Resolution 1838.[49] The Security Council expressed grave concerns about the serious threat posed by piracy off the coast of Somalia, and how piracy threatens "the prompt, safe and effective delivery of humanitarian aid to Somalia, to international navigation and safety of commercial maritime routes, and to [lawfully conducted] fishing activities."[50] The resolution also called upon states to take part in actively fighting piracy by deploying naval vessels and aircraft to the region. The Security Council finally reaffirmed that the United Nations Convention on the Law of the Sea (UNCLOS) embodies the rules applicable to countering piracy and armed robbery at sea. This pronouncement left no doubt that the conventional international law of the sea should be used to analyze legal issues associated with contemporary piracy. Resolution 1838 further urges states to promulgate guidance for their ships regarding precautionary measures to protect vessels from attack when sailing in waters off the coast of Somalia.[51]

Security Council Resolution 1846

Security Council Resolution 1846, which was adopted on December 2, 2008, further broadened international political support and legal capabilities to combat piracy off the Somali coast.[52] The resolution suggests, for the first time, that the 1988 Convention for the Suppression of Unlawful Acts against the Safety of Maritime Navigation (SUA) may be used by states to cooperate in the extradition and prosecution of pirates.

States that want to prosecute suspected pirates, but do not have national laws proscribing the crime, may charge suspects with the type of ship hijacking prevalent in the Horn of Africa under domestic legislation implementing SUA. The challenge of holding pirates accountable through criminal prosecutions has been repeatedly cited as the one of the most vexing challenges to contain piracy. The Security Council urged the 157 state parties of SUA to fully implement their obligations under the treaty and to build judicial capacity for the successful prosecution of suspected pirates.[53]

The Security Council action is regarded as an important legal capability to hold pirates accountable. American Ambassador Rosemary DiCarlo declared at the time, "We've had a major step today with this resolution. We need to continue working with the countries that are deeply engaged in this issue—and there are a number of them now, not only in Europe but elsewhere . . . [that are] dealing with pirates, once we have captured them."[54] She reiterated the U.S. view that the SUA Convention provides ample authority to cooperate.[55]

The 88 SUA Convention was created in response to the hijacking, hostage taking, and murder committed on board the Italian-flagged passenger liner *Achille Lauro* in 1985. The shocking incident is described by Michael Oren:

> [M]embers of the Palestine Liberation Front (PLF) overran the *Achille Lauro* and held its twelve American passengers at gunpoint. . . . the PLF gunmen did not merely incarcerate the Americans but decided to make an example of one of them. Their choice was a handicapped sixty-nine-year old New Yorker named Leon Klinghoffer, an American Jew. The terrorists pushed Klinghoffer's wheelchair to the edge of the deck, shot him in the back, and pitched his still-twitching body into the sea.[56]

At the time of the attack on the cruise ship, many states did not have criminal legislation for extradition or prosecution for vessel hijacking. Over a three-year period following the attack, member states at the IMO developed and adopted SUA. The treaty entered into force in 1992.[57] A key SUA offense is to unlawfully and intentionally seize or exercise control over a ship by force or threat or other form of intimidation. Further, the treaty provides that state parties shall either prosecute a violation committed under the treaty, or extradite the offender. This provision to "extradite or prosecute" is intended to ensure that ship hijackers do not escape criminal trial and justice. The treaty also provides that state parties shall make SUA offenses punishable by penalties that take into account their "grave nature."[58]

The Nairobi Report had noted that some believe the 1988 SUA Convention is an inappropriate instrument for counterpiracy because it was prepared in a counterterrorism context. But the articles in the SUA Convention make no reference to terrorism or piracy—instead, the treaty proscribes certain acts, including the acts of hostage taking and hijacking of ships. Somali pirates typically commit both offenses when they seize a ship. These two crimes are not covered under the traditional law of piracy.

After publication of the report, the Security Council resolved any doubt about the application of SUA to antipiracy enforcement off the coast of Somalia, when it explicitly endorsed the use of the SUA Convention in Security Council Resolution 1846.[59] Admiral Thad Allen, the Commandant of the U.S. Coast Guard, had promoted the use of the SUA Convention for counterpiracy operations off the coast of Somalia in his Internet blog journal, "iCommandant," during November 2008.[60] The SUA convention, Admiral Allen noted, applies to nearly all of the attacks occurring in the GOA. The 1988 treaty obligates state parties to criminalize attacks against vessels and establish jurisdiction over such offenses for ships flying their flag. He concluded that "[l]everaging states' SUA obligations in conjunction with existing international law against piracy provides an effective legal framework to deliver an 'endgame.'"[61] The UN Security Council would agree, following adoption of Resolution 1846 on December 2, with Resolution 1816 on December 16, 2008.

Prosecuting pirates under SUA will not obviate the challenges associated with disposition of persons under control. Until regional and bilateral agreements are executed, along with more structured coordination, disposition and logistics issues associated with persons picked up during counterpiracy operations will continue to exist. In part, this is because piracy prosecutions involve cases with suspects from one country and witnesses and victims from others. The vessel likely is registered in yet another state, and carries cargo owned by corporations from one or more additional countries. In addition, the flag state of the vessel and the warship that conducts the interdiction could vary. The coordination provisions of the original Resolution 1816, and that were highlighted in the subsequent Security Council resolutions on piracy that came after it, emphasize the importance of cooperation in repressing piracy.[62] In particular, states should cooperate through routine patrols to deter the crime, as well as take action to bring pirates to justice after they are caught. In the past, coordination on Somali piracy disposition and logistics issues was ad hoc, but the Security Council was working toward institutionalizing collaboration. Resolution 1851 would provide a much larger mechanism for international cooperation in the fight against piracy.

Security Council Resolution 1851

The Security Council adopted Resolution 1851 on December 16, 2008, which encouraged the establishment of a venue for regularized contact between states, similar to the ReCAAP model. The resolution also reauthorized "all necessary measures" to fight piracy, and for the first time, authorized military operations on Somali soil by the international community.[63] At the time of its adoption, some diplomats expressed concern over the authorization to enter Somalia and the potential impact that the decision might have on state sovereignty in other venues. The Indonesian Foreign Ministry's Director General for Legal and International Treaties, Arief Havas Oegroseno, for example, considered the resolution, "loosely worded, raising fears it could be generalized in future for application in other jurisdictions."[64]

Oegroseno's unease reflects Indonesia's long-standing hesitancy about permitting the Security Council to authorize international action in any country's territorial waters, a position that was evident from the beginning of the negotiations even on Resolution 1816. Jakarta's discomfort with Resolution 1816 was tied to its struggle to maintain adequate maritime patrols and maritime order throughout its vast archipelago. This challenge makes Indonesia especially sensitive to calls for the United Nations to authorize member states to intervene in "ungoverned" maritime space.

Oegroseno's comment reflects Jakarta's position on the three earlier UN resolutions, because those may serve as precedent for the Security Council to intervene in the Straits of Malacca and Singapore, the Lombok Strait, and the Sunda Strait—three of the world's 13 major straits.[65] In order to address Jakarta's concerns, the final draft of Resolution 1816 eliminates ambiguity regarding the application of the resolution beyond Somalia, by containing a provision indicating that the resolution applies only with respect to the situation in Somalia, and that it does not establish new customary international law.[66] That compromise from the summer of 2008 opened the door for Resolution 1851, which, significantly, permitted the international coalition to conduct military strikes inside Somalia to counter piracy.

Authority to enter Somalia is part of the broader focus to address the reasons that piracy is occurring. Pirates brazenly operate in a virtually lawless environment. Jonas Gahr Store, Norway's Minister for Foreign Affairs, stated that "the creation of safe havens for pirates in states with broken security sectors was unacceptable" and that "the efforts to 'resurrect' Somalia must continue with full force."[67] Then Secretary of State Condoleezza Rice has also stated that Resolution 1851 sent a "strong signal of commitment to combat the scourge of piracy that will help to end the impunity of Somali pirates."[68]

Resolution 1851 also reiterated that the 1988 SUA Convention could be employed in prosecuting maritime pirates. The resolution encourages states involved in suppressing piracy off the coast of Somalia to consider creating a tactical maritime command center in the region that could coordinate information sharing.[69] In regard to establishing such a center, Rice pledged that the United States would work with interested partner nations to create a "contact group" on Somali piracy. The contact group would serve as a mechanism to share intelligence, to coordinate activities, and to reach out to other partners, including those in shipping and insurance industries."[70] India, one of the states with the largest number of vessels attacked by Somali pirates in recent years, also endorsed creation of such a group. The Indian representative to the United Nations, Ambassador Nirupam Sen, said it would be necessary to institutionalize operational coordination among navies in the Horn of Africa (HOA) in order to have an effective international response.[71] The Contact Group on Piracy off the Coast of Somalia (CGPCS) was an outgrowth of Resolution 1851, and is discussed after Resolutions 1918 and 1950, immediately below.

Security Council Resolution 1918

The problem of "catch and release" of suspected pirates led the UN Security Council to act on April 27, 2010, to adopt a fifth resolution concerning piracy off the coast of Somalia. Piracy is a crime of opportunity, and one in which the potential costs (death in an attack or imprisonment if convicted at trial) are weighed against the potential benefits (gain of fabulous wealth). The international community has an interest in reshaping the decision-making calculus of pirates by increasing the costs, and thereby bolstering general deterrence. By releasing captured pirates, states have illustrated a weakness in deterrence that pirates exploit. In order to fill this gap, Resolution 1918 called on states to update and develop their domestic counterpiracy laws, and directs the United Nations to review the feasibility of creating an international piracy court.

The status of piracy as a crime of universal jurisdiction makes it an important exception to the norm of flag state jurisdiction. For many states, however, criminal law does not apply beyond the edge of the territorial sea. In such cases, even though all states *may* take action, if a particular state does not have domestic criminal codes proscribing the conduct, it will most likely not be able to initiate prosecution.[72] Difficulty associated with prosecuting maritime piracy has led states to avoid the courtroom. In two-thirds of the cases of pirates captured off the coast of Somalia, naval forces have simply released them.[73]

In one 2008 case, for example, the Danish government released pirates because it was not convinced it could convict them at trial, even though the men had been found with assault weapons and handwritten notebooks outlining how to split the spoils of their crime among warlords.[74] In that case, the ship and its crew were released, but it was a troubling outcome to many, including the commanding officer of the Danish vessel involved: "We catch them, confiscate their weapons, and then we let them go . . . it's frustrating."[75] The landscape is changing, however, as France, the United States, and other countries have begun to conduct criminal trials to prosecute Somali pirates.

The dilemma is real, however, since detaining pirates poses a host of logistical, legal, and diplomatic burdens. In one case in May 2010 that drew international scrutiny, for example, Russian marines from the warship *Marshal Shaposhnikov* captured 10 Somali pirates after a high-seas shootout involving the ship *Moscow University*, a small oil tanker carrying $50 million in crude oil through the Gulf of Aden (GOA). The crew was Russian, and they sought safety behind a barricade in the engine room. Russian commandos freed them. Colonel Alexei Kuznetzov stated that the pirates were released due to "imperfections in international law." Later, chief of the general staff, General Nikolai Y. Makarov, observed that it was "much easier to catch pirates than to decide what to do with them."[76] Like many countries, Russian law does not provide a legal cause of action or basis for detaining piracy committed by foreign nationals. In the case of the *Moscow University* interdiction, Russia ultimately set the 10 Somalis adrift, and then later reported, "it seems they all have died."[77]

Security Council Resolution 1950

On November 23, 2010, the Security Council extended Resolution 1897 for an additional year when it unanimously adopted Resolution 1950.[78] Resolution 1950 urged all states to take action against the illicit financing and money laundering associated with piracy, and sought cooperation with the International Criminal Police Organization (INTERPOL) to do so.

Resolution 1950 also was significant because it was the first time that the Security Council raised the issue of foreign illegal, unreported, and unregulated (IUU) fishing in Somalia's 200-nautical-mile exclusive economic zone (EEZ) as one factor in contributing to the rise in piracy. The Security Council acknowledged Somalia's sole right to exploit its offshore resources, including fisheries. Preventing "illegal fishing and illegal dumping, including toxic substances," is important for countering instability and poverty. Toward that end, the Security Council called on states, upon request of the coastal states, to provide technical assistance to Somalia and its neighbors to enhance maritime security forces.[79]

One prominent scholar has suggested the Security Council could do even more, including making the possession of large, high horse-power outboard engines on board skiffs prima facie evidence of piracy, and taking steps to enforce the two-decades-old Security Council Resolution 733, which imposed an arms embargo against Somalia.[80]

Table 1: Somalia Counterpiracy Resolutions of the UN Security Council[1]

1950 (2010): Stressed the need to combat piracy and its underlying causes, including instability in Somalia; noted with concern ransom payments and the lack of enforcement of the arms embargo; discussed the piracy prosecution options report (S/2010/394); stressed need to support investigation and prosecution of those who illicitly finance, plan, organize, or unlawfully profit from pirate attacks off the coast of Somalia; cited "illegal fishing" for the first time in a piracy-specific resolution.

1918 (2010): Welcomed creation of the Contact Group on Piracy off the Coast of Somalia (CGPCS); called for regional States to criminalize piracy and to consider the prosecution and imprisonment of pirates; commended Kenya for its piracy prosecutions; welcomed implementation of the Djibouti Code of Conduct.

1897 (2009): Invited consideration of special agreements to take custody of pirates; urged States, in collaboration with the shipping and insurance industries, and the IMO, to develop and implement avoidance, evasion, and defensive best practices when under attack or when sailing in the waters off the coast of Somalia, and urged States to make their citizens and vessels available for forensic investigation in port immediately following an attack.

1851 (2008): Encouraged establishment of an international cooperation mechanism for counterpiracy off Somalia—the Contact Group on Piracy off the Coast of Somalia (CGPCS) was established shortly thereafter, encouraged the creation of a regional counterpiracy coordination center; authorized States to take action against pirate safe havens within Somalia; invited States with maritime forces in the area and the regional States to conclude ship rider agreements.

1846 (2008): Noted the 1988 SUA Convention provides for parties to create criminal offenses, establish jurisdiction and extradition of suspects seizing or exercising control over a ship by force; urged States parties to SUA to fully implement their obligations and build judicial capacity for the successful prosecution of persons suspected of piracy and armed robbery at sea off Somalia.

1838 (2008): Called upon States interested in the security of maritime activities to take part in the fight against piracy by deploying naval vessels and aircraft, and reaffirmed that the Law of the Sea Convention sets out the legal framework to combating piracy.

1816 (2008): The first Somalia piracy resolution; authorized naval forces entry into Somalia's territorial waters to pursue pirates; urged States to cooperate with each other and the IMO and called on States to cooperate on counterpiracy logistics, jurisdiction, investigation, and prosecution of piracy.

Source: Captain Brian S. Wilson, JAGC, USN (ret.).

Contact Group on Piracy off the Coast of Somalia

The Contact Group on Piracy off the Coast of Somalia (CGPCS) was formed in response to UN Security Council Resolution 1851, which called on states to facilitate coordination of counterpiracy activities off the coast of Somalia.

The CGPCS is the broadest coalition of nations ever gathered to develop and coordinate practical solutions to the scourge of maritime piracy. The first meeting occurred at the United Nations on January 14, 2009, and 24 nations participated in the initial discussions.[81] Observers from the EU, NATO, and the African Union also attended the first meeting. India, one of the states most affected by Somali piracy, endorsed creation of the group at its founding. The Indian representative to the UN, Ambassador Nirupam Sen, presciently asserted that naval cooperation had to be institutionalized in order for the international community to be effective in its response.[82] By June 2010, 49 countries, seven international organizations, and three industry observers were participating in the CGPCS.

The Contact Group formed four working groups to develop collective action against different aspects of the effort against Somali piracy. These groups divided along functional lines. Working Group One addresses activities related to military operational collaboration and information sharing or "maritime domain awareness," and the establishment of a regional coordination center. Working Group One is chaired by the United Kingdom with support from the International Maritime Organization (IMO). Working Group Two is chaired by Denmark, and it focuses on improving the judicial process of prosecuting piracy. The Working Group works in conjunction with the United Nations Office on Drugs and Crime. The United States chairs Working Group Three, which focuses on strengthening merchant ship security. Working Group Four is chaired by Egypt, and it was established to enhance public diplomacy related to counterpiracy, including dissemination of information to the public and making media outreach more effective.

At a meeting in New York in September 2009, the CGPCS approved a terms of reference for creation of an International Trust Fund (CGPCS ITF) to help defray costs that are associated with prosecution of suspected pirates. The expense of transferring and extraditing suspects and delivering witnesses to testify at trial are covered by the ITF. In November 2010 at the seventh meeting of the CGPCS, the group issued a communiqué underscoring the importance of bolstering prosecution of piracy as part of a comprehensive counterpiracy strategy.[83] The CGPCS agreed to review the seven options on legal reform proposed by the Secretary-General and to make recommendations on the most feasible approach to prosecution. Finally, the group commended the Republic of Kenya and the Republic of Yemen for bringing pirates to justice, and the commitment of the Republic of Seychelles to continue prosecution of suspected prates. So far, the CGPCS has been successful in developing strategies for force generation, legal options, capacity building, and industry engagement. The forum also regularly informs the deliberations by national governments and multilateral organizations, to include the UN, NATO, EU,

AU, IMO, and UNODC, on counterpiracy options, operations, programs, and strategies.

Djibouti Code of Conduct

A November 2007 IMO Assembly resolution called upon regional states in East Africa to conclude an international agreement to prevent, deter, and suppress piracy.[84] The result was negotiation of the Code of Conduct concerning the Repression of Piracy and Armed Robbery against Ships in the Western Indian Ocean and the Gulf of Aden. The agreement, which is not legally binding, is the first regional understanding between Arab and African countries to address maritime piracy.

Seeking to replicate the success of counterpiracy agreements in Asia, the IMO sponsored meetings from 2005 to 2008 in Sana'a, Yemen,[85] Oman, and Dar es Salaam, Tanzania,[86] to facilitate negotiation of an antipiracy agreement among regional states.[87] A final meeting was held in Djibouti in January 2009, and it produced an agreement among 17 regional states to enhance cooperation in the prosecution and repatriation of captured Somali pirates.[88] The Djibouti Code of Conduct recognizes the extent of the problem of piracy and armed robbery against ships in the region, and the signatories declare their intention to cooperate to the fullest possible extent, and in a manner consistent with international law, in the repression of piracy and armed robbery against ships.

The agreement includes the goal of creating a Regional Maritime Information Centre or System.[89] Signatory states expressed a commitment to report relevant information through a system of national focal points and information centers, and to interdict ships suspected of engaging in acts of piracy or armed robbery against ships. States parties also agreed to apprehend and prosecute persons. Pirates that are prosecuted and convicted at trial and imprisoned are entitled to proper care and treatment, and the agreement also calls for states to repatriate seafarers, fishermen, and other shipboard passengers, and victims of piracy.

The Code of Conduct is open for signature to 21 states in the region. As of October 8, 2010, 16 nations had signed the Code.[90] Recognizing the limited capacity of most of the countries, however, the Code of Conduct is nonbinding. The nations are expected to act only in accordance with their available resources and related priorities, and in accordance with their respective national laws and regulations. The IMO is assisting the states in the region to meet their commitments under the Code.[91] Japan was an early leader in supporting the IMO's technical cooperation and capacity-building programs, and Tokyo's $13.5 million pledge started the IMO Djibouti Code of Conduct Trust Fund.[92]

In April 2010, the secretariat of the IMO developed a list of projects and activities to promote the Code of Conduct regionally,[93] and established a Project Implementation Unit (PIU) within the Maritime Safety Division. The PIU is funded through the Djibouti Code Trust Fund, and is helping to establish a training center in Djibouti and three regional counterpiracy information sharing centers (ISCs). The ISCs are located in Dar es Salaam, Mombasa, and Sana'a.[94] The PIU conducted a workshop on development of counterpiracy legislation and legal aspects of maritime law enforcement in Djibouti from October 11–13, 2010. Working in cooperation with the European Commission, Regional Agreement on Combating Piracy and Armed Robbery against Ships in Asia (ReCAAP) Information Sharing Center (ISC), United Nations Political Office for Somalia (UNPOS), the United Nations Office on Drugs and Crime (UNODC), and the International Criminal Police Organization (INTERPOL), the IMO is implementing a broad maritime security capacity-building program for the Code of Conduct signatories. National-level counterpiracy officials and other experts from countries that signed the Djibouti Code of Conduct are receiving training by ReCAAP-ISC. This approach fosters and transfers experience from Asia to Africa, and helps to harmonize state practice between the two regions.

Notes

1. Report of the Sub-Committee of the League of Nations Committee of Experts for the Progressive Codification of International Law, League of Nations Document C. 196 M. 70, 1927V, at 118–119.

2. Records of the Eighth Ordinary Session of the Assembly, Meetings of the Committees, Minutes of the First Committee (Constitutional and Legal Questions), League of Nations, Official Journal, Special Supplement #55 (Geneva, 1927), at 11.

3. Harvard Research in International Law, *Draft Convention on Piracy, with Comments*, 26 American Journal of International Law Supp.: Research in International Law 739, 764 (1932). See also excerpts from the jury charge, Sir Viscount Sankey L. D., In Re Piracy Jure Gentium [1934] A.C. 586, 592–600 and Carnegie Endowment for International Peace, Yearbook 115 (1932).

4. Convention on the High Seas, opened for signature April 29, 1958, 13 U.S.T. 2312 (1962), T.I.A.S. No. 5200, 450 UNT.S. 82.

5. Ken Cottril, *Asia Fights Maritime Piracy*, Traffic World, May 8, 2000, at 35.

6. The 16 countries are the People's Republic of Bangladesh, Brunei Darussalam, the Kingdom of Cambodia, the People's Republic of China, the Republic of India, the Republic of Indonesia, Japan, the Republic of Korea, the Lao People's Democratic Republic, Malaysia, the Union of Myanmar, the Republic of the Philippines, the Republic of Singapore, the Democratic Socialist Republic of Sri Lanka, the Kingdom of Thailand, and the Socialist Republic of Viet Nam.

7. Speech by Mr. Yoshiaki Ito, Executive Director, ReCAAP ISC, April 2007. http://www.recaap.org/news/pdf/news/Apr.07.pdf.

8. Speech by Mr. Yoshiaki Ito, Executive Director, ReCAAP ISC, April 2007.

9. Speech by Mr. Yoshiaki Ito, Executive Director, ReCAAP ISC, April 2007.

10. Joshua Ho, *Combating Piracy and Armed Robbery in Asia: RECAAP's Information Sharing Centre*, 33 Marine Policy 432–434 (March 2009).

11. Speech by Mr. Yoshiaki Ito, Executive Director, ReCAAP ISC, April 2007.

12. The ISC operates a secure, 24-hour Information Network (IFN) System that includes a web-based platform for collection, organization, analysis, and sharing of piracy and armed robbery information among ReCAAP states. The ISC is linked through the IFN with designated national Focal Points, such as coast guards and maritime authorities, of ReCAAP member countries to enable the dissemination and exchange of information.

13. Speech by Mr. Yoshiaki Ito, Executive Director, ReCAAP ISC, April 2007.

14. UN Doc. A/Res/60/30, Oceans and the Law of the Sea, November 29, 2005.

15. IMO Doc. A.1002(25), Piracy and Armed Robbery against Ships in Waters off the Coast of Somalia, ¶ 7, November 29, 2007.

16. Maritime and port authority representatives attended from Djibouti, Egypt, Eritrea, Ethiopia, Jordan, Oman, Saudi Arabia, Somalia, Sudan, and Yemen. IMO Doc. MSC 85/26, ¶ 18.13.

17. At the Oman Workshop, Djibouti, Egypt, Eritrea, Jordan, Oman, Somalia, and Yemen endorsed the draft Motion of Understanding, which is also called the Sana'a/Muscat MOU. IMO Doc. MSC 85/26, ¶ 18.14.

18. "[T]he Dar es Salaam meeting was to promote good maritime security on a regional basis, with a particular focus on the prevention, detection and suppression of piracy and armed robbery against ships in the Western Indian Ocean, Gulf of Aden and Red Sea." IMO Doc. MSC 85/26, ¶ 18.15.

19. IMO Doc. MSC 85/26, ¶ 18.14.

20. IMO Doc. IMO/KUL 1/4, Kuala Lumpur Statement on Enhancement on Safety, Security and Environmental Protection in the Straits of Malacca and Singapore, September 20, 2006.

21. IMO Doc. IMO/KUL 1/4, Kuala Lumpur Statement on Enhancement on Safety, Security and Environmental Protection in the Straits of Malacca and Singapore, September 20, 2006.

22. IMO Doc. IMO/KUL 1/4, Kuala Lumpur Statement on Enhancement of Safety, Security and Environmental Protection in the Straits of Malacca and Singapore, September 20, 2006. See also, UN Doc. A/61/584, November 17, 2006, for a report of the KL meeting.

23. IMO Doc. IMO/SGP 1/4, Singapore Statement on Enhancement of Safety, Security and Environmental Protection in the Straits of Malacca and Singapore, September 6, 2007.

24. IMO Doc. C ES.25/12/1, October 22, 2009, Protection of Vital Shipping Lanes, the 2nd Co-operation Forum and 2nd Project Coordination Committee Meeting.

25. Workshop Commissioned by the Special Representative of the Secretary-General of the UN to Somalia, Nairobi, Kenya, November 10–21, 2008, Piracy off the Somali Coast: Final Report: Detailed Recommendations [Hereinafter, "Nairobi Report"].

26. Nairobi Report, at 33, ¶ 6.

27. J. Peter Pham, *Book Briefs (Book Review of Martin N. Murphy's Somalia, the New Barbary? Piracy and Islam in the Horn of Africa)*, 32 American Foreign Policy Interests 403 (2010).

28. Nairobi Report, at 33, ¶ 6.

29. Nairobi Report, at ¶ 8.1.2, 8.1.3.

30. Nairobi Report, at ¶ 1.5.

31. Nairobi Report, at ¶ 3.1.2.

32. Nairobi Report, at ¶ 3.8.

33. Nairobi Report, at ¶ 8.1.2.

34. Nairobi Report, at ¶ 8.1.2.

35. Nairobi Report, at ¶ 8.1.2.

36. Nairobi Report, at ¶ 1.3.

37. Nairobi Report, at ¶ 1.3. Banning payment of ransom is endorsed by Ambassador John Norton Moore, Director, Center for Oceans Law and Policy, and Walter L. Brown, Professor of Law, University of Virginia School of Law. See, John Norton Moore, Toward a More Effective Counter-Piracy Policy, unpublished paper presented at the Maritime Piracy/Counter-Piracy Workshop, sponsored by Booz Allen Hamilton, June 12, 2009. Also see, Contemporary Piracy: Consequences and Cures: A Post-Workshop Report, October 2009, at 18 (American Bar Association Standing Committee on Law and National Security, et al.).

38. Nairobi Report, at ¶ 1.2 (Recommendation 13).

39. UN Doc. S/Res. 1851, The Situation in Somalia, December 16, 2008, at ¶ 3.

40. Nairobi Report, at ¶ 4.2.3

41. Nairobi Report, at ¶ 4.2.4.

42. UN Doc. S/Res. 1851, The Situation in Somalia, at ¶ 3.

43. Nairobi Report, ¶ 1.1 (Recommendation 8).

44. Nairobi Report, ¶ 1.1 (Recommendation 3).

45. John Kruzel, *Defense Department Welcomes UN Resolution Aimed at Pirates*, American Forces Press Service, December 17, 2008.

46. UN Doc. S/Res. 1816, The Situation in Somalia.

47. UN Doc. S/Res. 1816, at ¶ 11

48. UN Doc. S/Res. 1816, at ¶ 11.

49. UN Doc. S/Res. 1838, The Situation in Somalia.

50. UN Doc. S/Res. 1838, at 1.

51. UN Doc. S/Res. 1838, The Situation in Somalia, ¶ 6 (referring to IMO Assembly Resolution A.1002[25]).

52. UN Doc. S/Res. 1846, The Situation in Somalia.

53. Paulo Prada and Alex Roth, *On the Lawless Seas, It's Not Easy Putting Somali Pirates in the Dock*, Wall Street Journal, December 12, 2008. Regarding the 1988 SUA Convention, the article stated, "few signatories have enacted national legislation empowering their courts to prosecute foreigners for such acts outside their territory."

54. Press Release, U.S. Mission to the United Nations, Rosemary DiCarlo, United States Ambassador and Alternate Representative for Special Political Affairs Speaks on Anti-Piracy Resolution by Security Council, at Security Council Stakeout, US Federal News, December 2, 2008.

55. Press Release, U.S. Mission to the United Nations.

56. Michael B. Oren, *Power, Faith, and Fantasy* 556 (2007).

57. The Convention for the Suppression of Unlawful Acts against the Safety of Maritime Navigation was approved at the IMO in Rome on March 10, 1988, and entered into force on March 1, 1992.

58. In 2005 SUA was amended with two protocols that promulgate a new legal framework to combat the proliferation of weapons of mass destruction and their delivery systems on board vessels and platforms at sea. Amendments to the Suppression of Unlawful Acts (SUA) were approved at a diplomatic conference at the IMO in 2005 and the amendments entered into force on July 28, 2010. The SUA Amendments provide a framework for criminalizing the conduct of those who transport terrorists or use a ship as a weapon. They further provide enforcement mechanisms to facilitate nonflag state boarding of vessels suspected of being involved in such illicit activity, and mandate that a state party either prosecute or extradite suspected SUA offenders.

59. Despite the ability of states to prosecute Somali piracy under SUA, virtually all parties to the treaty that have seized Somali pirates have at one time or another released them. Germany, for example, released six Somali pirates captured by the frigate *Karlsruhe* on December 25, 2008. At that time, Berlin took no legal action because no German interests were involved in the piratical attack. See, *German Navy Foils Somali Pirates*, BBC News, December 25, 2008. Germany has proposed the establishment of an international piracy court to alleviate the difficulty of "catch and release."

60. iCommandant: Web Journal of Admiral Thad Allen, U.S. Coast Guard Internet website, December 1, 2008 [Former commandant, U.S. Coast Guard].

61. iCommandant: Web Journal of Admiral Thad Allen.

62. UN Doc. S/Res. 1816, The Situation in Somalia, December 16, 2008, at ¶ 3.

63. UN Doc. S/Res. 1851, The Situation in Somalia, at 1.

64. Tony Hotland, *RI Rejects U.S. Anti-Piracy Proposal*, The Jakarta Post, December 17, 2008.

65. Hotland, *RI Rejects U.S. Anti-Piracy Proposal.*

66. UN Doc. S/Res. 1816, The Situation in Somalia.

67. UN Doc. SC/9541.

68. Condoleezza Rice, Combating the Scourge of Piracy, December 16, 2008.

69. UN Doc. S/Res. 1851, The Situation in Somalia, December 16, 2008.

70. Rice, Combating the Scourge of Piracy.

71. UN Doc. SC/9541, Security Council Authorizes States to Use Land-Based Operations in Somalia as Part of Fight against Piracy Off Coast, December 16, 2008.

72. The 2008 United Nations Report on Somali Piracy discussed the lack of implementing legislation in some states: "Clearly a state that wishes to prosecute pirates and other such criminals needs to ensure that the relevant laws apply on the high seas too. If they wish to pursue pirates into another state's territorial sea with a view to prosecuting them in their domestic courts, then the law will need to apply there too." Nairobi Report, at 25.

73. Prada and Roth, *On the Lawless Seas.*

74. Prada and Roth, *On the Lawless Seas.*

75. Prada and Roth, *On the Lawless Seas* (aboard the HDMS *Absalon* [L 16]).

76. Ellen Barry, *Russia Frees Somali Pirates It Had Seized in Shootout*, New York Times, May 8, 2010, at 4.

77. David Cairns, *Russian Navy Sent Somali Pirates to Their Death*, The First Post, May 12, 2010, http://www.thefirstpost.co.uk/63244,news-comment,news-politics,russian-navy-sent-somali-pirates-to-their-death-from-the-moscow-university.

78. UN Doc. S/Res/1950, November 23, 2010, reproduced in IMO Doc. MSC 88/INF.21, November 25, 2010. The resolution, which was sponsored by all members of the Security Council and Canada, Denmark, Germany, Greece, Norway, Somalia, and Ukraine, was adopted without debate. It is available at http://www.un.org/News/Press/docs/2010/sc10092.doc.htm.

79. UN Doc. S/Res/1950, at ¶ 6.

80. UN Doc. S/Res/733, January 23, 1992. See also, J. Ashley Roach, *Suppressing Somali Piracy—Next Steps*, 14(39) ASIL Insights (American Society of International Law, December 1, 2010).

81. More information about CGPCS is available on the U.S. Department of State's website, at http://www.state.gov.

82. UN Doc. SC/9541, Security Council Authorizes States to Use Land-Based Operations in Somalia as Part of Fight against Piracy Off Coast, Unanimously Adopting Resolution 1851, 6046th Meeting (PM), December 16, 2008.

83. IMO Doc. MSC 88/INF.19, Annex 1, Communiqué, the 7th Plenary Session of the Contact Group on Piracy off the Coast of Somalia, New York, New York, November 10, 2010, at 3.

84. IMO Doc. A.1002(25) at ¶ 7.

85. Maritime and port authority representatives attended from Djibouti, Egypt, Eritrea, Ethiopia, Jordan, Oman, Saudi Arabia, Somalia, Sudan, and Yemen.

86. "The Dar es Salaam meeting was to promote good maritime security on a regional basis, with a particular focus on the prevention, detection and suppression of piracy and armed robbery against ships in the Western Indian Ocean, Gulf of Aden and Red Sea." IMO Doc. MSC 85/9, Draft Report of the Maritime Safety Committee on Its Eighty-Fifth Session, December 1, 2008, at 89. See also, IMO Doc. C 102/14, April 3, 2009, Protection of Vital Shipping Lanes, Sub-regional meeting to conclude agreements on maritime security, piracy and armed robbery against ships for States from the Western Indian Ocean, Gulf of Aden and Red Sea areas.

87. IMO Doc. MSC 75/24, Report of the Maritime Safety Committee on Its Seventy-Fifth Session, May 29, 2002, at ¶¶ 18.7–18.19.

88. Press Release, IMO, High-Level Meeting in Djibouti Adopts a Code of Conduct to Repress Acts of Piracy and Armed Robbery against Ships, January 30, 2009.

89. This accord is referred to as the Sana'a/Muscat MOU, and was endorsed by Djibouti, Egypt, Eritrea, Jordan, Oman, Somalia, and Yemen. IMO Doc. MSC 85/9, Draft Report of the Maritime Safety Committee on Its Eighty-Fifth Session, December 1, 2008, at 89.

90. IMO Doc. C 105/12/Add.1, October 8, 2010. The following nations have signed the code: Comoros, Djibouti, Egypt, Ethiopia, Jordan, Kenya, Madagascar, Maldives, Mauritius, Oman, Saudi Arabia, Seychelles, Somalia, the Sudan, the United Republic of Tanzania, and Yemen.

91. "States in the region" means Comoros, Djibouti, Egypt, Eritrea, Ethiopia, France, Jordan, Kenya, Madagascar, the Maldives, Mauritius, Mozambique, Oman, Saudi Arabia, the Seychelles, Somalia, South Africa, Sudan, the United Arab Emirates, the United Republic of Tanzania, and Yemen.

92. IMO Doc. C/ES.25/12, November 5, 2009.

93. IMO Doc. C 102/14/1 5 May 2009, Protection of Vital Shipping Lanes, Project profile for the implementation of the Djibouti Code of Conduct.

94. IMO Doc. C 105/12/Add.1, October 8, 2010.

CHAPTER 7

International Criminal Prosecution

Article 94(1) of UNCLOS requires that flag states adopt adequate criminal laws to prosecute the crime of maritime piracy committed against a ship flying their flag. Furthermore, all states parties to the SUA Convention have a duty to criminalize hijacking against one of their flagged vessels. If a flag state has not adequately criminalized piracy or hijacking, it could be seen as in breach of its international obligations. In order to fulfill their general duty to repress piracy, states should adopt appropriate legislation, especially legislation that facilitates the apprehension and prosecution of suspected pirates. In recent years, France, Germany, Maldives, the Netherlands, Seychelles, Somali Transitional Federal Government (TFG), Spain, the United States, and Yemen have prosecuted Somali pirates.

Suspected pirates that are apprehended beyond the territorial sea of any coastal state (or pursuant to UN Security Council Resolution 1816, inside Somalia's territorial sea) should be prosecuted under the domestic laws of the investigating state or another cooperating state. Some scholars suggest, however, that the provision in Article 105 of UNCLOS limits prosecution of a pirate to the "courts of the State which carried out the seizure." State practice, however, has softened this language, and states have transferred or extradited pirates from the country making the seizure to other states for prosecution. The investigating state may reach agreement with other nations, including the flag state of a ship victimized by piracy; a coastal state, if the attack occurred in the nation's territorial sea; or the state of nationality of the victims. Any state may cooperate with the flag state of a warship, which interdicted pirates under Article 100 of UNCLOS.

On December 23, 2008, the secretariat of the IMO requested member states to submit information concerning their counterpiracy laws.[1]

States were asked to provide information on a series of questions, including whether the nation is a party to UNCLOS, whether the definition of piracy incorporated into domestic criminal law is consistent with Article 101, UNCLOS, whether the provision of universal jurisdiction under Article 105, UNCLOS, is being implemented, whether the nation is a party to the SUA Convention, and whether the country's domestic laws reflect the crimes and jurisdiction set forth in SUA. Preliminary data was provided at the 96th session of the IMO Legal Committee.[2]

After nearly two years of collecting data and examining submissions from 40 nations and Hong Kong, China, the IMO reported that 31 of the states were parties to UNCLOS. Only 10 states had defined piracy in their domestic laws in accordance with Article 101 in UNCLOS, and only 6 had otherwise incorporated the definition into other areas of the criminal code.[3] Just 8 states adopted the scope of universal jurisdiction for the crime of piracy that is a feature of Article 105, UNCLOS, and 5 nations referred to the crime of piracy as flowing from the customary law of nations. More nations were party to SUA than to UNCLOS—37 of the 40 states were members of the SUA treaty, although the SUA Convention was in full force with just 7 states. Of the 10 nations that had incorporated the substantive criminal offenses of SUA into their domestic laws, only 4 applied the mandatory jurisdiction provisions of the treaty. In sum, the responses from the 40 states illustrate a lack of harmony among states combating piracy. This condition suggests that states ought to consider developing a Code for Uniformity of National Law in the Administration of Piracy Justice.

By February 2011, hundreds of Somali pirates had been prosecuted in criminal trials in the region, including 88 convictions in Somaliland, 200 convictions from 260 trials in Puntland, 120 convictions in Yemen, 34 suspected pirates in custody in Maldives, and 12 convictions in Oman. Outside the region, Belgium had convicted one Somali pirate, France 15, Germany 10, the Netherlands tried 10 and convicted 5, and Spain and the United States each had convicted 2 pirates. But the difficulty of criminal trial for pirates has led states to simply "catch and release" suspects at sea—disarming suspected pirates and setting them free. In addition to the financial cost and logistical hurdles involved in prosecuting pirates, some nations worry that either suspects or convicted pirates may be able to secure political asylum or preferred refugee status. In at least one case, pirates apparently were dealt with extrajudicially when the Russian Navy released 10 captured pirates who "may have died."

In November 2010, Kenya's second-highest court ruled that it did not have jurisdiction over pirates captured outside of the country's territorial waters. The decision cast into doubt the ability of Kenya to accept pirates captured by foreign naval forces. The jurisdictional question remains in a state of flux. But the treatment of pirates as *hostis humani generis* (enemies of all mankind) in international law could enable Kenya's courts to continue to prosecute suspects. The practical and legal difficulty in prosecution by individual states has led to a number of calls for creation of an international piracy court. The UN Security Council has authority under Chapter VII of the UN Charter to maintain international peace and security, and it has been suggested that establishment of an international piracy tribunal is manifestly within the ambit of Security Council authority. An international tribunal distributes costs of prosecution and imprisonment across the international community. The imprimatur of a UN court also likely would attract support from nations to agree to incarcerate convicted pirates in their territory. The International Criminal Tribunals for Yugoslavia and Rwanda, for example, have convicted criminals who were then sent to prison in more than 20 nations.

Code of Practice

The IMO Maritime Safety Committee (MSC) has assisted member states to develop a Code of Practice to aid in investigation of maritime piracy.[4] The Code of Practice recommends that states adopt legislation to establish their jurisdiction over piracy and armed robbery against ships, including laws to apprehend and prosecute persons suspected of committing the offenses.[5] In particular, states are urged to implement through domestic legislation the provisions of UNCLOS and SUA relating to piracy. The Code of Practice also provides guidelines for training investigators and investigative strategy. In the end, piracy is like any other crime, and conventional "detective methods offer the best chance of identifying and apprehending pirates and perpetrators of armed robbery."[6] Consequently, the Code provides a frame work for the careful and systematic collection of evidence, including photographs and videotape, individual witness accounts, detailed forensic examination of the scenes of crime, and search of intelligence databases.[7]

States also are encouraged to link counterpiracy naval patrols to broader efforts at ensuring maritime security. Efforts to suppress illegal smuggling and narcotics trafficking, for example, can be utilized to deter and defeat piracy.

In July 2009, UN Office on Drugs and Crime (UNODC) issued guidance for countries requesting transfer of piracy suspects to Kenya.[8] The guidance was developed in conjunction with the Kenya Department of Public Prosecutors, the EU/Kenya liaison officer for EU NAVFOR, the legal advisor to the Combined Maritime Forces, and a representative from the U.S. Naval Criminal Investigative Service, during a workshop held on June 25, 2009. The guidance includes a communication checklist specifying information to be provided to Kenyan prosecutors, as well as evidentiary standards to ensure successful prosecution. The guidance sets forth appropriate points of contact in Kenya and evidence handling procedures associated with the transfer of piracy suspects to Kenyan authorities.

Months after the adoption of the IMO Code of Practice, UNODC issued additional guidelines for transferring suspected pirates from foreign warships to Mombasa, Kenya.[9] Commanding officers of naval vessels should, if possible, ensure that all evidentiary exhibits are bagged, labeled, and photographed; witness statements have been prepared and translated into English; pirates identified (to the extent feasible); and food and basic emergency medical care provided to the pirates. UNODC also recommends that pirates not be brought topside or be visible on the ship as it approaches the jetty. Kenyan officials meet the warships at the pier with a team of prosecutors and up to 10 police officers. The suspected pirates and evidence are taken to the Port Police Station.

As the warship transfers the pirates and evidentiary exhibits, it also may deliver a presentation to Kenyan authorities of the facts surrounding the case, and the legal theory for seizing the suspects. Based on the evidence and presentation, Kenya may decide to accept or decline jurisdiction over the pirates. Acceptance of the pirates is contingent upon successful interviews of the suspects by Kenyan authorities that the pirates have not been mistreated. If Kenya accepts the suspects, the physical and demonstrative evidence will be removed from the warship by a local police exhibit handling team. The pirate suspects are formally arrested on the wharf, not the warship. Since the warship is protected by sovereign immunity in customary international law and Article 32, UNCLOS, Kenyan authorities may not exercise legal jurisdiction on board the foreign ship.[10]

In order to facilitate Kenya's role in piracy law enforcement, UNODC has provided funds for Kenyan police training, installation of secure exhibit rooms, and reconditioning of police vehicles and information technology systems. Likewise, Kenyan courts have received aid from UNODC in transportation logistics for witnesses, reviews of cases on remand, courtroom security, provision of online legal resources and judicial training, interpreters and office equipment, and defense legal counsel.

The UNODC strategic plan for piracy is to support a regional center for prosecution in Kenya and Seychelles as a means to ensure fair and efficient trials and imprisonment. That piece is already in place. But the organization also plans on expanding, creating a third and fourth regional center for piracy prosecution in order to spread the burden. Meanwhile, a Somalia corrections program is being pursued in order to ensure humane and secure imprisonment of Somali pirates inside Somalia. This effort entails raising the capabilities of Somali prosecutors, judges, and legal defense counsel and pursuing substantive legal reform in the country, all with the objective of developing the capacity to conduct fair and efficient trials in Somalia.

Prosecution options will continue to be severely limited unless and until regional, and specifically Somali, prison capacity is substantially increased and nations able to prosecute pirates are assured through political agreements and protocols that Somalis can be incarcerated in African (preferably Somali) prisons. As long as nations cannot count on being able to repatriate Somalis apprehended in pirate incidents back to Somalia or elsewhere in Africa, they will continue to resist taking potential asylum seekers into their national court and prison systems.

2010 Report of the UN Secretary-General

Given the choices available for conducting piracy criminal trials, the UN Security Council requested the UN Secretary-General to report on the options available for prosecuting the crime of maritime piracy. The remit of the Security Council included a request for an assessment of the option of creating special domestic chambers possibly with international components, a regional tribunal, or an international tribunal and corresponding imprisonment arrangements.[11]

In reply to the Security Council dispatch, in July 2010, the UN Secretary-General issued a report that identified seven options for consideration: (1) build regional capacity; (2) create a Somali court in a regional state; (3) create a special tribunal in a regional state without UN support; (4) create a special tribunal in a regional state with UN support; (5) create a regional tribunal; (6) establish an international tribunal; and (7) create an UN Security Council piracy court. The July 2010 report does not advocate any single approach, but rather is a neutral compendium of the options available and the comparative advantages and disadvantages of each. The extraordinary time and costs of establishing and operating international courts, however, and the small volume of suspects they would prosecute, augurs in favor of national courts as a more efficient option.

Build Regional Capacity

The first option for increasing piracy trials in Africa is to enhance UN assistance to build the capacity of regional states to prosecute and imprison persons responsible for acts of piracy and armed robbery at sea off the coast of Somalia. A perennial problem for the nations that are conducting counterpiracy naval patrols is the uncertainty surrounding the options available for prosecution. By increasing the capacity of states in the region to prosecute Somali piracy suspects, the international community can contain the problem and aid the regional authorities in becoming more effective in maintaining law and order.

Assisting the states in the Horn of Africa to develop domestic judicial and law enforcement capacity is key to a long-term solution to the threat of Somali piracy. There already is some success with pursuing this option, as illustrated by the new high-security courtroom in Shimo La Tewa, Mombasa, which was created to try piracy cases and other serious criminal offenses. Building partnership capacity throughout the Horn of Africa requires concerted political engagement and steady funding, such as the International Trust Fund to Support Initiatives of States Countering Piracy. Improving logistics is especially important since substantial resources are required to imprison those convicted, and repatriate those adjudged "not guilty." Judicial capacity and prison standards in Puntland are particularly minimal, and any effort to secure greater Somali participation in piracy criminal prosecutions would require long-term investments in the criminal legal system of the country.

Create a Somali Court in a Regional State

The second option is to create a new Somali court, placing it within the territory of a third state in the region. The court could be created either with or without UN sponsorship. Such a court would enable Somalis to adjudicate piracy cases from a secure venue, helping Somalis to maintain legal jurisdiction and political control of the process, while providing a safe location in which to conduct trials, hear witnesses, and issue judicial decisions. The court would require development of a restatement of Somali substantive criminal law and criminal procedure, and thus serve as a motivation for the country to update its legislative framework necessary for conducting piracy prosecutions. Assistance to the Somali court under this option would not benefit the host state's criminal justice system. This option may provide essential experience and help to poise the Somali judicial system to conduct trials inside Somalia.

France and Portugal support the second option, as does Mr. Jack Lang, who served as the Special Adviser on Legal Issues Related to Piracy off the Coast of Somalia.[12] Russia has also supported creation of a special Somali piracy court to be located outside of Somalia, but numerous nations oppose the idea, including Canada, China, Greece, India, Japan, the United Kingdom, and the United States. The greatest downside to the idea is that prosecution of pirates by numerous nations generates positive externalities throughout the legal systems, especially in nations such as Kenya, which has limited capacity. Furthermore, establishing a court outside an existing national justice system could weaken the commitment of other states to prosecute pirates in their domestic courts.

Create a Special Chamber in a Regional State

Creating a special chamber to prosecute pirates in a regional state—either with or without UN support—constituted the third and fourth options. For the time being, if the challenges of launching an effective Somali criminal court are too great, another option is to establish a special chamber within the national jurisdiction of a state within the region, and this may be done with or without UN participation. It is uncertain whether there is sufficient number of piracy prosecutions in a regional state to justify creation of a special chamber dedicated to such trials. Kenya has the greatest number of Somali piracy prosecutions underway. International donors have insufficient confidence in the Somali judicial system to provide additional funding for expansion of piracy prosecutions inside the country. Consequently, other regional states receive greater UN assistance funding, which would make it easier to establish a special chamber within an existing judicial system. Piracy prosecutions, however, might siphon resources away from an already fragile criminal jurisdiction, or an influx of pirate defendants could create a "two tier" system of justice inside the neighboring country. Participation in the cases by the United Nations, or by judges, prosecutors, and staff selected by the UN, would bring additional expertise and resources, but also likely slow down the judicial process.

Create a Regional Tribunal

Many commentators and observers find establishment of a regional tribunal as a promising option, although creation of such a court is likely to be very costly and take years of negotiations. A court akin to the International Criminal Court would require agreement of a multilateral treaty. If the court made use of UN judges, prosecutors, and staff, a separate agreement with the United Nations would be needed. Such a court would help to build the judicial capacity in the regional state in which it were located, and the court would enjoy close proximity to Somalia.

Establish an International Tribunal

The sixth option is establishment of an international tribunal on the basis of an agreement between a host nation in the region and the United

Nations. The tribunal would tend to broaden the capacity of the host nation, but also likely would require greater resources, a long time to stand up, and complex negotiations to transfer and prosecute suspected pirates.

Popular with law school students and academic researchers everywhere, the option of establishing an international tribunal is easier said than done. Creating an international tribunal is a daunting task likely to take a decade or more. First, states would have to convene (and pay for) preparatory meetings to develop a draft statute for creation of the court. There will be no shortage of thorny questions, including the role of the decider of fact and law, the organization (a single judge, a panel of judges, etc.), evidentiary standards to be applied to the evidence, funding of the tribunal and counsel, incarceration of suspects before trial and after trial, if convicted, disposition of acquitted defendants, funding for individual trials, location of the court, and composition and nationality of the permanent staff, to name just a few.

After several years of negotiation, if states were able to develop a statute, they then would have to convene a diplomatic conference to adopt the convention. Once the convention is adopted, a critical mass of states—generally specified in the statute—would have to accept the treaty in order for it to enter into force. But that is not the end of the story, because each nation that seeks to be bound in a treaty relationship with the other state parties would have to either ratify or accede to the treaty. This action places the state under legal obligation to adhere to the treaty statute. Simultaneously, each state that becomes a party to the international piracy tribunal would have to ensure that its domestic criminal laws conform to the statute of the international court. The substantive law of piracy and procedural criminal law may have to be amended. Thus, the average period of time from inception to effective operation of an international piracy tribunal can be expected to be a decade or more.

The difficulty in finding a jurisdiction willing and able to prosecute pirates captured by the international naval coalition operating off the coast of Somalia has led some lawyers to suggest that suspected pirates should be prosecuted at the International Tribunal for the Law of the Sea (ITLOS), which is based in Hamburg, Germany.

ITLOS was established under UNCLOS to address disputes between states arising from the terms of the Convention. But Blank Rome LLP, one of the world's finest maritime law firms, has recommended that the forum be available as a criminal tribunal to prosecute pirates. In an article in *Mainbrace*, a newsletter produced for clients, the admiralty law firm stated ITLOS should be used to try and punish pirates, thereby reducing the burden on states in having to deal with the problem.[13] "To effectively implement this resource," Blank Rome asserts, "the rules of jurisdiction concerning

ITLOS would have to be revised to give it the power to deal with such disputes."

But ITLOS has no competence to serve as a criminal venue, and broadening the jurisdiction of the Tribunal to address criminal matters is, again, easier said than done. Furthermore, seafarers convicted of piracy by any future ITLOS would still have to be incarcerated somewhere—guarded, housed, and fed—so attempts to shift the burden to the international tribunal do not facilitate or streamline prosecution, but merely add yet another layer of inertia and complexity to an already challenging situation.

Create a UN Security Council Tribunal

Establishment of an international piracy prosecution tribunal by Security Council resolution, preferably under Chapter VII of the UN Charter, would place the issue of piracy squarely in the category of problems that pose a threat to international peace and security. Such a tribunal would be similar to the International Tribunal for the Former Yugoslavia (ICTY) and the International Criminal Tribunal for Rwanda (ICTR), which are subsidiary organs of the Security Council. An international tribunal may enjoy greater capacity and wider jurisdiction than a domestic court, and be aided by the Security Council's ability to require cooperation from third states under Chapter VII.

Another popular idea is to amend the statute of the International Criminal Court (ICC), granting the body jurisdiction over the crime of piracy.[14] After years of negotiation, the ICC was stood up in 2002. As of October 2010, there are 114 state parties to the Rome Statute.[15] The court presently has jurisdiction over the crimes of genocide, crimes against humanity, and war crimes. The ICC was created with the aim of ending impunity for the perpetrators of "the most serious crimes of concern to the international community as a whole." There is some question as to whether piracy is one of the "most serious" crimes on the order of genocide, or whether states could just as easily address the threat.

Piracy does not fit well within the ICC mandate, and any attempt to stretch the Rome Statute to include piracy would be controversial.[16] Under Article 3 of the Rome Statute, the ICC may sit either in The Hague or at another location, so if the ICC state parties could agree to use the court to conduct piracy trials, the court could locate its chambers in Asia or Africa. Whatever form an international tribunal might take, the costs are likely to be comparatively high in relation to other options. Furthermore, establishment and management of an international piracy court is likely to be rather cumbersome, burdened by multilateral or UN Security Council oversight.[17]

CGPCS Working Group Two

The Contact Group on Piracy off the Coast of Somalia (CGPCS) was established as a collaborative forum to aid nations in antipiracy activities and operations in the Horn of Africa (HOA). Much of the diplomatic action has been focused on the endgame—the prosecution of pirates in domestic courts. Nearly 600 suspected pirates had been prosecuted or were in the process of being prosecuted by September 2010.[18] Trials had or were occurring in 10 jurisdictions during 2008–2010. CGPCS Working Group Two (WG2) was established to explore and implement more effective legal procedures to bring pirates to justice. From the time WG2 first met in January 2009 through November 2010, it has held six sessions. The purpose of the meetings was to facilitate prosecution and the imprisonment of pirate suspects within domestic criminal law systems.

States are sharing how they approach decision making for prosecution and extradition of suspects, posttrial transfer issues, how to ensure that seafarer witnesses who may be traveling throughout the world are able to appear to testify at trial, and implementing basic human rights of suspected and convicted pirates.[19] By sharing experiences regarding legal and practical challenges to national prosecutions, nations can better overcome the difficulties associated with apprehending and detaining suspects captured at sea.

In order to have practical value, the WG2 meetings developed a collection of legal resources and guidance that is called a "legal toolbox." The toolbox was constructed from discussions and written input to a UNODC questionnaire on the legal and practical challenges to national piracy prosecutions. The findings of the UNODC report indicate that how nations criminalize piracy and armed robbery at sea, the liability of persons for committing the offenses (or attempts to commit the offenses), rules concerning court jurisdiction, and evidentiary and procedural requirements affect the outcome of trial.[20]

Legal Toolbox

The legal toolbox contains, among other items, three documents concerning the collection of evidence. The three documents are the US Counter Piracy Evidence Collection Guidance, which the author helped to develop while serving with the Joint Staff; the Kenya Transfer Guidance for Piracy Suspects; and the Seychelles Transfer Guide.[21] The legal toolkit also contains guidance for ensuring national decision-making frameworks are in place to enable states to make rapid decisions on prosecution and extradition of suspected pirates, best practices for posttrial transfer of pirates, criminalization of piracy and the possession of piracy-related equipment, improvements in data collection and processing of suspects, to include biometrics, and legal aspects of human rights and piracy financing.

At the Copenhagen meeting in November 2010, WG2 focused on completing a number of tasks to facilitate prosecution of piracy. First, the participants explored the possibility of creating a legal framework for the transfer of convicted pirates from prosecuting states in the region, such Kenya and Seychelles, to Somalia to serve their sentences in the newly constructed UN prison that opened at Hargeisa, Somaliland, on November 22, 2010. A model bilateral prisoner transfer agreement could tie the criminal courts in neighboring nations to the prison facility in Somalia. One feature of such agreement is that the prisoners must accept the transfer to Somaliland. Post-trial transfer back to Somalia, however, still involves significant expense. A long-term solution would be to develop the capabilities inside Somalia to handle the entire criminal law process, from indictment through trial and imprisonment. The cost of developing such an independent penal and judicial capacity in Somaliland and Puntland is about $20 million.

The US Counter-Piracy Evidence Collection Guidance, formerly called the US Disposition and Logistics Guidance, is designed for tactical at-sea processing of pirate suspects by commanding officers of warships patrolling off the Horn of Africa. The original version was coordinated among the Pentagon, the Department of State, and the U.S. Coast Guard, and subsequently released to commander, U.S. Central Command by the Joint Staff in 2006.[22] The revised document states that law enforcement should be contacted to begin the investigation and intelligence-gathering procedures as soon as the initial scene of the incident is secured.[23] The warship conducting a counter-piracy interdiction should prepare a summary report, indicating the location of the incident, the actions taken to disrupt the piracy, indicia of piracy (such as observing a display of weapons or other piracy paraphernalia, including high horse-power outboard engines on board skiffs), nature of the contact with the suspected pirates, and any other piracy incidents reported in the area over the previous 48 hours.

Investigators should try to accurately identify the suspects, including obtaining the name (and variations on the spelling of the name and family name), age, race, nationality, language spoken, place of birth (identified by a parish, village, settlement, or landmark), and obtain photographs of the suspect. Diagrams and documentation outlining the piracy attack often are helpful to the court. Statements should be obtained from victim witnesses and government witnesses, who must be made available at trial in order to conduct a successful prosecution. All evidence must be secured to ensure a proper chain of custody, including documentation of the communications equipment, list of boarding equipment, such as ladders and hooks, and a list of weapons—all supplemented by photographs.

The nation of Kenya has borne a disproportionate amount of the burden of prosecuting Somali pirates. In 2006, Kenya conducted its first piracy prosecution by taking to trial 10 pirates that were picked up by the USS *Churchill*. All defendants were convicted.[24] In December 2008, the United Kingdom and Kenya signed a memorandum of agreement to facilitate the disposition and prosecution of Somali pirates seized by the British Navy. The United States and Kenya signed a similar agreement in January 2009. In March 2009, the EU and Kenya also signed an MOU.

Although since the time of signature the memorandums of agreement have expired, Kenya has continued to accept cases on a case-by-case basis under the general duty of states to cooperate to repress piracy. By November 2010, Kenya had accepted 17 cases, with 142 suspected pirates. The primary challenge in the cases has been the logistical and practical difficulty of ensuring the appearance of seafarer witnesses at trial. Mauritius is also considering an MOU with the EU for the transfer of suspected pirates.

Kenya has prosecuted more Somali pirates than all other nations combined. Under the (now repealed) Penal Code of Kenya, the crime of piracy was proscribed as having been committed by "any person who, in territorial waters or upon the high seas, commits any act of piracy *jure gentium* is guilty of the offence of piracy."[25] The statute does not contain a more complete definition, but since Kenya became a party to UNCLOS in 1989, the nation imports the definition of piracy reflected in Article 101 of the treaty, which is regarded as customary international law. Kenya released the Transfer Guidance for Piracy Suspects to help inform and to facilitate coordination between Kenya and foreign maritime security forces.[26] Under Kenyan criminal law, prosecutors must show that suspected pirates participated in the commission of the offense of piracy as either a principal or joint offender. Article 20(1) of the Penal Code indicates that every person who actually does an act which constitutes an offense, or who does an act that enables another to do an act that constitutes an offense, or who aids, abets, or counsels another committing such act, may be charged either with commission of the offense or attempted commission of the offense. The Seychelles has promulgated similar guidance for the transfer of piracy suspects.[27]

Conclusion

On December 31, 2010, the UN Office on Drugs and Crime reported that 738 suspected or convicted Somali pirates were being detained in 13 countries. Somalia held 338 individuals, including 78 in Somaliland and 260 in Puntland. But Jack Lang, in a report to the Secretary-General on the legal issues related to piracy in the Horn of Africa, reported that in May 2010,

90 percent of all pirates captured had evaded the judicial process. Typically, naval forces have opted for a "catch and release" policy that immediately turns loose captured pirates after destroying skiffs and weapons. In order to avoid this practice, the process of transferring captured suspects to nations appropriate for prosecution should become standardized. Some countries still have not criminalized piracy in domestic criminal codes in harmony with the definition of piracy and general duty set forth in UNCLOS. Belgium, France, Japan, the Maldives, the Seychelles, Spain, and the United Republic of Tanzania have embarked on a review of their counter-piracy laws.

The international law of the sea, as embodied in UNCLOS, also provides ample jurisdiction for nations to exercise control over suspected pirates. Other bases for jurisdiction over suspected pirates exist. Active personality jurisdiction is available to Somalia to prosecute its nationals who have committed acts of piracy. Passive personality jurisdiction may be used by the nations that have nationals who have been the victims of piracy attack. State jurisdiction over ships flying its flag may be asserted by a nation over pirates that hijack such vessels. Nations that interdict or disrupt acts of piracy also may prosecute perpetrators in domestic court in accordance with Article 105 of UNCLOS. Finally, the Convention for the Suppression of Unlawful Acts against the Safety of Maritime Navigation enshrines the duty to prosecute or extradite persons suspected of committing ship hijacking.

Notes

1. IMO Circ. Ltr. No. 2933, December 23, 2008. The United Nations Division of Ocean Affairs and Law of the Sea (DOALOS) also embarked on a complementary effort to assess national legislation to counter piracy. See, National Legislation on Piracy, October 7, 2010, http://www.un.org/depts/los/piracy/piracy_national_legislation.htm.
2. IMO Doc. LEG 96/7, Piracy: Review of National Legislation, August 20, 2009, and LEG 96/7/Corr.1 and IMO Doc. LEG 96/13, Report of the Legal Committee, October 14, 2009, ¶ 7.2.
3. IMO Doc. LEG 97/9, Piracy: Review of National Legislation, September 10, 2010.
4. IMO Doc. A.1025(26), Code of Practice for Investigation of Crimes of Piracy and Armed Robbery against Ships, January 18, 2010. The document updates IMO Doc. A.922(22), Code of Practice for the Investigation of Crimes of Piracy and Armed Robbery against Ships, January 22, 2002. See, Chapter 3.
5. IMO Doc. A.1025(26), ¶ 3.1.
6. IMO Doc. A.1025(26), ¶ 5.2.
7. IMO Doc. A.1025(26), ¶ 7.

8. Alan Cole, Counter Piracy Programme Coordinator, Guidance for the Transfer of Suspected Pirates, Armed Robbers and Seized Property to Kenya, United Nations Office on Drugs and Crime, Nairobi, Kenya, July 1, 2009.

9. United Nations Office on Drugs and Crime, Piracy Suspect Transfer Procedures for Mombasa, Kenya, November 18, 2009.

10. Articles 32 and 95, UNCLOS.

11. UN Doc. S/Res. 1918, The Situation in Somalia, April 27, 2010.

12. UN Doc. SG/A/1260, Bio 4230, L3162, Secretary-General Appoints Jack Lang of France Special Adviser on Legal Issues Related to Piracy off the Coast of Somalia, August 26, 2010.

13. *Pirates of Somalia*, Mainbrace No. 1 (January 2009).

14. Yvonne M. Dutton, *Bringing Pirates to Justice: A Case for Including Piracy within the Jurisdiction of the International Criminal Court*, 11 Chicago Journal of International Law 197 (Summer 2010).

15. The States Parties to the Rome Statute, http://www.icc-cpi.int/Menus/ASP/states+parties/The+States+Parties+to+the+Rome+Statute.htm. The states included 31 African states, 15 Asian states, 18 Eastern European nations, 25 Latin American and Caribbean states, and 25 Western European nations.

16. Preamble, Rome Statute of the International Criminal Court ("Rome Statute"), July 17, 1998, UN Doc. A/CONF.183/9 (1998), *reprinted in* 37 ILM 999.

17. UN Doc. S/2010/394, Report of the Secretary-General on possible options to further the aim of prosecuting and imprisoning persons responsible for acts of piracy and armed robbery at sea off the coast of Somalia, including, in particular, options for creating special domestic chambers possibly with international components, a regional tribunal or an international tribunal and corresponding imprisonment arrangements, taking into account the work of the Contact Group on Piracy off the Coast of Somalia, the existing practice in establishing international and mixed tribunals, and the time and resources necessary to achieve and sustain substantive results, July 26, 2010.

18. IMO Doc. LEG 97/9/1, Piracy: Review of National Legislation, September 30, 2010.

19. IMO Doc. LEG 97/9/1, Piracy: Review of National Legislation.

20. IMO Doc. MSC 88/18/4, Piracy and Armed Robbery against Ships: Working Group 2 of the Contact Group on Piracy off the Coast of Somalia, September 20, 2010.

21. IMO Doc. MSC 88/INF.10, Piracy and Armed Robbery against Ships: Working Group 2 of the Contact Group on Piracy off the Coast of Somalia, September 20, 2010.

22. The original version of the US Disposition and Logistics Guidance was reprinted in James Kraska, *Developing Piracy Policy for the National Strategy for Maritime Security and the International Maritime Organization*, *in* Legal Challenges in Maritime Security 331 (Myron H. Nordquist, et al., eds., 2008).

23. IMO Doc. MSC 88/INF.10, Annex 1, Piracy and Armed Robbery against Ships.

24. Republic v. Hassan Mohamud Ahmed, Crim. No. 434, 2006, Chief Magistrate Court, November 1, 2006, *as cited in* James Thuo Gathi, *Kenya's Piracy Prosecutions*,

104 American Journal of International Law 416, 417 (2010). The pirates each received 10 years' confinement as punishment for their crime, and the convictions were upheld on appeal.

25. Gathi, *Kenya's Piracy Prosecutions*, at 416, 421–424.

26. IMO Doc. MSC 88/INF.10, Annex 2, Piracy and Armed Robbery against Ships.

27. IMO Doc. MSC 88/INF.10, Annex 3, Piracy and Armed Robbery against Ships.

APPENDIX

Primary Documents

United Nations Convention on the Law of the Sea (1982)

Article 100 Duty to Cooperate in the Repression of Piracy

All States shall cooperate to the fullest possible extent in the repression of piracy on the high seas or in any other place outside the jurisdiction of any State.

Article 101 Definition of Piracy

Piracy consists of any of the following acts:

(a) any illegal acts of violence or detention, or any act of depredation, committed for private ends by the crew or the passengers of a private ship or a private aircraft, and directed:

  (i) on the high seas, against another ship or aircraft, or against persons or property on board such ship or aircraft;
  (ii) against a ship, aircraft, persons or property in a place outside the jurisdiction of any State;

(b) any act of voluntary participation in the operation of a ship or of an aircraft with knowledge of facts making it a pirate ship or aircraft;
(c) any act of inciting or of intentionally facilitating an act described in subparagraph (a) or (b).

Article 102 Piracy by a Warship

Piracy by a warship, government ship or government aircraft whose crew has mutinied

The acts of piracy, as defined in Article 101, committed by a warship, government ship or government aircraft whose crew has mutinied and taken control of the ship or aircraft are assimilated to acts committed by a private ship or aircraft.

Article 103 Definition of a Pirate Ship or Aircraft

A ship or aircraft is considered a pirate ship or aircraft if it is intended by the persons in dominant control to be used for the purpose of committing one of the acts referred to in Article 101. The same applies if the ship or aircraft has been used to commit any such act, so long as it remains under the control of the persons guilty of that act.

Article 104 Retention or Loss of the Nationality of a Pirate Ship or Aircraft

A ship or aircraft may retain its nationality although it has become a pirate ship or aircraft. The retention or loss of nationality is determined by the law of the State from which such nationality was derived.

Article 105 Seizure of a Pirate Ship or Aircraft

On the high seas, or in any other place outside the jurisdiction of any State, every State may seize a pirate ship or aircraft, or a ship or aircraft taken by piracy and under the control of pirates, and arrest the persons and seize the property on board. The courts of the State which carried out the seizure may decide upon the penalties to be imposed, and may also determine the action to be taken with regard to the ships, aircraft or property, subject to the rights of third parties acting in good faith.

Article 106 Liability for Seizure without Adequate Grounds

Where the seizure of a ship or aircraft on suspicion of piracy has been effected without adequate grounds, the State making the seizure shall be liable to the State the nationality of which is possessed by the ship or aircraft for any loss or damage caused by the seizure.

Article 107 Ships and Aircraft Which Are Entitled to Seize on Account of Piracy

A seizure on account of piracy may be carried out only by warships or military aircraft, or other ships or aircraft clearly marked and identifiable as being on government service and authorized to that effect.

Article 110 Right of Visit [In Case of Piracy]

1. Except where acts of interference derive from powers conferred by treaty, a warship which encounters on the high seas a foreign ship, other than a ship entitled to complete immunity in accordance with articles 95 and 96, is not justified in boarding it unless there is reasonable ground for suspecting that:

   (a) the ship is engaged in piracy;

   * * *

   (d) the ship is without nationality; or
   (e) though flying a foreign flag or refusing to show its flag, the ship is, in reality, of the same nationality as the warship.

2. In the cases provided for in paragraph 1, the warship may proceed to verify the ship's right to fly its flag. To this end, it may send a boat under the command of an officer to the suspected ship. If suspicion remains after the documents have been checked, it may proceed to a further examination on board the ship, which must be carried out with all possible consideration.
3. If the suspicions prove to be unfounded, and provided that the ship boarded has not committed any act justifying them, it shall be compensated for any loss or damage that may have been sustained.
4. These provisions apply mutatis mutandis to military aircraft.
5. These provisions also apply to any other duly authorized ships or aircraft clearly marked and identifiable as being on government service.

Article 111 Right of Hot Pursuit

1. The hot pursuit of a foreign ship may be undertaken when the competent authorities of the coastal state have good reason to believe that the ship has violated the laws and regulations of that State. Such pursuit must be commenced when the foreign ship or one of its boats is within the internal waters, the archipelagic waters, the territorial sea or the contiguous zone of the pursuing State, and may only be continued outside the territorial sea or the contiguous zone if the pursuit has not been interrupted. It is not necessary that, at the time when the foreign ships within the territorial sea or the contiguous zone receives the order to stop, the ship giving the order should likewise be within the territorial sea or contiguous zone. If the foreign ship is within the contiguous zone, as defined in article 33, the pursuit may only be undertaken if there has been a violation of the rights for the protection of which the zone was established.
2. The right of hot pursuit shall apply mutatis mutandis to violations in the exclusive economic zone or on the continental shelf, including safety zones around continental shelf installations, of the laws and regulations of the coastal State applicable in accordance with this Convention to the exclusive economic zone or the continental shelf, including such safety zones.

3. The right of hot pursuit ceases as soon as the ship pursued enters the territorial sea of its own State or of a third State.
4. Hot pursuit is not deemed to have begun unless the pursuing ship has satisfied itself by such practicable means as may be available that the ship pursued or one of its boats or other craft working as a team and using the ship pursued as a mother ship is within the limits of the territorial sea, or, as the case may be, within the contiguous zone or the exclusive economic zone or above the continental shelf. The pursuit may only be commenced after a visual or auditory signal to stop has been given at a distance, which enables it to be seen or heard by the foreign ship.
5. The right of hot pursuit may be exercised only by warships or military aircraft, or other ships or aircraft clearly marked and identifiable as being on government service and authorized to that effect.
6. Where hot pursuit is effected by an aircraft:

    (a) the provisions of paragraphs 1 to 4 shall apply mutatis mutandis;
    (b) the aircraft giving the order to stop must itself actively pursue the ship until a ship or another aircraft of the coastal State, summoned by the aircraft, arrives to take over the pursuit, unless the aircraft is itself able to arrest the ship. It does not suffice to justify an arrest outside the territorial sea that the ship was merely sighted by the aircraft as an offender or suspected offender, if it was not both ordered to stop and pursued by the aircraft itself or other aircraft or ships which continue the pursuit without interruption.

7. The release of a ship arrested within the jurisdiction of a State and escorted to a port of that State for the purposes of an inquiry before the competent authorities may not be claimed solely on the ground that the ship, in the course of its voyage, was escorted across a portion of the exclusive economic zone or the high seas, if the circumstances rendered this necessary.
8. Where a ship has been stopped or arrested outside the territorial sea in circumstances which do not justify the exercise of the right of hot pursuit, it shall be compensated for any loss or damage that may have been thereby sustained.

Convention on the High Seas 1958

Article 14

All States shall co-operate to the fullest possible extent in the repression of piracy on the high seas or in any other place outside the jurisdiction of any State.

Article 15

Piracy consists of any of the following acts:

1. Any illegal acts of violence, detention or any act of depredation, committed for private ends by the crew or the passengers of a private ship or a private aircraft, and directed:
   (a) On board such ship or aircraft;
   (b) Against a ship, aircraft, persons or property in a place outside the jurisdiction of any State;
2. Any act of voluntary participation in the operation of a ship or of an aircraft with knowledge of facts making it a pirate ship or aircraft;
3. Any act of inciting or of intentionally facilitating an act described in sub-paragraph 1 or sub-paragraph 2 of this Article.

Article 16

The acts of piracy, as defined in Article 15, committed by a warship, government ship or government aircraft whose crew has mutinied and taken control of the ship or aircraft are assimilated to acts committed by a private ship.

Article 17

A ship or aircraft is considered a pirate ship or aircraft if it is intended by the persons in dominant control to be used for the purpose of committing one of the acts referred to in Article 15. The same applies if the ship or aircraft has been used to commit any such act, so long as it remains under the control of the persons guilty of that act.

Article 18

A ship or aircraft may retain its nationality although it has become a pirate ship or aircraft. The retention or loss of nationality is determined by the law of the State from which such nationality was derived.

Article 19

On the high seas, or in any other place outside the jurisdiction of any State, every State may seize a pirate ship or aircraft, or a ship taken by piracy and under the control of pirates, and arrest the persons and seize the property on board. The courts of the State which carried out the seizure may decide upon the penalties to be imposed, and may also determine the action to be taken with regard to the ships, aircraft or property, subject to the rights of third parties acting in good faith.

Article 20

Where the seizure of a ship or aircraft on suspicion of piracy has been effected without adequate grounds, the State making the seizure shall be liable to the State the nationality of which is possessed by the ship or aircraft, for any loss or damage caused by the seizure.

Article 21

A seizure on account of piracy may only be carried out by warships or military aircraft, or other ships or aircraft on government service authorized to that effect.

Article 22

1. Except where acts of interference derive from powers conferred by treaty, a warship which encounters a foreign merchant ship on the high seas is not justified in boarding her unless there is reasonable ground for suspecting:

   (a) That the ship is engaged in piracy; or
   (b) That the ship is engaged in the slave trade; or
   (c) That though flying a foreign flag or refusing to show its flag, the ship is, in reality, of the same nationality as the warship.

2. In the cases provided for in sub-paragraphs (a), (b) and (c) above, the warship may proceed to verify the ship's right to fly its flag. To this end, it may send a boat under the command of an officer to the suspected ship. If suspicion remains after the documents have been checked, it may proceed to a further examination on board the ship, which must be carried out with all possible consideration.
3. If the suspicions prove to be unfounded, and provided that the ship boarded has not committed any act justifying them, it shall be compensated for any loss or damage that may have been sustained.

Guidance to Shipowners and Ship Operators, MSC.1/Circ.1334

Guidance to shipowners and ship operators, shipmasters and crews on preventing and suppressing acts of piracy and armed robbery against ships (MSC.1/Circ.1334, June 23, 2009)

* * *

Annex

GUIDANCE TO SHIPOWNERS, COMPANIES, SHIP OPERATORS, SHIPMASTERS AND CREWS ON PREVENTING AND SUPPRESSING ACTS OF PIRACY AND ARMED ROBBERY AGAINST SHIPS

Introduction

1. This circular aims at bringing to the attention of shipowners, companies, ship operators masters and crews the precautions to be taken to reduce the risks of piracy on the high seas and armed robbery against ships at anchor, off ports or when underway through a coastal State's territorial waters. It outlines steps that should be taken to reduce the risk of such attacks, possible responses to them and the vital need to report attacks, both successful and unsuccessful, to the authorities of the relevant coastal State and to the ships' own maritime Administration. Such reports are to be made as soon as possible, to enable necessary action to be taken.

2. It is important to bear in mind that shipowners, companies, ship operators, masters and crews can and should take measures to protect themselves

and their ships from pirates and armed robbers. While security forces can often advise on these measures, and flag States are required to take such measures as are necessary to ensure that owners and masters accept their responsibility, ultimately it is the responsibility of shipowners, companies, ship operators, masters and crews to take seamanlike precautions when their ships navigate in areas where the threat of piracy and armed robbery exists. Planning should give consideration to the crew's welfare during and after a period of captivity by pirates or armed robbers. Before operating in waters where attacks have been known to occur, it is imperative for shipowners, companies, ship operators and masters concerned to gather accurate information on the situation in the area. To this end the information on attacks and attempted attacks gathered, analyzed and distributed by the IMO, IMB's Piracy Reporting Centre and the ReCAAP Information Sharing Centre (ReCAAP ISC), the Maritime Security Centre, Horn of Africa, Governments and others is vital information, upon which precautionary measures should be based.

* * *

Discretion by Masters and Members of the Crew

6. Masters should bear in mind the possibility that attackers are monitoring ship-to-shore communications and using intercepted information to select their targets. Masters should however also be aware that switching off AIS in high-risk areas reduces ability of the supporting naval vessels to track and trace vessels, which may require assistance. Caution should also be exercised when transmitting information on cargo or valuables on board by radio in areas where attacks occur.

7. It is up to the master's professional judgment to decide whether the AIS system should be switched off, in order for the ship not to be detected, when entering areas where piracy is an imminent threat, however the master should balance the risk of attack against the need to maintain the safety of navigation and, in particular, the requirements of COLREG Rule 7 on Risk of collision, and should act in accordance with the guidance in resolutions A.917(22) and A.956(23). The master should also be aware that other ships operating in high-risk areas may have taken a decision to switch off the AIS system. In the event of an attack, masters should ensure to the extent feasible that AIS is turned on again and transmitting to enable security forces to locate the vessel.

8. Members of the crew going ashore in ports in affected areas should be advised not to discuss the voyage or cargo particulars with persons unconnected with the ship's business.

* * *

The Pre-Piracy/Armed Robbery Phase

13. Written procedures on how to prevent or suppress attacks of pirates and armed robbers should be found either in the ship's Safety Management System or in the ship security plan.

14. The entry into force of the ISPS Code and the ISM Code have made security assessments and risk assessments an integral part of the safety and security precautions. Measures to prevent and suppress piracy and armed robbery against ships should be part of either the emergency response procedures in the safety management system, or as a situation that requires increased alertness, should become a part of the procedures in the ship security plan.

15. All ships operating in waters or ports where attacks occur should carry out a security assessment as a preparation for development of measures to prevent attacks of pirates or armed robbers against ships and on how to react should an attack occur. This should be included as a part of the emergency response procedures in the safety management system or a part of the procedures in the ship security plan. The security assessment should take into account the basic parameters of the operation including:

1. the risks that may be faced including any information given on characteristics of piracy or armed robbery in the specific area;
2. the ship's actual size, freeboard, maximum speed, and the type of cargo;
3. the number of crew members available, their proficiency and training;
4. the ability to establish secure areas on board ship; and
5. the equipment on board, including any surveillance and detection equipment that has been provided.

* * *

Routeing and Delaying Anchoring

20. If at all possible, ships should be routed away from areas where attacks are known to have taken place and, in particular, seek to avoid bottlenecks. When deciding on a ship's route the company should take into consideration the type of ship, the size and maximum speed as well as the freeboard and the dangerous nature of the cargo. If convoys are offered such a measure should also be considered to avoid serious attacks on ships at sea. If ships are approaching ports where attacks have taken place on ships at anchor, rather than ships underway, and it is known that the ship will have to anchor off port for some time, consideration should be given to delaying anchoring by longer routeing to remain well off shore or other methods by which the period during which the ship will be at risk is reduced. Contact with port authorities should ensure that berthing priorities are not affected. Charter party agreements should recognize that ships may need to delay arrival at ports

where attacks occur either when no berth is available for the ship or offshore loading or unloading will be delayed for a protracted period.

* * *

Practice the Implementation of the Ship Security Plan

21. Prior to entering an area, where attacks have occurred, the ship's crew should have practiced the procedures set down in the ship security plan. Alarm signals and procedures should have been thoroughly practised and training and drills carried out.

* * *

Precautions at Anchor or In Port

24. In areas where attacks occur, the ships' masters should exercise vigilance when their ships are preparing to anchor or while at anchor. Furthermore, it is important to limit, record and control those who are allowed access to a ship when in port or at anchor. Photographing those who board the ship can be a useful deterrent or assist the identification of attackers who may have had access to the ship prior to their attack. Given that attackers may use knowledge of cargo manifests to select their targets, every effort should be made to limit the circulation of documents which give information on the cargoes on board or their location on the ship. Similar precautions should be taken in regard to the circulation of information on crew members' personal valuables and ship's equipment, as these items are also targeted by attackers.

25. Prior to leaving port, the ship should be thoroughly searched and all doors or access points secured or controlled. This is particularly important in the case of the bridge, engine-room, steering space and other vulnerable areas.

* * *

29. It is particularly important to maintain a radar and visual watch for craft which may be trailing the ship when underway but which could close in quickly when mounting an attack. Small craft which appear to be matching the speed of the ship on a parallel or following course should always be treated with suspicion. When a suspect craft has been noticed, it is important that an effective all-round watch is maintained for fear the first craft is a decoy with the intention to board the ship from a second craft while attention is focused on the first.

* * *

39. If suspicious movements are identified which may result in an imminent attack, the ship is advised to contact the relevant RCC, the flag State or other relevant information centres such as the IMB Piracy Reporting Centre or the ReCAAP ISC. Where the master believes these movements could

constitute a direct danger to navigation, consideration should be given to broadcasting an "All stations (CQ)" "danger message" as a warning to other ships in the vicinity as well as advising the appropriate RCC. A danger message should be transmitted in plain language using the "safety" priority. All such measures shall be preceded by the safety signal (Sécurité).[1]

* * *

Lighting

45. Ships should use the maximum lighting available consistent with safe navigation, having regard in particular to the provisions of Rule 20(b) of the 1972 Collision Regulations. Bow and overside lights should be left on if it can be done without endangering navigation. Ships must not keep on deck lights when underway, as it may lead other ships to assume the ship is at anchor. Wide beam floods could illuminate the area astern of the ship. Signal projector lights can be used systematically to probe for suspect craft using the radar guidance if possible. So far as is practicable crew members on duty outside the ship's secure areas when in port or at anchor should avail themselves of shadow and avoid being silhouetted by deck lights as this may make them targets for seizure by approaching attackers.

* * *

Use of Defensive Measures

55. Experiences show that robust actions from the ship, which is approached by pirates, may discourage the attackers. Outrunning attacks may be an appropriate preventive maneuver. If the situation permits, the speed should be increased and maintained at the maximum level. Provided that navigational safety allows, masters should also consider "riding off" attackers' craft by heavy wheel movements and turning into wind so as to remove any lee from either side of the ship. Heavy wheel movements should only be used when attackers are alongside and boarding is imminent. The effect of the bow wave and wash may deter would-be attackers and make it difficult for them to attach poles or grappling irons to the ship. Maneuvers of this kind should not be used in confined or congested waters or close inshore or by ships constrained by their draught in the confined deep water routes found, for example, in the Straits of Malacca and Singapore.

Use of Passive and Non-Lethal Devices

56. The use of passive and non-lethal measures such as netting, wire, electric fencing, and long-range acoustic devices may be appropriate preventive measures to deter attackers and delay boarding.

57. The use of water hoses should also be considered though they may be difficult to train if evasive maneuvering is also taking place. Water pressures of 80 lb per square inch and above have deterred and repulsed attackers. Not only does the attacker have to fight against the jet of water but the flow may swamp his/her boat and damage engines and electrical systems. Special fittings for training hoses could be considered which would also provide protection for the hose operator. A number of spare fire hoses could be rigged and tied down to be pressurized at short notice if a potential attack is detected.

58. Employing evasive maneuvers and hoses must rest on a determination to successfully deter attackers or to delay their boarding to allow all crew members to gain the sanctuary of secure areas. Continued heavy wheel movements with attackers on board may lessen their confidence that they will be able to return safely to their craft and may persuade them to disembark quickly. However, responses of this kind could lead to reprisals by the attackers if they seize crew members and should not be engaged in unless the master is convinced he can use them to advantage and without risk to those on board. They should not be used if the attackers have already seized crew members.

Firearms

59. With respect to the carriage of firearms on board, masters, shipowners and companies should be aware that ships entering the territorial sea and/or ports of a State are subject to that State's legislation. It should be borne in mind that importation of firearms is subject to port and coastal State regulations. It should also be borne in mind that carrying firearms may pose an even greater danger if the ship is carrying flammable cargo or similar types of dangerous goods.

Non-Arming of Seafarers

60. The carrying and use of firearms by seafarers for personal protection or for the protection of a ship is strongly discouraged. Seafarers are civilians and the use of firearms requires special training and aptitudes and the risk of accidents with firearms carried on board ship is great. Carriage of arms on board ship may encourage attackers to carry firearms or even more dangerous weapons, thereby escalating an already dangerous situation. Any firearm on board may itself become an attractive target for an attacker.

61. It should also be borne in mind that shooting at suspected pirates may impose a legal risk for the master, shipowner or company, such as collateral damages. In some jurisdictions, killing a national may have unforeseen consequences even for a person who believes he or she has acted in self defense. Also the differing customs or security requirements for the carriage and

importation of firearms should be considered, as taking a small handgun into the territory of some countries may be considered an offence.

***

Appendix 4

Extract from UN Guidance on Surviving as a Hostage

Introduction

Over the past few years the number of seafarers who have been kidnapped or taken hostage has increased substantially. Every hostage or kidnap situation is different. There are no strict rules of behavior; however, there are a number of steps which you can take to minimize the effects of detention and enhance your ability to cope and to see the incident through to a successful release.

Survival Considerations

These techniques have been successfully employed by others who have been taken hostage:

- No one can tell an individual whether he or she should resist or not if taken hostage/kidnapped. This decision must be made by each person's own assessment of the circumstances. Resisting the attempt may be extremely risky. You may be injured if you attempt to resist armed individuals. It is possible that you will immediately be blindfolded and drugged.
- Being taken hostage is probably one of the most devastating experiences a seafarer can undergo. The first 15 to 45 minutes of a hostage situation are the most dangerous. Follow the instructions of your captors. They are in a highly emotional state, regardless of whether they are psychologically unstable or caught in an untenable situation. They are in a fight or flight reactive state and could strike out. Your job is to survive. After the initial shock wears off, your captors are able to better recognize their position. Be certain you can explain everything on your person.
- Immediately after you have been taken, pause, take a deep breath and try to relax. Fear of death or injury is a normal reaction to this situation. Recognizing your reactions may help you adapt more effectively. A hostage usually experiences greatest anxiety in the hours following the incident. This anxiety will begin to decline when the person realizes he/she is still alive—at least for now—and a certain routine sets in. Feelings of depression and helplessness will continue throughout captivity and most hostages will feel deeply humiliated by what they undergo during captivity. Most hostages, however, will quickly adapt to the situation. Remember your responsibility is to survive.
- Do not be a hero; do not talk back or act "tough". Accept your situation. Any action on your part could bring a violent reaction from your captors. Past

experiences show that those who react aggressively place themselves at greater risk than those who behave passively.

- Keep a low profile. Avoid appearing to study your abductors, although, to the extent possible, you should make mental notes about their mannerisms, clothes and apparent rank structure. This may help the authorities after your release.

Try to think of persuasive reasons why hostage-takers should not harm you. Encourage them to let authorities know your whereabouts and condition. Suggest ways in which you may benefit your captors in negotiations that would free you. It is important that your abductors view you as a person worthy of compassion and mercy. Never beg, plead or cry. You must gain your captors' respect as well as sympathy.

- If you end up serving as a negotiator between hostage-takers and authorities, make sure the messages are conveyed accurately. Be prepared to speak on the radio or telephone.
- Escape only if you are sure you will be successful. If you are caught, your captors may use violence to teach you and others a lesson.
- At every opportunity, emphasize that, as a seafarer you are neutral and not involved in politics.
- If there is a rescue attempt by force, drop quickly to the floor and seek cover. Keep your hands over your head. When appropriate, identify yourself. In many cases, former hostages feel bitter about the treatment they receive after their release. Most hostages feel a strong need to tell their story in detail. If assistance in this regard is not provided, request a post-traumatic stress debriefing. Bear in mind that the emotional problems of a former hostage do not appear immediately. Sometimes they appear months later. Whatever happens, readjustment after the incident is a slow process requiring patience and understanding. As soon as the hostage realizes that he or she is a normal person having a normal reaction to an abnormal situation, the healing process can begin.
- Be patient.

***

Appendix 7

Decalogue of Safety

1. Watch over the ship and the cargo.

It is the duty of every Master to take care of the cargo and take precautionary measures for the complete safety of the ship, as well as that of the activities carried out on board by the crew or other persons employed on board. . . .

2. Illuminate the ship and its side

Keep the ship illuminated, particularly, the outer side and the whole length of the deck, using high-powered floodlights. Bad visibility impedes the action of the watchmen, constituting a favorable factor for unlawful activities. . . .

3. Establish communication for outside support

Whenever possible, install a telephone line with easy access for the watchman or crew member on duty. Ask for assistance by the telephone. Remember also the list of stations, which will be on permanent watch on VHF Channel 16. These stations can forward the request for assistance to the competent authorities.

4. Control of accesses to the cargo and to living quarters

The Master's cabin is one of the main objectives of the assailants who are looking for money and the master keys to other living quarters, to steal the crew's personal effects of value and nautical equipment from the bridge. The cabins and other living quarters should be kept locked whenever their occupants are absent. . . .

5. Keep the portholes closed

. . . Try also to keep the accesses to internal areas locked, guaranteeing the entry and exit by the gangway watchman.

6. Do not leave valuables exposed

Try to reduce the opportunities of robbery by putting all portable equipment, which is not in use to its place of storage. . . .

7. Keep the gangways raised

At anchorages and in port, make the access difficult by keeping the gangways and rope ladders raised. In port, only leave the gangway to the dockside down.

8. In case of an assault

Do not hesitate to sound the ship's general alarm in case of a threat of assault; try to keep adequate lighting to permanently dazzle the opponents, in case of an attempt by strangers to climb the ship's side; raise the alarm, by VHF Channel 16, to the ships in the area and to the permanent watch system of the authorities ashore (cite the existing structure in the port). . . . [I]f appropriate, to protect the lives of those onboard, use measures to repel the boarding by employing powerful floodlights for dazzling the aggressors or using jets of water or signaling rockets against the areas of boarding; and do not attempt any heroic acts.

9. Keep the contracted watchmen under the control of the officer of the watch

. . . Do not allow the watchman to leave the gangway, unless he is relieved by another watchman or a crew member.

10. Communicate to the police any occurrence relating to robbery, theft or assault

Occurrences involving assault or robbery should be communicated to the Security forces, for the pertinent legal steps to be taken.

Note

1. Specific guidance in respect of waters off the coast of Somalia has been issued as MSC.1/Circ.1332 and also MSC.1/Circ.1302.

Recommendations to Governments, MSC.1/Circ.1333

Recommendations to Governments for preventing and suppressing piracy and armed robbery against ships (MSC.1/Circ.1333, June 26, 2009)

* * *

Annex Recommendations to Governments for Preventing and Suppressing Piracy[1] and Armed Robbery against Ships[2]

Piracy and Armed Robbery against Ships

1. Before embarking on any set of measures or recommendations, it is imperative for governmental or other agencies concerned to gather accurate statistics of the incidents of piracy and armed robbery against ships, to collate these statistics under both type and area and to assess the nature of the attacks with special emphasis on types of attack, accurate geographical location and *modus operandi* of the wrongdoers and to disseminate or publish these statistics to all interested parties in a format that is understandable and usable. Advanced intelligence could also prove useful in obtaining information to Governments in order to be able to act in a coordinated manner even before an attack occurs. Based on the statistics of the incidents and any intelligence of piracy and armed robbery against ships Governments should issue to ships entitled to fly their flag, as necessary, advice and guidance on any appropriate additional precautionary measures ships may need to put in place to protect themselves from attack. Governments should involve representatives of shipowners and seafarers in developing these measures to prevent and suppress piracy and armed robbery against ships.

2. In any ongoing campaign against piracy and armed robbery, it is necessary, wherever possible, to neutralize the activities of pirates and armed robbers. As these people are criminals under both international law and most national laws, this task will generally fall to the security forces of the States involved. Governments should avoid engaging in negotiations with these criminals and seek to bring perpetrators of piracy and armed robbery against ships to justice. Negotiating with criminals in a case regarding hijacking of a ship may encourage potential perpetrators to seek economic revenue through piracy.

Self Protection

3. Ships can and should take measures to protect themselves from pirates and armed robbers. These measures are recommended in MSC.1/Circ.1334. While security forces can often advise on these measures, and flag States are required to take such measures as are necessary to ensure that owners and masters accept their responsibility, ultimately it is the responsibility of owners, companies, ship operators and masters to take seamanlike precautions when their ships navigate in areas where the threat of piracy and armed robbery exists. Flag States should make shipowners/companies aware of any UN Security Council, IMO, or any other UN resolutions on piracy and any recommendations therein relevant for the shipowner, ship operator, the master and crew when operating in areas where piracy or armed robbery against ships occur.

4. With respect to the carriage of firearms on board, the flag State should be aware that merchant ships and fishing vessels entering the territorial sea and/or ports of another State are subject to that State's legislation. It should be borne in mind that importation of firearms is subject to port and coastal State regulations. It should also be borne in mind that carrying firearms may pose an even greater danger if the ship is carrying flammable cargo or similar types of dangerous goods.

Non-arming of Seafarers

5. For legal and safety reasons, flag States should strongly discourage the carrying and use of firearms by seafarers for personal protection or for the protection of a ship. Seafarers are civilians and the use of firearms requires special training and aptitudes and the risk of accidents with firearms carried on board ship is great. Carriage of arms on board ships may encourage attackers to carry firearms or even more dangerous weapons, thereby escalating an already dangerous situation. Any firearm on board may itself become an attractive target for an attacker.

Use of Unarmed Security Personnel

6. The use of unarmed security personnel is a matter for individual shipowners, companies, and ship operators to decide. It should be fully acceptable to provide an enhanced lookout capability this way.

Use of Privately Contracted Armed Security Personnel

7. The use of privately contracted armed security personnel on board ships may lead to an escalation of violence. The carriage of such personnel and their weapons is subject to flag State legislation and policies and is a matter for flag States to determine in consultation with shipowners, companies, and ship operators, if and under which conditions this will be allowed. Flag States should take into account the possible escalation of violence, which could result from carriage of armed personnel on board merchant ships, when deciding on its policy.

Military Teams or Law Enforcement Officers Duly Authorized by Government

8. The use of military, or law enforcement officers duly authorized by the Government of the flag State to carry firearms for the security of the ship is a matter for the flag State to authorize in consultation with shipowners, companies, and ship operators. Flag States should provide clarity of their policy on the use of such teams on board vessels entitled to fly their flag.

* * *

14. Article 100 of the 1982 United Nations Convention on the Law of the Sea (UNCLOS) requires all States to cooperate to the fullest possible extent in the repression of piracy. In this regard, States interested in the security of maritime activities should take an active part in repression of and fight against piracy, particularly in areas where the United Nations Security Council expresses concern about the imminent threat of attacks by pirates and calls upon States to do so. This could be done by prosecuting suspected pirates, contributing to capacity building efforts and by deploying naval vessels and aircraft in accordance with international law to patrol the affected areas.

15. On communication and cooperation between various agencies, and the response time after an incident has been reported to the coastal State:

1. an incident command system for tactical as well as operational response should be adopted in each country concerned to provide a common terminology; integrated communications; a unified command structure; consolidated action

plans; a manageable span of control; designated incident facilities; and comprehensive resource management;
2. existing mechanisms for dealing with other maritime security matters, e.g., smuggling, drug-trafficking and terrorism, should be incorporated into the incident command system in order to allow for efficient use of limited resources;
3. procedures for rapidly relaying alerts received by communication centres to the entity responsible for action should be developed or, if existing, kept under review; and
4. Governments should by bilateral or multilateral agreements cooperate in establishing, when appropriate, a single point of contact for ships to report piracy threats or activities in specific high threat areas.

* * *

24. On investigation into reported incidents and prosecution of pirates and armed robbers when caught:

1. it should be firmly established which entity in each country has responsibility and legal authority for carrying out post-attack investigations, since lack of clarity during the hours after an incident may result in missed investigative opportunities and loss or deterioration of evidence;
2. the appointed investigation agency should have personnel trained in standard investigative techniques and who are familiar with the legal requirements of the courts of their countries, as it is widely assumed that prosecution, conviction and confiscation of assets of offenders are the most effective means of discouraging would-be offenders;
3. as offenders may be involved in other kinds of offences, piracy and armed robbery against ships should not be viewed in isolation and useful information should, therefore, be sought in existing criminal records; and
4. systems should be in place to ensure that potentially useful information is disseminated to all appropriate parties, including investigators.

* * *

Criminal Jurisdiction

26. A person apprehended at sea outside the territorial sea of any State for committing acts of piracy or armed robbery against ships, should be prosecuted under the laws of the investigating State by mutual agreement with other substantially interested States.

Substantially interested State means a State:

1. which is the flag State of a ship that is the subject of an investigation; or
2. in whose territorial sea an incident has occurred; or

3. where an incident caused, or threatened, serious harm to the environment of that State, or within those areas over which the State is entitled to exercise jurisdiction as recognized under international law; or
4. where the consequences of an incident caused, or threatened, serious harm to that State or to artificial islands, installations or structures over which it is entitled to exercise jurisdiction; or
5. where, as a result of an incident, nationals of that State lost their lives or received serious injuries; or
6. that has at its disposal important information that may be of use to the investigation; or
7. that, for some other reason, establishes an interest that is considered significant by the lead investigating State; or
8. that was requested by another State to assist in the repression of violence against crews, passengers, ships and cargoes or the collection of evidence; or
9. that intervened under UNCLOS article 100, exercised its right of visit, under UNCLOS article 110, or effected the seizure of a pirate/armed robber, ship or aircraft under UNCLOS article 105 or in port or on land.

***

29. Flag States should require all ships operating in waters where attacks occur to have measures to prevent attacks and attempted attacks of piracy and armed robbery against ships and on how to act if such an attack or attempted attack occurs, as part of the emergency response procedures in the safety management system, or part of the ship security plan. Such measures should include a full spectrum of appropriate passive and active security measures. The ship security plan and emergency response plans should be based on a risk assessment which take into account the basic parameters of the operation including:

1. the risks that may be faced;
2. the ship's actual size, freeboard, maximum speed and the type of cargo, which is being transported;
3. the number of crew members available, their capability and training;
4. the ability to establish secure areas on board ship; and
5. the equipment on board, including any surveillance and detection equipment that has been provided.

***

32 Coastal States Situated in Areas Affected by Piracy and Armed Robbery

1. in order to be able to respond, as quickly as possible, to any report from ships on piracy and armed robbery attacks, every piracy or armed robbery

threat area should be adequately covered by Coast Earth Stations which are continuously operational, and which preferably are situated in the littoral State responsible for the area or in neighboring States;

2. neighboring countries having common borders in areas which can be characterized as piracy and armed robbery threat areas should establish cooperation agreements with respect to preventing and suppressing piracy and armed robbery[1]. Such agreements should include the coordination of patrol activities in such areas. An example of a model agreement is attached as appendix 6;

3. on further development of regional cooperation, a regional agreement to facilitate coordinated response at the tactical as well as the operational level should be concluded between the countries concerned:

3.1. such an agreement should specify how information would be disseminated; establish joint command and control procedures (a regional incident command system); ensure efficient communications; set policies for joint operations and entry and pursuit; establish the links between entities involved in all maritime security matters; establish joint specialized training of and the exchange of views between investigators; and establish joint exercises between tactical and operational entities . . . :

* * *

Appendix 6

Draft[3] Regional Agreement on Cooperation in Preventing and Suppressing Acts of Piracy and Armed Robbery Against Ships

* * *

Program for law enforcement officials aboard another Party's vessels

1. The Parties shall establish a law enforcement liaison officer program among their law enforcement authorities. Each Party may designate a coordinator to organize its program activities and to notify the other Parties of the types of vessels and officials involved in the program.

* * *

3. Subject to the law of the Parties involved, these liaison officers may, in appropriate circumstances:

1. embark on the law enforcement vessels of other Parties;
2. authorize the pursuit, by the law enforcement vessels on which they are embarked, of suspect vessels fleeing into the territorial waters of the liaison officer's Party;
3. authorize the law enforcement vessels on which they are embarked to conduct patrols to suppress acts of armed robbery against ships in the liaison officer's Party's national waters; and

4. enforce the laws of the Parties in national waters, or seaward there from in the exercise of the right of hot pursuit or otherwise in accordance with international law.

4. When a liaison officer is embarked on another Party's vessel, and the enforcement action being carried out is pursuant to the liaison officer's authority, any search or seizure of property, any detention of a person, and any use of force pursuant to this Agreement, whether or not involving weapons, shall be carried out by the liaison officer, except as follows:

1. crew members of the other Party's vessel may assist in any such action if expressly requested to do so by the liaison officer and only to the extent and in the manner requested. Such request may only be made, agreed to, and acted upon in accordance with the applicable laws and policies; and
2. such crew members may use force in self-defense, in accordance with the applicable laws and policies.

5. Parties may only conduct operations to suppress piracy and armed robbery in the waters of another Party with the permission of that Party in any of the following circumstances:

1. an embarked liaison officer so authorizes;
2. on those exceptional occasions when a suspect vessel, detected seaward of national waters, enters the national waters of another Party and no liaison officer is embarked in a law enforcement vessel, and no law enforcement vessel from the Party whose national waters have been entered by a suspect vessel is immediately available to investigate, the law enforcement vessel may follow the suspect vessel into national waters, in order to board the suspect vessel and secure the scene, while awaiting expeditious instructions and the arrival from law enforcement authorities of the Party in whose national waters the event took place;
3. on those equally exceptional occasions when a suspect vessel is detected within a Party's national waters, and no liaison officer is embarked from that Party and no law enforcement vessel is immediately available to investigate from that Party, the law enforcement vessel from another Party may enter the national waters, in order to board the suspect vessel and secure the scene, while awaiting expeditious instructions from the law enforcement authorities and the arrival of law enforcement officials of the Party in whose national waters the event has occurred; and
4. Parties shall provide prior notice to the law enforcement authority of the Party in whose national waters the event took place of action to be taken under subparagraphs.2 and.3 of this paragraph, unless it is not operationally feasible

to do so. In any case, notice of the action shall be provided to the relevant law enforcement authority without delay.

* * *

Jurisdiction over Detained Vessel

1. In all cases arising in national waters, or concerning vessels flying the flag of a Party seaward of any State's territorial sea, the Party whose flag is being flown by the suspect vessel shall have the primary right to exercise jurisdiction over a detained vessel, cargo and/or persons on board (including seizure, forfeiture, arrest, and prosecution), provided, however, that the Party may, subject to its constitution and laws, waive its primary right to exercise jurisdiction and authorize the enforcement of another Party's law against the vessel, cargo and/or persons on board.

* * *

Implementation

1. Operations to suppress piracy and armed robbery pursuant to this Agreement shall be carried out only against suspect vessels, including vessels without nationality, and vessels assimilated to vessels without nationality.
2. All Parties shall utilize the Incident Command System when operating in conjunction with another Party in an operation within the scope of this Agreement.
3. All Parties undertake to agree on uniform reporting criteria in order to ensure that an accurate assessment of the threat is developed. Furthermore, all Parties shall endeavour to ensure that reporting ships are not unduly detained for investigative purposes. A summary of reports to each Party shall be shared at least annually with the other Parties.
4. A Party conducting a boarding and search pursuant to this Agreement shall promptly notify the flag State of the results thereof. The relevant Party shall timely report to the other Party, consistent with its laws, on the status of all investigations, prosecutions and judicial proceedings resulting from enforcement action taken pursuant to this Agreement where evidence of piracy and armed robbery has been found.
5. Each Party shall ensure that its law enforcement officials, when conducting boardings and searches [and air interception] activities pursuant to this Agreement, act in accordance with the applicable national laws and policies of that Party and with the applicable international law and accepted international practices.
6. Boardings and searches pursuant to this Agreement shall be carried out by law enforcement officials from law enforcement vessels [or aircraft]. The

boarding and search teams may operate from such ships [and aircraft] of the relevant Parties, and seaward of the territorial sea of any State, from such ships of other Parties as may be agreed upon by the Parties. The boarding and search team may carry standard law enforcement small arms.

Notes

1. The following definition of piracy is contained in Article 101 of the 1982 United Nations Convention on the Law of the Sea (UNCLOS) (Article 101):

> Piracy consists of any of the following acts:
>
> (a) any illegal acts of violence or detention, or any act of depredation, committed for private ends by the crew or the passengers of a private ship or a private aircraft, and directed:
>
> (i) on the high seas, against another ship or aircraft, or against persons or property on board such ship or aircraft;
>
> (ii) against a ship, aircraft, persons or property in a place outside the jurisdiction of any State;
>
> (b) any act of voluntary participation in the operation of a ship or of an aircraft with knowledge of facts making it a pirate ship or aircraft;
>
> (c) any act inciting or of intentionally facilitating an act described in subparagraph (a) or (b).

2. The subregional meeting on piracy and armed robbery against ships in the Western Indian Ocean, Gulf of Aden, and Red Sea area, held in Dar es Salaam, United Republic of Tanzania, from April 14–18, 2008, agreed to modify this definition. Consistent with the ReCAAP Agreement, the private ends motive has been added to the definition. The formulation within internal waters, archipelagic waters, and territorial sea replaced within a state's jurisdiction. The new formulation reflects the views of France, supported by other states participating in the meeting, that the definition for armed robbery against ships should not be applicable to acts committed seaward of the territorial sea. The new definition reads: "Armed robbery against ships means any unlawful act of violence or detention or any act of depredation, or threat thereof, other than an act of piracy, committed for private ends and directed against a ship or against persons or property on board such a ship, within a State's internal waters, archipelagic waters and territorial sea."

3. Note: Attention should also be given to existing regional agreements such as the Djibouti Code of Conduct, the ReCAAP, and the IMO/MOWCA Memorandum of Understanding on the Establishment of a Regional Integrated Coast Guard Network in West and Central Africa.

National Strategy for Maritime Security

U.S. National Strategy for Maritime Security (2005)[1]

Section I—Introduction to Maritime Security

The safety and economic security of the United States depend in substantial part upon the secure use of the world's oceans. The United States has a vital national interest in maritime security. We must be prepared to stop terrorists and rogue states before they can threaten or use weapons of mass destruction or engage in other attacks against the United States and our allies and friends. Toward that end, the United States must take full advantage of strengthened alliances and other international cooperative arrangements, innovations in the use of law enforcement personnel and military forces, advances in technology, and strengthened intelligence collection, analysis, and dissemination.

Salt water covers more than two-thirds of the Earth's surface. These waters are a single, great ocean, an immense maritime domain[2] that affects life everywhere. Although its four principal geographical divisions—Atlantic, Arctic, Indian, and Pacific—have different names, this continuous body of water is the Earth's greatest defining geographic feature.

The oceans, much of which are global commons under no State's jurisdiction, offer all nations, even landlocked States, a network of sea-lanes or highways that is of enormous importance to their security and prosperity. They are likewise a source of food, mineral resources, and recreation, and they support commerce among nations. They also act as both a barrier to and a conduit for threats to the security of people everywhere. Like all other countries, the United States is highly dependent on the oceans for its security and the welfare of its people and economy.

In today's economy, the oceans have increased importance, allowing all countries to participate in the global marketplace. More than 80 percent of the world's trade travels by water and forges a global maritime link. About half the world's trade by value, and 90 percent of the general cargo, are transported in containers. Shipping is the heart of the global economy, but it is vulnerable to attack in two key areas. Spread across Asia, North America, and Europe are 30 megaports/cities that constitute the world's primary, interdependent trading web. Through a handful of international straits and canals pass 75 percent of the world's maritime trade and half its daily oil consumption. International commerce is at risk in the major trading hubs as well as at a handful of strategic chokepoints.

The infrastructure and systems that span the maritime domain, owned largely by the private sector, have increasingly become both targets of and potential conveyances for dangerous and illicit activities. Moreover, much of what occurs in the maritime domain with respect to vessel movements, activities, cargoes, intentions, or ownership is often difficult to discern. The oceans are increasingly threatened by illegal exploitation of living marine resources and increased competition over nonliving marine resources. Although the global economy continues to increase the value of the oceans' role as highways for commerce and providers of resources, technology and the forces of globalization have lessened their role as barriers. Thus, this continuous domain serves as a vast, ready, and largely unsecured medium for an array of threats by nations, terrorists, and criminals.

Defeating this array of threats to maritime security—including the threat or use of weapons of mass destruction (WMD)[3]—requires a common understanding and a joint effort for action on a global scale. Because the economic well-being of people in the United States and across the globe depends heavily upon the trade and commerce that traverses the oceans, maritime security must be a top priority. Maritime security is required to ensure freedom of the seas; facilitate freedom of navigation and commerce; advance prosperity and freedom; and protect the resources of the ocean. Nations have a common interest in achieving two complementary objectives: to facilitate the vibrant maritime commerce that underpins economic security, and to protect against ocean-related terrorist, hostile, criminal, and dangerous acts. Since all nations benefit from this collective security, all nations must share in the responsibility for maintaining maritime security by countering the threats in this domain.

* * *

The safety and economic security of the United States depends upon the secure use of the world's oceans. Since the attacks of September 11, 2001, the Federal government has reviewed and strengthened all of its strategies to combat the evolving threat in the War on Terrorism. Various departments have each carried out maritime security strategies, which have provided an effective layer of security since 2001. In December 2004, the President directed the Secretaries of the Department of Defense and Homeland Security to lead the Federal effort to develop a comprehensive National Strategy for Maritime Security, to better integrate and synchronize the existing Department-level strategies and ensure their effective and efficient implementation.

Maritime security is best achieved by blending public and private maritime security activities on a global scale into an integrated effort that addresses all maritime threats. The new National Strategy for Maritime Security aligns all Federal government maritime security programs and initiatives into a comprehensive and cohesive national effort involving appropriate Federal, State, local, and private sector entities.

In addition to this Strategy, the Departments have developed eight supporting plans to address the specific threats and challenges of the maritime environment. While the plans address different aspects of maritime security, they are mutually linked and reinforce each other. The supporting plans include:

- National Plan to Achieve Domain Awareness
- Global Maritime Intelligence Integration Plan
- Interim Maritime Operational Threat Response Plan
- International Outreach and Coordination Strategy
- Maritime Infrastructure Recovery Plan
- Maritime Transportation System Security Plan
- Maritime Commerce Security Plan
- Domestic Outreach Plan

Development of these plans was guided by the security principles outlined in this National Strategy for Maritime Security. These plans will be updated on a periodic basis in response to changes in the maritime threat, the world environment, and national security policies.

Together, the National Strategy for Maritime Security and its eight supporting plans present a comprehensive national effort to promote global economic stability and protect legitimate activities while preventing hostile or illegal acts within the maritime domain.

***

Section II—Threats to Maritime Security

Transnational Criminal and Piracy Threats

The continued growth in legitimate international commerce in the maritime domain has been accompanied by growth in the use of the maritime domain for criminal purposes. The smuggling of people, drugs, weapons, and other contraband, as well as piracy and armed robbery against vessels, pose a threat to maritime security. Piracy and incidents of maritime crime tend to be concentrated in areas of heavy commercial maritime activity, especially where there is significant political and economic instability, or in regions with little or no maritime law enforcement capacity. Today's pirates and criminals are usually well organized and well equipped with advanced communications, weapons, and high-speed craft. The capabilities to board and commandeer large underway vessels—demonstrated in numerous piracy incidents—could also be employed to facilitate terrorist acts.

Just as the world's oceans are avenues for a nation's overseas commerce, they are also the highways for the import or export of illegal commodities. Maritime drug trafficking[4] generates vast amounts of money for international organized crime syndicates and terrorist organizations. Laundered through the international financial system, this money provides a huge source of virtually untraceable funds. These monetary assets can then be used to bribe government officials, bypass established financial controls, and fund additional illegal activities, including arms trafficking, migrant smuggling, and terrorist operations. Further, these activities can ensure a steady supply of weapons and cash for terrorist operatives, as well as the means for their clandestine movement.

***

Section III—Strategic Objectives

Today's transnational threats have the potential to inflict great harm on many nations. Thus, the security of the maritime domain requires comprehensive and cohesive efforts among the United States and many cooperating nations to protect the common interest in global maritime security. This Strategy describes how the United States Government will promote an international maritime security effort that will effectively and efficiently enhance the security of the maritime domain while preserving the freedom of the domain for legitimate pursuits.[5] This approach does not negate the United States' inherent right to self-defense or its right to act to protect its essential national security interests. **Defending against enemies is the first and most fundamental commitment of the United States Government. Preeminent among our national security priorities is to take all necessary steps to prevent WMD from entering the country and to avert an attack on the homeland.** This course of action must be undertaken while respecting the constitutional principles upon which the United States was founded.

Three broad principles provide overarching guidance to this Strategy. First, *preserving the freedom of the seas* is a top national priority. The right of vessels to travel freely in international waters, engage in innocent and transit passage, and have access to ports is an essential element of national security. The free, continuing, unthreatened intercourse of nations is an essential global freedom and helps ensure the smooth operation of the world's economy.

Second, the United States Government must *facilitate and defend commerce* to ensure this uninterrupted flow of shipping. The United States is a major trading nation, and its economy, environment, and social fabric are inextricably linked with the oceans and their resources. The adoption of a just-in-time delivery approach to shipping by most industries, rather than stockpiling or maintaining operating reserves of energy, raw materials, and key components, means that a disruption or slowing of the flow of almost any item can have widespread implications for the overall market, as well as upon the national economy.

Third, the United States Government must *facilitate the movement of desirable goods and people across our borders, while screening out dangerous people and material.* There need not be an inherent conflict between the demand for security and the need for facilitating the travel and trade essential to continued economic growth. This Strategy redefines our fundamental task as one of good border management rather than one that pits security against economic well-being. Accomplishing that goal is more manageable to the extent that screening can occur before goods and people arrive at our physical borders.

***

Section IV—Strategic Actions

The United States recognizes that, because of the extensive global connectivity among businesses and governments, its maritime security policies affect other nations, and that significant local and regional incidents will have global effects. Success in securing the maritime domain will not come from the United States acting alone, but through a powerful coalition of nations maintaining a strong, united, international front. The need for a strong and effective coalition is reinforced by the fact that most of the maritime domain is under no single nation's sovereignty or jurisdiction. Additionally, increased economic interdependency and globalization, largely made possible by maritime shipping, underscores the need for a coordinated international approach. Less than 3 percent of the international waterborne trade of the United States is carried on vessels owned, operated, and crewed by U.S. citizens. The United States also recognizes that the vast majority of actors and activities within the maritime domain are legitimate. Security of the maritime domain can be accomplished only by seamlessly employing all instruments of national power in a fully coordinated manner in concert with other nation-states consistent with international law.

Maritime security is best achieved by blending public and private maritime security activities on a global scale into a comprehensive, integrated effort that addresses all maritime threats. Maritime security crosses disciplines, builds upon current and future efforts, and depends on scalable layers of security to prevent a single point of failure. Full and complete national and international coordination, cooperation, and intelligence and information sharing among public and private entities are required to protect and secure the maritime domain. Collectively, these five strategic actions achieve the objectives of this Strategy:

- Enhance International Cooperation
- Maximize Domain Awareness
- Embed Security into Commercial Practices
- Deploy Layered Security
- Assure Continuity of the Marine Transportation System

These five strategic actions are not stand-alone activities. Domain awareness is a critical enabler for all strategic actions. Deploying layered security addresses not only layers of prevention (interdiction and preemption) and protection (deterrence and defense) activities, but also the integration of domestic and international layers of security provided by the first three strategic actions.

***

Section V—Conclusions

This National Strategy presents a vision for the achievement of maritime security for the people and interests of the United States while respecting the information privacy and other legal rights of Americans. Moreover, it underscores our commitment to strengthening our international partnerships and advancing economic well-being around the globe by facilitating commerce and abiding by the principles of freedom of the seas.

As a vision for the future, it certainly faces some serious challenges. The sheer magnitude of the maritime domain complicates the arduous and complex task of maintaining maritime security. The United States confronts a diverse set of adversaries fully prepared to exploit this vast milieu for nefarious purposes. The seas serve as the medium for a variety of transnational threats that honor no national frontier and that seek to imperil the peace and prosperity of the world. Many of these threats mingle with legitimate commerce, either to provide concealment for carrying out hostile acts, or to make available weapons of mass destruction, their delivery systems, and related materials to nations and non-state actors of concern.

Notes

1. Bold and italics in original.

2. The maritime domain is defined as all areas and things of, on, under, relating to, adjacent to, or bordering on a sea, ocean, or other navigable waterway, including all maritime-related activities, infrastructure, people, cargo, and vessels and other conveyances. Note: The maritime domain for the United States includes the Great Lakes and all navigable inland waterways such as the Mississippi River and the Intra-Coastal Waterway.

3. The term "weapon of mass destruction" (WMD) is defined in 18 U.S. Code § 2332a(c) as including any destructive device as defined in [18 U.S. Code] § 921 . . .; any weapon that is designed or intended to cause death or serious bodily injury through the release, dissemination, or impact of toxic or poisonous chemicals, or their precursors; any weapon involving a biological agent, toxin, or vector (as those terms are defined in [18 U.S. Code] § 178 . . .); or any weapon that is designed to release radiation or radioactivity at a level dangerous to human life.

4. The National Drug Control Strategy outlines U.S. goals in this area.

5. The National Strategy for Maritime Security is guided by the objectives and goals contained in the National Security Strategy and the National Strategy for Homeland Security. This Strategy also draws upon the National Strategy for Combating Terrorism, the National Strategy to Combat Weapons of Mass Destruction, the National Strategy for the Physical Protection of Critical Infrastructure and Key Assets, the National Defense Strategy, the National Military Strategy, and the National Drug Control Strategy.

U.S. Piracy Policy

United States Maritime Security (Piracy) Policy (2007)
(Annex B to the National Strategy for Maritime Security)

June 14, 2007

MEMORANDUM FOR THE VICE PRESIDENT
THE SECRETARY OF STATE
THE SECRETARY OF THE TREASURY
THE SECRETARY OF DEFENSE
THE ATTORNEY GENERAL
THE SECRETARY OF COMMERCE
THE SECRETARY OF TRANSPORTATION
THE SECRETARY OF ENERGY
THE SECRETARY OF HOMELAND SECURITY
ASSISTANT TO THE PRESIDENT AND CHIEF OF STAFF
DIRECTOR OF THE OFFICE OF MANAGEMENT AND BUDGET
DIRECTOR OF NATIONAL INTELLIGENCE
ASSISTANT TO THE PRESIDENT FOR NATIONAL SECURITY AFFAIRS
COUNSEL TO THE PRESIDENT
ASSISTANT TO THE PRESIDENT FOR HOMELAND SECURITY AND COUNTERTERRORISM
DIRECTOR OF THE CENTRAL INTELLIGENCE AGENCY
CHAIRMAN OF THE JOINT CHIEFS OF STAFF
DIRECTOR OF THE FEDERAL BUREAU OF INVESTIGATION
DIRECTOR, NATIONAL COUNTERTERRORISM CENTER

SUBJECT: Maritime Security (Piracy) Policy

The attached Policy for the Repression of Piracy and Other Criminal Acts of Violence at Sea (Piracy Policy) is approved for immediate implementation. . . . This policy responds to the emergence of high-risk maritime areas that threaten US interests. Recent instances of piracy have highlighted the need for this policy in order to coordinate US Government response and to promote international solutions. This policy advances our commitment to cooperate with other states, regional and international organizations, and the maritime industry in order to counter this threat. The United States has long been a leader in the protection of navigational rights and freedoms. Our objectives consistently have been to promote and facilitate peaceful international uses of the oceans. We recognize that all nations have an interest and responsibility in protecting those rights and freedoms.

/s/

GEORGE W. BUSH

Attachment Tab 1

Policy for the Repression of Piracy and Other Criminal Acts of Violence at Sea

I. Purpose

This document establishes United States Government policy and implementation actions to cooperate with other states and international and regional organizations in the repression of piracy and other criminal acts of violence against maritime navigation.[1]

II. Background

Piracy is any illegal act of violence, detention, or depredation committed for private ends by the crew, or the passengers, of a private ship and directed against a ship, aircraft, persons, or property on the high seas or in any other place outside the jurisdiction of any state. Piracy also includes inciting or facilitating an act of piracy, and any act of voluntary participation in the operation of a ship with knowledge of facts making it a pirate ship. Piracy is a universal crime, and all states are obligated to cooperate to the fullest possible extent in the repression of piracy.[2]

Piracy threatens US national security interests and the freedom and safety of maritime navigation throughout the world, undermines economic security, and contributes to the destabilization of weak or failed state governance. The combination of illicit activity and violence at sea might also be associated with other maritime challenges, including illegal, unlawful, and unregulated fishing, international smuggling, and terrorism.

Criminal and terrorist activities not defined as piracy also occur at sea and similarly threaten US economic and national security interests. These acts of violence endanger the safety of maritime navigation and may involve weapons of mass destruction. The prevention, interdiction, and punishment of those acts occurring in territorial seas are generally the responsibility of the coastal state. Prevention and punishment of acts occurring in international waters likely will require international cooperation and adequate domestic legal systems, most recently reflected in the 2005 Protocols to the 1988 Convention for the Suppression of Unlawful Acts against the Safety of Maritime Navigation and the Protocol for the Suppression of Unlawful Acts against the Safety of Fixed Platforms located on the Continental Shelf. The policy set forth in this annex fosters both increased coordination and international cooperation and is consistent with, supports, and builds upon existing maritime security efforts for piracy repression.

III. Policy

The United States strongly supports efforts to repress piracy and other criminal acts of violence against maritime navigation. The physical and economic security of the United States—a major global trading nation with interests across the maritime spectrum—relies heavily on the secure navigation of the world's oceans for unhindered legitimate commerce by its citizens and its partners. Piracy and other acts of violence against maritime navigation endanger sea lines of communication, interfere with freedom of navigation and the free flow of commerce, and undermine regional stability.

Piracy endangers maritime interests on a global scale, and the responsibility for countering this threat does not belong exclusively to the United States. Consequently, the United States will engage states and international and regional organizations to develop greater resources, capacity, and authorities to repress piracy and maximize inclusion of coalition assets in piracy repression operations.

Piracy repression should include diplomatic, military, intelligence, economic, law enforcement, and judicial actions. Effectively responding to piracy and criminal activity sends an important deterrent message and requires coordination by all departments and agencies of the US Government in order to ensure that those responsible are brought to justice in a timely manner.

It is the policy of the United States to repress piracy, consistent with US law and international obligations, and to cooperate with other nations in repressing piracy through the following actions:

- Prevent pirate attacks and other criminal acts of violence against US vessels, persons, and interests;

- Interrupt and terminate acts of piracy consistent with international law and the rights and responsibilities of coastal and flag states;
- Reduce the vulnerability of the maritime domain to such acts and exploitation when US interests are directly affected;
- Ensure that those who commit acts of piracy are held accountable for their actions by facilitating the prosecution of suspected pirates and ensure that persons suspected of committing acts of violence against maritime navigation are similarly held accountable by flag and littoral states and, in appropriate cases, the United States;
- Preserve the freedom of the seas, including high seas freedoms;
- Protect sea lines of communication; and
- Continue to lead and support international efforts to repress piracy and other acts of violence against maritime navigation and urge other states to take decisive action both individually and through international efforts.

Responses to these threats will vary according to geographic, political, and legal environments. The scope of the mission and the defined nature of the threat also will affect the choice of response.

IV. Implementation

The Assistant to the President for National Security Affairs and the Assistant to the President for Homeland Security and Counterterrorism shall lead an interagency process to accomplish the following tasks:

- Incorporate this policy into the Maritime Operational Threat Response Plan (Protocols), as appropriate;
- Oversee the development of specific guidance and protocols for the prevention of and response by the United States Government to piracy and other acts of violence against the safety of maritime navigation;
- Review existing US laws against or relating to piracy and prepare for consideration such amendments as may be necessary to enhance our ability to prosecute pirates in US courts;[3] and
- Seek international cooperation, consistent with the International Outreach and Coordination Strategy of the National Strategy for Maritime Security, to enhance the ability of other states to repress piracy and other criminal acts of violence against maritime navigation and to support US anti-piracy actions.

Notes

1. The National Security Strategy (2006) and the National Strategy for Maritime Security (2005) identify maritime threats.
2. Articles 14–15, Convention on the High Seas (1958), and Articles 100–101, Law of the Sea Convention (1982).

3. US Constitution, Article I, § 8; 18 USC §7 (1) (Special Maritime and Territorial Jurisdiction of the United States); 18 USC § 111 (Assault on Federal Officials); 18 USC § 113 (Assault on the high seas); 18 USC § 371 (Conspiracy); 18 USC § 844(i) (Use of explosive against property used in foreign commerce of the United States or against any property used in an activity affecting foreign commerce of the United States); 18 USC § 1651 (Piracy on the high seas); 18 USC § 1659 (Plundering a ship); 18 USC § 2111 (Robbery on high seas); 18 USC § 2280(a)(1)(A),(B), and/or (H) (Maritime violence/hijacking of a ship); 18 USC § 2232 (Assaults on US nationals overseas); 18 USC § 2232a (Use of WMD against US nationals outside of the United States).

UN Security Council Resolution 1816, The Situation in Somalia

United Nations Security Council Resolution 1816 (2008)

Adopted by the Security Council at Its 5902nd Meeting, on June 2, 2008

The Security Council,

Recalling its previous resolutions and the statements of its President concerning the situation in Somalia,

Gravely concerned by the threat that acts of piracy and armed robbery against vessels pose to the prompt, safe and effective delivery of humanitarian aid to Somalia, the safety of commercial maritime routes and to international navigation,

* * *

Affirming that international law, as reflected in the United Nations Convention on the Law of the Sea of 10 December 1982 ("the Convention"), sets out the legal framework applicable to combating piracy and armed robbery, as well as other ocean activities,

Reaffirming the relevant provisions of international law with respect to the repression of piracy, . . . including but not limited to boarding, searching, and seizing vessels engaged in or suspected of engaging in acts of piracy, and to apprehending persons engaged in such acts with a view to such persons being prosecuted,

Determining that the incidents of piracy and armed robbery against vessels in the territorial waters of Somalia and the high seas off the coast of Somalia exacerbate the situation in Somalia, which continues to constitute a threat to international peace and security in the region,

* * *

***Acting* under Chapter VII of the Charter of the United Nations**

* * *

2. *Urges* States whose naval vessels and military aircraft operate on the high seas and airspace off the coast of Somalia to be vigilant to acts of piracy and armed robbery and, in this context, *encourages*, in particular, States interested in the use of commercial maritime routes off the coast of Somalia, to increase and coordinate their efforts to deter acts of piracy and armed robbery at sea. . . .;

* * *

7. *Decides* that for a period of six months from the date of this resolution, States cooperating with the TFG in the fight against piracy and armed robbery at sea off the coast of Somalia, for which advance notification has been provided by the TFG to the Secretary-General, may:

(a) Enter the territorial waters of Somalia for the purpose of repressing acts of piracy and armed robbery at sea, in a manner consistent with such action permitted on the high seas with respect to piracy under relevant international law; and

(b) Use, within the territorial waters of Somalia, in a manner consistent with action permitted on the high seas with respect to piracy under relevant international law, all necessary means to repress acts of piracy and armed robbery;

8. *Requests* that cooperating states take appropriate steps to ensure that the activities they undertake pursuant to the authorization in paragraph 7 do not have the practical effect of denying or impairing the right of innocent passage to the ships of any third State;

9. *Affirms* that the authorization provided in this resolution applies only with respect to the situation in Somalia. . . .

* * *

11. *Calls upon* all States, and in particular flag, port and coastal States, States of the nationality of victims and perpetrators of piracy and armed robbery, and other States with relevant jurisdiction under international law and national legislation, to cooperate in determining jurisdiction, and in the investigation and prosecution of persons responsible for acts of piracy and armed robbery off the coast of Somalia, consistent with applicable international law including international human rights law, and to render assistance by, among other actions, providing disposition and logistics assistance with respect to persons under their jurisdiction and control, such victims and witnesses and persons detained as a result of operations conducted under this resolution;

* * *

UN Security Council Resolution 1838, The Situation in Somalia

United Nations Security Council Resolution 1838 (2008)

Adopted by the Security Council at Its 5987th Meeting, on October 7, 2008

The Security Council,

* * *

Reaffirming that international law, as reflected in the United Nations Convention on the Law of the Sea of 10 December 1982 ("the Convention"), sets out the legal framework applicable to combating piracy and armed robbery at sea, as well as other ocean activities,

Commending the contribution made by some States since November 2007 to protect the World Food Program ("WFP") maritime convoys, . . .,

Noting recent humanitarian reports that as many as three-and-a-half million Somalis will be dependent on humanitarian food aid . . .,

Reaffirming its respect for the sovereignty, territorial integrity, political independence and unity of Somalia,

* * *

***Acting* under Chapter VII of the Charter of the United Nations**

* * *

2. *Calls upon* States interested in the security of maritime activities to take part actively in the fight against piracy on the high seas off the coast of Somalia, in particular by deploying naval vessels and military aircraft. . . .;

* * *

8. *Affirms* that the provisions in this resolution apply only with respect to the situation in Somalia. . . .;

UN Security Council Resolution 1846, The Situation in Somalia

United Nations Security Council Resolution 1846 (2008)

Adopted by the Security Council at Its 6026th Meeting, on December 2, 2008

The Security Council,

* * *

Expressing again its determination to ensure the long-term security of World Food Program (WFP) maritime deliveries to Somalia,

* * *

Commending the key role played by the African Union Mission to Somalia (AMISOM) in facilitating delivery of humanitarian assistance to Somalia through the port of Mogadishu and the contribution that AMISOM has made towards the goal of establishing lasting peace and stability in Somalia, and *recognizing* specifically the important contributions of the Governments of Uganda and Burundi to Somalia,

Acting under Chapter VII of the Charter of the United Nations

1. *Reiterates* that it condemns and deplores all acts of piracy and armed robbery against vessels in territorial waters and the high seas off the coast of Somalia;

* * *

7. *Calls upon* States and regional organizations to coordinate, including by sharing information through bilateral channels or the United Nations,

their efforts to deter acts of piracy and armed robbery at sea off the coast of Somalia. . . .;

* * *

9. *Calls upon* States and regional organizations that have the capacity to do so, to take part actively in the fight against piracy and armed robbery at sea off the coast of Somalia, in particular, consistent with this resolution and relevant international law, by deploying naval vessels and military aircraft, ...
10. *Decides* that for a period of 12 months from the date of this resolution States and regional organizations cooperating with the TFG in the fight against piracy and armed robbery at sea off the coast of Somalia, for which advance notification has been provided by the TFG to the Secretary-General, may:

    (a) Enter into the territorial waters of Somalia for the purpose of repressing acts of piracy and armed robbery at sea, in a manner consistent with such action permitted on the high seas with respect to piracy under relevant international law; and

    (b) Use, within the territorial waters of Somalia, in a manner consistent with . . . international law, all necessary means to repress acts of piracy and armed robbery at sea;

* * *

13. *Requests* that cooperating States take appropriate steps to ensure that the activities they undertake pursuant to the authorization in paragraph 10 do not have the practical effect of denying or impairing the right of innocent passage to the ships of any third State;

* * *

15. *Notes* that the 1988 Convention for the Suppression of Unlawful Acts Against the Safety of Maritime Navigation ("SUA Convention") provides for parties to create criminal offences, establish jurisdiction, and accept delivery of persons responsible for or suspected of seizing or exercising control over a ship by force or threat thereof or any other form of intimidation; *urges* States parties to the SUA Convention to fully implement their obligations under said Convention. . . .;

UN Security Council Resolution 1851, The Situation in Somalia

United Nations Security Council Resolution 1851 (2008)

Adopted by the Security Council at Its 6046th Meeting, on December 16, 2008

The Security Council,

* * *

Again taking into account the crisis situation in Somalia, and the lack of capacity of the Transitional Federal Government (TFG) to interdict, or upon interdiction to prosecute pirates or to patrol and secure the waters off the coast of Somalia, including the international sea lanes and Somalia's territorial waters, *Noting* the several requests from the TFG for international assistance to counter piracy off its coast, . . . expressing the TFG's willingness to consider working with other States and regional organizations to combat piracy and armed robbery off the coast of Somalia,

* * *

Noting with concern that the lack of capacity, domestic legislation, and clarity about how to dispose of pirates after their capture, has hindered more robust international action against the pirates off the coast of Somalia and in some cases led to pirates being released without facing justice, . . .

* * *

Determining that the incidents of piracy and armed robbery at sea in the waters off the coast of Somalia exacerbate the situation in Somalia, which continues to constitute a threat to international peace and security in the region,

***Acting* under Chapter VII of the Charter of the United Nations**

* * *

2. *Calls* upon States, regional and international organizations that have the capacity to do so, to take part actively in the fight against piracy and armed robbery at sea off the coast of Somalia . . . by deploying naval vessels and military aircraft . . .

3. *Renews* its call upon States and regional organizations that have the capacity to do so, to . . . [deploy] naval vessels, arms and military aircraft and through seizures and disposition of boats, vessels, arms and other related equipment used in the commission of piracy and armed robbery at sea off the coast of Somalia, or for which there are reasonable grounds for suspecting such use;

4. *Encourages* all States and regional organizations fighting piracy and armed robbery at sea off the coast of Somalia to establish an international cooperation mechanism to act as a common point of contact between and among states, regional and international organizations on all aspects of combating piracy and armed robbery at sea off Somalia's coast; and *recalls* that future recommendations on ways to ensure the long-term security of international navigation off the coast of Somalia, including the long-term security of WFP maritime deliveries to Somalia and a possible coordination and leadership role for the United Nations in this regard to rally Member States and regional organizations to counter piracy and armed robbery at sea off the coast of Somalia are to be detailed in a report by the Secretary-General no later than three months after the adoption of resolution 1846;

5. *Further encourages* all states and regional organizations fighting piracy and armed robbery at sea off the coast of Somalia to consider creating a centre in the region to coordinate information relevant to piracy and armed robbery at sea off the coast of Somalia, . . .

6. . . . *[E]ncourages* Member States to continue to cooperate with the TFG in the fight against piracy and armed robbery at sea, *notes* the primary role of the TFG in rooting out piracy and armed robbery at sea, and *decides* that for a period of twelve months from the date of adoption of resolution 1846, States and regional organizations cooperating in the fight against piracy and armed robbery at sea off the coast of Somalia for which advance notification has been provided by the TFG to the Secretary-General may undertake all necessary measures that are appropriate in Somalia, for the purpose of suppressing acts of piracy and armed robbery at sea, . . . consistent with applicable international humanitarian and human rights law;

* * *

8. *Welcomes* the communiqué issued by the International Conference on Piracy around Somalia held in Nairobi, Kenya, on 11 December 2008 and *encourages* Member States to work to enhance the capacity of relevant states in the region to combat piracy, including judicial capacity;

UN Security Council Resolution 1897, The Situation in Somalia

United Nations Security Council Resolution 1897 (2009)

Adopted by the Security Council at Its 6226th Meeting, on November 30, 2009

The Security Council,

* * *

Reaffirming its respect for the sovereignty, territorial integrity, political independence and unity of Somalia, ...

Further reaffirming that international law, as reflected in the United Nations Convention on the Law of the Sea of 10 December 1982 ("The Convention"), sets out the legal framework applicable to combating piracy and armed robbery at sea, as well as other ocean activities,

* * *

Acting under Chapter VII of the Charter of the United Nations

* * *

2. *Notes* . . . that escalating ransom payments and the lack of enforcement of the arms embargo established by resolution 733 (1992) are fuelling the growth of piracy off the coast of Somalia. . . . ;

3. *Renews* its call upon States and regional organizations that have the capacity to do so, to . . . [deploy] naval vessels, arms and military aircraft and through seizures and disposition of boats, vessels, arms and other related equipment used in the commission of piracy and armed robbery at sea off the coast of Somalia, or for which there are reasonable grounds for suspecting such use;

* * *

6. *Invites* all States and regional organizations fighting piracy off the coast of Somalia to conclude special agreements or arrangements with countries willing to take custody of pirates in order to embark law enforcement officials ("shipriders") from the latter countries, in particular countries in the region, to facilitate [. . .] investigation and prosecution of [suspected pirates. . . .]

***

11. *Calls on* Member States to assist Somalia, . . . [and] to strengthen capacity in Somalia, including regional authorities, to bring to justice those who are using Somali territory to plan, facilitate, or undertake criminal acts of piracy and armed robbery at sea. . . . ;

UN Security Council Resolution 1918, The Situation in Somalia

United Nations Security Council Resolution 1918 (2010)

Adopted by the Security Council at Its 6301st Meeting, on April 27, 2010

The Security Council,

Recalling its previous resolutions concerning the situation in Somalia, especially resolutions 1814 (2008), 1816 (2008), 1838 (2008), 1844 (2008), 1846 (2008), 1851 (2008) and 1897 (2009),

* * *

Being concerned over cases when persons suspected of piracy are released without facing justice and *determined* to create conditions to ensure that pirates are held accountable,

1. *Affirms* that the failure to prosecute persons responsible for acts of piracy and armed robbery at sea off the coast of Somalia undermines anti-piracy efforts of the international community;

2. *Calls on* all States, including States in the region, to criminalize piracy under their domestic law and favourably consider the prosecution of suspected, and imprisonment of convicted, pirates apprehended off the coast of Somalia, consistent with applicable international human rights law;

3. *Welcomes* in this context the progress being made to implement the IMO Djibouti Code of Conduct, and *calls upon* its participants to implement it fully as soon as possible;

4. *Requests* the Secretary-General to present to the Security Council within 3 months a report on possible options to further the aim of prosecuting and imprisoning persons responsible for acts of piracy and armed robbery at sea off the coast of Somalia, . . . and the time and the resources necessary to achieve and sustain substantive results;

* * *

UN Security Council Resolution 1950, The Situation in Somalia

United Nations Security Council Resolution 1950 (2010)

Adopted by the Security Council at Its 6429th Meeting, on November 23, 2010

* * *

Acting **under Chapter VII of the Charter of the United Nations**

* * *

6. *Acknowledges* Somalia's rights with respect to offshore natural resources, including fisheries, in accordance with international law, *recalls* the importance of preventing, in accordance with international law, illegal fishing and illegal dumping, including toxic substances, and *calls upon* States and interested organizations, including the IMO, to provide technical assistance to Somalia, including regional authorities, and nearby coastal States upon their request to enhance their capacity to ensure coastal and maritime security, including combating piracy and armed robbery at sea off the Somali and nearby coastlines, and stresses the importance of coordination in this regard through the CGPCS;

Regional Cooperation Agreement on Combating Piracy (ReCAAP)

Regional Cooperation Agreement on Combating Piracy and Armed Robbery against Ships in Asia (ReCAAP) (2006)

* * *

Article 3 General Obligations

1. Each Contracting Party shall, in accordance with its national laws and regulations and applicable rules of international law, make every effort to take effective measures in respect of the following:

   (a) to prevent and suppress piracy and armed robbery against ships;
   (b) to arrest pirates or persons who have committed armed robbery against ships;
   (c) to seize ships or aircraft used for committing piracy or armed robbery against ships, to seize ships taken by and under the control of pirates or persons who have committed armed robbery against ships, and to seize the property on board such ships; and
   (d) to rescue victim ships and victims of piracy or armed robbery against ships.

2. Nothing in this Article shall prevent each Contracting Party from taking additional measures in respect of subparagraphs (a) to (d) above in its land territory.

Part II Information Sharing Center

Article 4 Composition

1. An Information Sharing Center, hereinafter referred to as "the Center", is hereby established to promote close cooperation among the Contracting Parties in preventing and suppressing piracy and armed robbery against ships.
2. The Center shall be located in Singapore.

* * *

Article 7 Functions

The functions of the Center shall be:

(a) to manage and maintain the expeditious flow of information relating to incidents of piracy and armed robbery against ships among the Contracting Parties;

(b) to collect, collate and analyze the information transmitted by the Contracting Parties concerning piracy and armed robbery against ships, including other relevant information, if any, relating to individuals and transnational organized criminal groups committing acts of piracy and armed robbery against ships;

* * *

Part III Cooperation through the Information Sharing Center

Article 9 Information Sharing

1. Each Contracting Party shall designate a focal point responsible for its communication with the Center, and shall declare its designation of such focal point at the time of its signature or its deposit of an instrument of notification provided for in Article 18.
2. Each Contracting Party shall, upon the request of the Center, respect the confidentiality of information transmitted from the Center.

* * *

Article 10 Request for Cooperation

1. A Contracting Party may request any other Contracting Party, through the Center or directly, to cooperate in detecting any of the following persons, ships, or aircraft:

   (a) pirates;

   (b) persons who have committed armed robbery against ships;

(c) ships or aircraft used for committing piracy or armed robbery against ships, and ships taken by and under the control of pirates or persons who have committed armed robbery against ships; or
(d) victim ships and victims of piracy or armed robbery against ships.

2. A Contracting Party may request any other Contracting Party, through the Center or directly, to take appropriate measures, including arrest or seizure, against any of the persons or ships mentioned in subparagraph (a), (b), or (c) of paragraph 1 of this Article, within the limits permitted by its national laws and regulations and applicable rules of international law.
3. A Contracting Party may also request any other Contracting Party, through the Center or directly, to take effective measures to rescue the victim ships and the victims of piracy or armed robbery against ships.

***

Part IV Cooperation

Article 12 Extradition

A Contracting Party shall, subject to its national laws and regulations, endeavor to extradite pirates or persons who have committed armed robbery against ships, and who are present in its territory, to the other Contracting Party which has jurisdiction over them, at the request of that Contracting Party.

Arab-East African Djibouti Code of Conduct

Arab-East African Djibouti Code of Conduct (2009)

***

Annex

Code of Conduct Concerning the Repression of Piracy and Armed Robbery against Ships in the Western Indian Ocean and the Gulf of Aden, January 29, 2009

The Governments of Comoros, Djibouti, Egypt, Eritrea, Ethiopia, France, Jordan, Kenya, Madagascar, Maldives, Mauritius, Mozambique, Oman, Saudi Arabia, Seychelles, Somalia, South Africa, Sudan, the United Arab Emirates, the United Republic of Tanzania and Yemen

***

Have agreed as follows:

***

1. Consistent with their available resources and related priorities, their respective national laws and regulations, and applicable rules of international law, the Participants intend to co- operate to the fullest possible extent in the repression of piracy and armed robbery against ships with a view towards:

   (a) sharing and reporting relevant information;
   (b) interdicting ships and/or aircraft suspected of engaging in piracy or armed robbery against ships;
   (c) ensuring that persons committing or attempting to commit piracy or armed robbery against ships are apprehended and prosecuted; and

(d) facilitating proper care, treatment, and repatriation for seafarers, fishermen, other shipboard personnel and passengers subject to piracy or armed robbery against ships, particularly those who have been subjected to violence.

2. The Participants intend this Code of conduct to be applicable in relation to piracy and armed robbery in the Western Indian Ocean and the Gulf of Aden.

Article 3 Protection Measures for Ships

The Participants intend to encourage States, ship owners, and ship operators, where appropriate, to take protective measures against piracy and armed robbery against ships, taking into account the relevant international standards and practices, and, in particular, recommendations 1, 2 adopted by IMO.

Article 4 Measures to Repress Piracy

1. The provisions of this Article are intended to apply only to piracy.
2. For purposes of this Article and of Article 10, "pirate ship" means a ship intended by the persons in dominant control to be used for the purpose of committing piracy, or if the ship has been used to commit any such act, so long as it remains under the control of those persons.
3. Consistent with Article 2, each Participant to the fullest possible extent intends to co- operate in:

   (a) arresting, investigating, and prosecuting persons who have committed piracy or are reasonably suspected of committing piracy;
   (b) seizing pirate ships and/or aircraft and the property on board such ships and/or aircraft; and
   (c) rescuing ships, persons, and property subject to piracy.

4. Any Participant may seize a pirate ship beyond the outer limit of any State's territorial sea, and arrest the persons and seize the property on board.
5. Any pursuit of a ship, where there are reasonable grounds to suspect that the ship is engaged in piracy, extending in and over the territorial sea of a Participant is subject to the authority of that Participant. No Participant should pursue such a ship in or over the territory or territorial sea of any coastal State without the permission of that State.
6. Consistent with international law, the courts of the Participant which carries out a seizure pursuant to paragraph 4 may decide upon the penalties to be imposed, and may also determine the action to be taken with regard to the ship or property, subject to the rights of third parties acting in good faith.
7. The Participant, which carried out the seizure pursuant to paragraph 4, may, subject to its national laws, and in consultation with other interested entities, waive its primary right to exercise jurisdiction and authorize any other Participant to enforce its laws against the ship and/or persons on board.

8. Unless otherwise arranged by the affected Participants, any seizure made in the territorial sea of a Participant . . . should be subject to the jurisdiction of that Participant.

* * *

Article 7 Embarked Officers

1. In furtherance of operations contemplated by this Code of conduct, a Participant may nominate law enforcement or other authorized officials (hereafter referred to as "the embarked officers") to embark in the patrol ships or aircraft of another Participant (hereafter referred to as "the host Participant") as may be authorized by the host Participant.
2. The embarked officers may be armed in accordance with their national law and policy and the approval of the host Participant.
3. When embarked, the host Participant should facilitate communications between the embarked officers and their headquarters, and should provide messing and quarters for the embarked officers aboard the patrol ships or aircraft in a manner consistent with host Participant personnel of the same rank.
4. Embarked officers may assist the host Participant and conduct operations from the host Participant ship or aircraft if expressly requested to do so by the host Participant, and only in the manner requested. Such request may only be made, agreed to, and acted upon in a manner that is not prohibited by the laws and policies of both Participants.

Article 8 Coordination and Information Sharing

1. Each Participant should designate a national focal point to facilitate coordinated, timely, and effective information flow among the Participants consistent with the purpose and scope of this Code of conduct. In order to ensure coordinated, smooth, and effective communications between their designated focal points, the Participants intend to use the piracy information exchange centers [in] Kenya, United Republic of Tanzania, and Yemen (hereinafter referred to as "the Centers"). The Centers in Kenya and the United Republic of Tanzania will be situated in the maritime rescue coordination center in Mombasa and the sub-regional co-ordination center in Dar es Salaam, respectively. The Center in Yemen will be situated in the regional maritime information center to be established in Yemen based on the outcomes of the sub-regional meetings held by IMO in Sana'a in 2005 and Muscat in 2006 and Dar es Salaam. Each Center and designated focal point should be capable of receiving and responding to alerts and requests for information or assistance at all times.

* * *

Article 11 Review of National Legislation

In order to allow for the prosecution, conviction and punishment of those involved in piracy or armed robbery against ships, and to facilitate extradition or handing over when prosecution is not possible, each Participant intends to review its national legislation with a view towards ensuring that there are national laws in place to criminalize piracy and armed robbery against ships, and adequate guidelines for the exercise of jurisdiction, conduct of investigations, and prosecutions of alleged offenders.

Index

About the Author

Commander JAMES KRASKA is the Howard S. Levie Chair of Operational Law at the U.S. Naval War College in Newport, Rhode Island. A member of the faculty of the International Law Department and a Senior Associate in the Center for Irregular Warfare and Armed Groups at the Naval War College, he also holds appointments as a Senior Fellow at the Foreign Policy Research Institute and as a Guest Investigator at the Marine Policy Center, Woods Hole Oceanographic Institution. Kraska served as legal adviser for joint and naval task force flag rank commanders in the Asia-Pacific, served as a Navy criminal prosecutor for forward deployed naval forces in Japan, and completed four Pentagon major staff assignments with the Office of the Navy Judge Advocate General, the Deputy Chief of Naval Operations, and Global Security Affairs, Strategic Plans & Policy, the Joint Staff. In his last Pentagon assignment he served as the principal military drafter of the president's U.S. Piracy Policy and the first UN Security Council resolution on maritime piracy. His books include *Maritime Power and Law of the Sea* from Oxford University Press and *Arctic Security in an Age of Climate Change* from Cambridge University Press. He also serves as series editor of the Nijhoff Oceans Law Handbooks. Commander Kraska earned a research doctorate in law and a master's degree in law from the University of Virginia, a professional doctorate in law from Indiana University Bloomington, and a master's degree in defense policy from Claremont.